Puerto Ricans

Puerto Ricans
Born in the U.S.A.

Clara E. Rodríguez
FORDHAM UNIVERSITY

Westview Press
BOULDER • SAN FRANCISCO • OXFORD

Copyright © 1991 by Westview Press, Inc.

Published in 1991 in the United States of America by Westview Press, Inc., 5500 Central Avenue, Boulder, Colorado 80301, and in the United Kingdom by Westview Press, 36 Lonsdale Road, Summertown, Oxford OX2 7EW

First published by Unwin Hyman in 1989

Library of Congress Cataloging-in-Publication Data
Rodríguez, Clara E.
  Puerto Ricans: born in the U.S.A. / Clara E. Rodríguez
  p.   cm.
  Bibliography: p.
  Includes index.
  ISBN 0-8133-1267-1 — ISBN 0-8133-1268-X (pbk.)
    1. Puerto Ricans—United States—Social conditions.
2. Puerto Ricans—United States—Economic conditions.
3. United States—Race relations. I. Title.
E184.P85R59   1989
305.8′687295′073—dc19

Printed and bound in the United States of America

The paper used in this publication meets the requirements
of the American National Standard for Permanence of Paper
for Printed Library Materials Z39.48-1984.

10   9   8

CONTENTS

LIST OF TABLES

LIST OF FIGURES

PREFACE

In writing this book, I was constantly struck by how much Puerto Ricans seem to be at the center of the significant events of today. I was also struck by how little this is generally acknowledged. The South Bronx, which has the largest concentration of Puerto Ricans in New York, has been visited by a president, presidential candidates, the pope, actors, and foreign dignitaries, yet never once in the televised coverage of these visits did anyone comment upon the impact of the urban decay of the South Bronx on the Puerto Rican community. In the policy arena, Puerto Ricans are at the epicenter of battles over welfare reform, urban enterprise zones, and urban schools. Yet, to cite only the most recent example in the policy arena, Puerto Ricans in New York, "the poorest of American groups" in one of the richest states in the country, received only one line in the latest report of the Task Force on Poverty and Social Welfare (New York State, 1986).

Similarly, when the governor of New York, professors at Harvard, MIT, and Berkeley, and policymakers in Washington discuss deindustrialization, the new service economy, and the globalization of the economy, they usually ignore the fact that these trends affected Puerto Ricans more than most, and hit them sooner. When high-level policymakers and such mainstream media as the *New York Times*, the *Los Angeles Times*, and the *Wall Street Journal* do consider Puerto Ricans, they usually frame the discussion either in terms of the "plight" of Puerto Ricans, making it "their" problem, or in terms of the problem "they" present for "us."

On a global scale, Puerto Ricans also play critical yet unacknowledged roles. Puerto Ricans are at the center of U.S. efforts to "stabilize" the Caribbean. Puerto Rico is the anchor of the Caribbean Basin Initiative and the prime line of defense for the United States in Latin America. Yet the U.S. government has seldom acknowledged the strategic and crucial military and political importance of the island. Thus, despite being at the center of the issues discussed, the main actors are ignored. Puerto Ricans are effectively marginalized in the public view.

Today we are in an era of "renegotiated" social contracts—between management and labor, between men and women, between members of majority and minority groups, and especially between government and the recipients of government funds. Surrounding these renegotiations are disturbing questions about why certain groups have not progressed in the American class structure, particularly at a time of relative economic growth. Some answers may be found in the nature of this new economic growth. For instance, much of the growth may be illusory; that is, many of the transactions associated with growth are purely financial, and may not contribute to real economic performance or significant job growth. It is also possible that the economic growth that has occurred has favored upper-level service professionals and low-skilled labor in the informal sector. Thus, those between these extremes, like most Puerto Ricans, may have benefited little. No matter what the explanation, the Puerto Rican experience has much to teach us about the political, economic, and cultural reasons certain groups remain so far removed from the American dream.

The Puerto Rican community must be understood in a broad historical and comparative framework. It is not enough to take a superficial view of the data, ask a few "captive" or well-chosen Puerto Ricans to assess the situation of Puerto Ricans, and consider this an adequate assessment of the condition of Puerto Ricans in the United States, as journalists often do. An appropriately broad, in-depth view must bear in mind that Puerto Ricans are both the only colonial group to arrive en masse and the first racially heterogeneous group to migrate to the United States on a large scale.[1] These facts are basic to an understanding of the experience of Puerto Ricans in the United States, yet they have received little attention from scholars or policy analysts.[2]

Organization of the Book

Contextual Analysis

This book examines the contexts into which Puerto Rican immigrants to the United States stepped, and the results of their interaction within those contexts. Essentially a social history of the post-World War II Puerto Rican community, the book focuses mainly on New York City, which has the largest concentration of Puerto Ricans in the United States. However, the issues addressed transcend the borders of New York.

The first chapter examines the migration of Puerto Ricans from a historical perspective. The second chapter examines the context in which the data for this study were gathered. Separate chapters then analyze race, education, housing, economic structure, and the media in terms of how they affect and are affected by the Puerto Rican community. This subject-area approach differs from the chronological approach generally used in the study of Puerto Ricans.

The subject areas addressed in this volume were chosen because they are important to a complete picture of the Puerto Rican experience in the United States. The historical context is presented so that the reader might better understand the factors leading to the migration of Puerto Ricans. The role of the political and economic relationship between Puerto Rico and the United States is seen to influence migration as well as Puerto Ricans' choice of communities in the United States. Puerto Ricans are then examined within the data context—a context that is often used by those attempting to explain the Puerto Rican experience. The data picture drawn by using standard statistical indicators is critically reviewed on a number of methodological bases, and common interpretations of the data are questioned.

Chapter 3 focuses on race because this has been a critical, but generally neglected, area in the scientific literature. Bernardo Vega gave numerous examples of racial discrimination and divisive racial experiences in the pre-World War II Puerto Rican community in New York (Iglesias, 1980). Race has been a different kind of factor and experience for Puerto Ricans than it has been for any other group. As Vega notes: "That 'despreocupacion racial' [lack of racial worry] among Puerto Ricans was early on not well received—not even by other immigrants, who might themselves have been the objects of discrimination by pure North Americans" (Iglesias, 1980: 28; my translation). The recent words of a Puerto Rican female lawyer raised in the United States echo this observation: "Because Puerto Ricans don't discriminate in the way North Americans do, they are discriminated against." Chapter 3 takes an in-depth, multifaceted look at this issue.

The time of arrival is an important consideration in the insertion of any new group (Pedraza-Bailey, 1985; Bean and Tienda, 1988). Thus, the political-economic context is the focus of Chapter 4, which details how the greatest numbers of Puerto Ricans arrived during New York's transition from a major manufacturing center to a postindustrial economy based on service industries. Concentrated in the most vulnerable of the manufacturing areas (durable goods and the garment sector), Puerto Ricans became enmeshed in the economic and social dislocations inherent in the city's transition. They also became enmeshed in a race-ethnic order that was reproduced through restrictive union policies and practices, an educational system that tended to channel Puerto Ricans into the declining blue-collar areas, and the relative exclusion of Puerto Ricans from government employment.

Chapter 4 also details how, subsequently, new features of the economy further intensified a difficult economic situation. The features discussed include New York City's fiscal crisis; more austere federal policies; government's pulling out (in the 1980s) of training programs, affirmative action, and social spending; credentialism, plus the proliferation of more "credentialed" workers; labor competition as a result of the entrance of new immigrants working at lower wages; and diminishing middle-level jobs. It is argued that these factors have made up the troubled political and economic context into which Puerto Ricans stepped and within which they continue to live.

Chapter 5 focuses on housing, also an important but often neglected area for Puerto Ricans, and one closely related to the issue of race. Urban decay, urban renewal, and now gentrification are seen as having destroyed major Puerto Rican communities and consequently disrupted community and family ties. Data are reviewed that suggest Puerto Ricans may have had to relocate more often than others in New York City. It is also observed that the actions of the city, state, and federal authorities were insufficient to avert the decline of the largest Puerto Rican community—that in the South Bronx. The chapter details how Puerto Ricans made (and are making) valiant efforts to reconstruct their neighborhoods and to survive against great odds. Despite these efforts, displacement had and continues to have negative effects on education, jobs and income, family and other social support networks, and community organizations, as well as on psychic energies.

The educational context is covered in Chapter 6 because it is the most troubling of all. The proportion of Hispanic students performing at grade level lags behind that of other groups, particularly in predominantly Hispanic districts. The number of students with limited proficiency in English has increased. Dropout rates have increased and are at alarmingly high levels throughout the educational structure. Segregation persists, as do its correlations with low educational achievement. It does not seem likely that these problems will disappear; in fact, it is predicted that the dropout problem will increase because of new standards of passage (Hodgkinson, 1985).[3] In addition, the public school system will apparently have to deal with greater numbers of Latinos in the future—in New York the proportion of Hispanics in the early grades is currently larger than that of Blacks or Whites.[4] If this trend continues, the public school system may be faced with a predominantly Hispanic student body.

Chapter 6 discusses the explanations often given for the low educational attainment of Hispanic children: lack of money, poor job opportunities, bad data, and low expectation levels, as well as more macro and historical rationales, are examined. A review of the relevant empirical literature is offered, and the struggles waged by Puerto Ricans and other Latinos within the school system are presented. Finally, the chapter advances some recommendations for improvement of the educational situation of Puerto Ricans.

This book covers many areas, but it covers only a very small portion of the Puerto Rican reality, and an even smaller portion of the dreams of the Puerto Rican community. I do not pretend to depict "the Puerto Rican experience" here; that would clearly require more than this text could encompass. Presentation of the detail necessary to portray the rich and vibrant history of the community was not possible within the limitations of this volume; many critical areas have not been touched—politics, health, crime, the success stories. Chapter 7 attempts to convey, in a very small way, that beneath the surfaces only skimmed in the previous chapters lies a vibrant, vital world of relatively undiscovered and unacknowledged talents. This chapter focuses on the cultural context of Puerto Ricans in New York today, by examining a small dimension of the cultural ambience that has evolved within the Puerto Rican community. A case study analysis of the impact of a popular folk-rock group called Menudo provides the illustration.

The Reason for a Focused Approach

The decision to focus on one group, the Puerto Ricans, as opposed to the increasingly popular comparative approach (i.e., comparing one ethnic group to another) was made purposely. I felt that an in-depth focus on this very unique group was necessary because, in many cases, the literature had not adequately or accurately represented Puerto Ricans. The problem with such an approach is that it tends to highlight the uniqueness of the group and to understate the clear similarities and parallels that do exist between it and other groups. This can lead some to overemphasize the singularity of the group and its characteristics. The possibility that this might occur is particularly disturbing for me, because a major intent of the book is to examine the contexts into which Puerto Ricans stepped when they came to the United States, not the characteristics of Puerto Ricans. These contexts have undoubtedly also affected other groups similarly. It is my hope that the contextual approach taken here will have utility for the analysis of other groups. The book should be read with these possible comparisons in mind—although they are not made explicitly in the book.

Despite the specific focus on Puerto Ricans, this book should be seen as closely aligned with the ongoing research and literature in world systems theory. I view the most recent Puerto Rican migration as one of the earliest examples of the international flows of labor and capital that have characterized the post-World War II period. Puerto Rico's economic development program had an earlier genesis than those in most other developing countries. What was at the time a novel experiment was to be replicated in developing countries throughout the world. In country after country, this type of development was to yield a surplus population of displaced labor that would migrate or immigrate to other areas. The industrial restructuring of core areas, plus the continuing migration of capital and labor to low-wage sectors would make many of these migrants eventually redundant in their new homes.

The focus of the book is nonetheless on the settlement of Puerto Ricans in the United States, that is, on the postmigration period. It focuses on what happened after Puerto Ricans arrived. An assumption underlying the text is that many of the issues confronted by Puerto Ricans in the United States are (or were) similarly met by other colonial (im)migrants to more industrialized Western European nations.[5] The core-to-periphery relations are reproduced in many forms within the host country as well as within the periphery. This tends to be true regardless of whether the host is a former or a current colonial power.

Accessible Style and Modular Construction

The book has also been written in an accessible style, aimed at students and policymakers who have little familiarity with the Puerto Rican experience in the United States. Therefore, a conscious attempt has been made to keep the prose as simple and straightforward as possible. Statistical tables and discussions have been kept to a minimum, although there is a strong emphasis on research. The finer and more abstract or complex points have been relegated to the chapter endnotes. As a consequence, the notes in some chapters are quite extensive.

The book is constructed so that each chapter can be read separately, although there is a logical order and development in the chapters. To some degree, the reader may detect some changes in style in the different chapters; this is a reflection of the different approaches taken. Multiple methods have been used in this book; these include the case study, participant-observer approach, descriptive data analysis of secondary data sets, statistical techniques involving more inferential quantitative tests, the use of literary sources, and reviews of secondary source material. The variety of methods used reflects the highly interdisciplinary approach taken to the study of different aspects of the Puerto Rican community. In some cases it also reflects the nature of the materials in the area studied; for example, for the chapter on race, where there is not a large established body of scientific research, census data were researched, as well as themes in fictional and nonfictional literature.

The Utility of the Book

The book can serve as a text for students interested in the Puerto Rican migration and the history of the Puerto Rican community in the United States. It will be similarly useful to policymakers and others working with, or concerned with, Puerto Ricans or other urban Latino populations, for it provides an extensive description and analysis of the economic and social situation of Puerto Ricans. It will also be useful to those interested in developing new ways of understanding migration, race, education, housing and the South Bronx, minorities and the media, the intersection of race, class, and gender, and the influence of political economic forces on the absorption of racial-ethnic groups.

For international scholars concerned with the movement of people from the Third to the First World, it provides a contextual analysis of a unique experience—the only major migration to the United States from a U.S. territory. It will also serve as a useful resource for more comparative approaches to the study of immigrants. For everyone concerned with race and race relations, it tells about a people who represent American ideals in that they are unicultural and multiracial; it tries to bring new light to the areas of race and racial perceptions and attitudes. Finally, it will be of interest to those concerned about the history and future of America, for, in many ways, it is as much about the United States as it is about Puerto Ricans.

The Experience and the Purpose

This has been a very difficult, but exciting, book to write. It has been difficult because, according to the data, Puerto Ricans in the United States are disadvantaged to a far greater degree than other groups. After decades of researching the Puerto Rican community in the United States, I was not surprised by what I found, but I was saddened to be reminded that the situation continues to be a grave one. I have been reminded of two facts researchers should always bear in mind when working with data about Puerto Ricans: (1) we need more and different data (see Chapter 2), and (2) the data are not the people. My knowledge of and experience with the Puerto Rican people have reinforced this fact for me. My children, my family, and I have all been nurtured, supported, sheltered, and encouraged by the Puerto Rican community. There is much warmth and humanity in this community that is not captured in the data.

This book has been exciting to write because I have come to see more clearly the inherent strength and vitality of the Puerto Rican community, despite the adversities the people face. I have also come to a greater appreciation of the confidence, determination, and strength of those who have survived the confrontation in the United States victoriously—to paraphrase the young Puerto Rican poet, Sandra Maria Esteves (1987: 168).

During the time I was writing this book, a number of my non-Puerto Rican colleagues and friends visited Puerto Rico for the first time. They all reported that their impressions had been quite favorable. The people, like the climate, were warm, friendly, outgoing, and gracious, I was told. Indeed, some of my friends even reported that their less favorably predisposed companions also had very positive impressions of Puerto Rico. Indeed, it was these visitors who were the most pleased and surprised. They began to wonder why Puerto Ricans ever left such a wonderful place, and why the Puerto Rican experience in New York has been so "difficult." The following chapters attempt to answer both these questions.

No single book on such a large topic can be definitive. This book builds on work that has come before. It will serve as a point of departure for people just beginning to learn about Puerto Ricans. For those already familiar with the story of Puerto Ricans in the United States, it may provide a more solid foundation for continuing work. It is my hope that this book will also contribute to the movement toward universal justice.

Notes

1 There is considerable debate on whether Puerto Rico is or is not a colony of the United States; this debate is reviewed in Chapter 1. At this point, suffice it to say that del Valle's (1984: 14) extensive analysis of legislation in this area leads him to conclude that Puerto Rico is still an "unincorporated territory of the United States." This is the same legal status Puerto Rico held when the United States first assumed control in Puerto Rico.

2 For a variety of reasons, not the least of which is the warm, tropical climate of Puerto Rico, Puerto Ricans have been the subject of considerable, sometimes unwanted, research attention (Lewis, 1963). However, Puerto Ricans still hold the dubious distinction of being among the most researched and least understood people in the United States, if not in the world.

3 McDill et al. (1985) conclude, after reviewing the literature in this area, that raising standards may have positive as well as negative consequences for potential dropouts.

4 According to Gordon Ambach, New York State commissioner of education, Hispanics today represent 13.6% of all students in New York State and 33% of all students in the New York City schools—or one out of every three children (*New York Times*, February 9, 1986). Whites constituted 22.8% of all students in the New York City public school system in 1984 (New York City Board of Education, 1984a; see this work also for figures on Hispanics in the early grades).

5 The term (im)migrants reflects the experience of people who move from one culture to another (immigrants) but stay within a similar political sphere (migrant).

ACKNOWLEDGMENTS

In thinking of the many people who have helped to make this book a reality, I am reminded of the words of that wonderful Puerto Rican poet, Tato Laviera, who said, ". . . with every word I write I give thanks to 50 people." The debt that he feels for his inspiration is similar to the one I feel to all those who have assisted me in this project. It would be impossible to name them all, but in my talks with all of you I have already conveyed my gratitude. You know who you are and you know how much and how deeply I appreciate all that we have shared. In addition to that personal and intellectual support, I received important financial assistance from the Inter-University Program for Contemporary Latino Research/Social Science Research Council and from the Business and Professional Women's Association; this made possible the statistical analyses in the book.

Finally, I would like to dedicate this book to Clarita, Jimmy, Gel, Minnie, Lina, Jr., Tony, Gelvinita, China, Janet, Michelle, José and María. This book was written for them and for all those who know the beauty of the rainbow in their minds and hearts.

1

THE COLONIAL RELATIONSHIP:
MIGRATION AND HISTORY

Since 1898, all Puerto Ricans have been born in the U.S.A., for that was the year that the United States invaded Puerto Rico as part of its war with Spain and proceeded to make Puerto Rico an unincorporated territory of the United States. All Puerto Ricans born in Puerto Rico since that time have been born on U.S. soil. This book, however, focuses on Puerto Ricans who were born and/or live in the fifty states. For these Puerto Ricans, being "born in the U.S.A." has had quite a different meaning. This book will explore this meaning.

Looked at in historical perspective, Puerto Rican migration and immigration have always been greatly influenced by economic developments in Puerto Rico. In turn, these developments have been influenced by the political and economic ties that have existed between Puerto Rico and its colonial power, first Spain and then the United States.[1] This chapter will address these relationships, as well as the migration itself: who came, why they came, and where they settled. The second part of this chapter analyzes the impacts of Puerto Rico's colonial history on the post-World War II Puerto Rican communities in the United States.

The Migration

Despite the tendency in the literature to view the Puerto Rican migration as homogeneous, in real terms, the migration was quite diverse. It included many from the *campos*, the rural areas, where the farming pursuits of many were rendered economically marginal; these migrants were, essentially, displaced farmers and farm laborers. They migrated directly to New York City, to other large cities, or to small towns and farming communities, where they first worked as agricultural laborers and then moved to more urban areas. Others came from the *pueblos* (towns) in Puerto Rico. For many of these the trek to the states was a second migration. They were often only a generation or less removed from campo living and were under- or unemployed in the small towns or large urban areas to which they had migrated in Puerto Rico. They followed the same paths as those from the campos. After 1965, those who arrived were generally already highly urbanized; they had, in many cases, already become urban proletarians and were familiar with the ways of urban living. (Today the agricultural sector is so minor in Puerto Rico, and the urban-suburban residential patterns so pronounced, that the distinction between rural and urban that formed the basis of much earlier research has lost much meaning.)

Lost in most analyses of immigrants is a real qualitative sense of the diversity and richness of the migrant population. Often the data used in academic studies identify certain patterns of class and skill background, but, because they are based on standardized classifications of jobs developed for use in the United States, they misclassify or fail to identify the varied skills and talents of those who migrate from different cultures. For example, in the migration of Puerto Rican peasants and urban workers alike, there were sugar cane cutters and common laborers, but there were also accomplished musicians, fine needlecraft workers, country doctors and midwives, small entrepreneurs, botanists, spiritualists, practical agronomists, skilled artisans (in wood, cement, and leather), artists, singers, and able political workers long involved in the legal and political systems of Puerto Rico. The skills these migrants brought with them were seldom utilized for their livelihood; in many cases, these skills went entirely unnoticed in the new land.

Just as the migrants brought nontransferable skills, they also brought transferable skills that were not transferred. As Handlin (1959: 70) points out, as newcomers "they had to accept whatever jobs were available. Even those who arrived with skills or had training in white collar occupations had to take whatever places were offered to them." Many who had been schoolteachers in Puerto Rico migrated and became factory workers, cab drivers, and restaurant workers. Thus, although some statistical measures may reflect a fairly uniform class structure, the measures do not adequately account for nontransferable skills and the downward mobility initially experienced by many migrants. The Puerto Rican population is a heterogeneous one that reflects the distinct classes found on the island plus the development of new class positions and perspectives in the United States.

Patterns of Settlement

There have been Puerto Ricans, and even Puerto Rican organizations, in New York since the nineteenth century (Iglesias, 1980; Sánchez-Korrol, 1983). However, it was only after 1900 that significant numbers of Puerto Ricans came, with the bulk of the migration occurring in the 1950s and 1960s (see Figure 1.1). The migration of Puerto Ricans after the U.S. takeover has been classified into three major periods (Stevens-Arroyo and Díaz-Ramírez, 1982). During the first period, 1900–1945, the pioneers arrived. The majority of these *pioneros* settled in New York City, in the Atlantic St. area of Brooklyn, El Barrio in East Harlem, and other sections of Manhattan (e.g., the Lower East Side, the Upper West Side, Chelsea, and the Lincoln Center area), while some began to populate sections of the South Bronx. During this period, contracted industrial and agricultural labor also arrived and "provided the base from which sprang many of the Puerto Rican communities" outside of New York City (Maldonado, 1979: 103).

The second phase of migration, 1946–1964, is known as "the great migration" because the largest numbers of Puerto Ricans arrived. During this period the already established Puerto Rican communities of East Harlem, the South Bronx, and the Lower East Side increased their numbers and expanded their borders. Settlements in new areas of New York, New Jersey, Connecticut, Chicago, and other areas of the country appeared and grew, but the bulk of the Puerto Rican population continued to reside in New York.

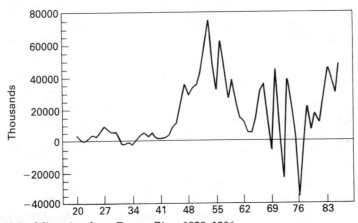

Figure 1.1   Migration from Puerto Rico, 1920–1986

Sources: For data from 1920 to 1940: U.S. Commission on Civil Rights (1976). For data from 1940 to 1986: Junta de Planificación de Puerto Rico, Negociado de Análisis Económico, 1940–1986.

3

The last period is termed "the revolving-door migration." It is dated 1965 to the present and involves a fluctuating pattern of net migration as well as greater dispersion to other parts of the United States. As Figure 1.1 illustrates, the last few years have shown net outflows from Puerto Rico that begin to rival those experienced in the early 1950s. By 1980, the majority of Puerto Ricans in the United States were living outside of New York State (U.S. Bureau of the Census, 1982: 6).

Contract Laborers

Contract laborers have been another stream in the Puerto Rican migration, but they have generally received little attention in the literature. This may be because many returned to Puerto Rico after their contracts were completed, while others moved quickly out of agricultural contract labor and settled in more urban areas. Initially recruited by companies and then by the "family intelligence service," these migrants formed the nucleus of Puerto Rican communities that would subsequently develop in less urban areas or in areas outside of the New York metropolitan area, such as Hawaii, California, and Arizona and other southwestern states. Communities in Gary, Indiana, and Lorain, Cleveland, and Youngstown, in Ohio, began in this way (Senior and Watkins, 1966). Contract labor migration began soon after 1898 and has continued throughout the twentieth century. Indeed, the very first group to migrate to the states after the 1898 takeover was a group of contract laborers who went to Hawaii. For many, the farm labor system was the "stepping stone to residence in the U.S. usually in urban areas" (Maldonado, 1979: 117).

Class and Selectivity

The class composition of the Puerto Rican communities has changed over time, but they have always retained a distinctive diversity. We know that the nineteenth-century Puerto Rican community was generally made up of well-to-do merchants, political activists closely allied with the Cuban revolutionary movement, and skilled workers, many of whom were *tabaqueros* (skilled tobacco workers) (Iglesias, 1980; Sánchez-Korrol, 1983). By the first quarter of the twentieth century, the Puerto Rican community was described by a number of scholars as consisting of people who were employed in predominantly working-class occupations (Chenault, 1938; Gosnell, 1945; Handlin, 1959). In the post-World War II period, migration from Puerto Rico to the United States accelerated, causing the

4

communities to grow rapidly. The composition of these communities continued to reflect diversity, but with a strong working-class base.

A related question that has preoccupied researchers is who exactly migrated to the United States; that is, were those who came the best or worst of the lot? With increasing numbers of immigrants from Asia and Latin America currently coming to the United States, and with evidence of differential group outcomes, there has been a renewed interest in this question. Implicit in this question (today) is whether differential group outcomes are the result of who came.[2] Further, there is concern over the declining quality of immigrants; the question is asked whether there is negative selectivity with regard to those who come and those who return (Borjas, 1987; Chiswick, 1977; Jasso and Rosenzweiz, 1982).[3]

Research interest in the human capital characteristics of Puerto Rican migrants has fluctuated over time. Throughout the post-World War II period, there were a number of scattered cross-sectional studies that give us partial but intriguing answers to the question of who came. The early studies seemed to emphasize the superiority of the migrants relative to those who did not migrate. For example, a 1948 study of more than 1,000 Puerto Rican migrants in New York found that the migrants had higher literacy rates (93%) than those who stayed in Puerto Rico (74%), that the migrants were predominantly skilled and semiskilled (only 26% were unskilled), that most of the migrants had been employed prior to migrating (69% of the men had been in the labor force), and that few had come from agricultural areas—indeed, 82% had been born and raised in the three largest cities on the island (Mills et al., 1950: 22–42; Senior and Watkins, 1966: 708 ff.).[4] An analysis of the 1940 census found that Puerto Ricans living in the United States had twice the average years of schooling of those in Puerto Rico (Senior and Watkins, 1966: 709).

Thus, up until the period of "the great migration," the "superiority of the migrant" was confirmed in the literature. However, subsequent studies that examined the post-1950 communities did not echo the "superior migrant" thesis, but focused more on the problems experienced by the migrants in the cities (see, for example, Wakefield, 1959; Padilla, 1958; Rand, 1958; Glazer and Moynihan, 1970; Sexton, 1966). Indeed, Senior and Watkins (1966) note that the average years of schooling ratio (between migrants and those still in Puerto Rico) was reduced in the 1950 and 1960 censuses.[5] They attribute this to increased numbers of "followers" as opposed to "deciders" coming as a result of the "family intelligence service." These followers were younger and from more rural backgrounds. In short, in the 1940s the migration was seen to be an urban, skilled migration, involving a predominance of women. In the 1950s, the migration was described as a predominantly male, unskilled, and rural migration.

5

Although the literature on Puerto Ricans in the states changed in focus, the evidence suggested that aside from higher proportions of rural migrants, the educational level (or "quality") of the migrants continued to be superior. For example, the ramp surveys conducted by the Planning Office in Puerto Rico between 1957 and 1962 found that each year showed increasing English proficiency and higher literacy levels among migrants than among the population as a whole, despite the fact that the majority of migrants during these years were coming from rural areas (Senior and Watkins, 1966).[6] Two subsequent islandwide surveys, made between 1962 and 1964, also found the migrants to have higher literacy rates than those on the island, and than previous migrants, and to come in the main (62%) from rural areas. Sandis's (1970) analysis of the Puerto Rican migrant population in the United States during the 1960s also showed educational and occupational selectivity relative to the island population. Finally, a U.S. Department of Labor (1974: 373) study of Puerto Ricans in poverty areas of New York in 1968–69 found that migrants still exhibited higher educational levels and English proficiency than those on the island.

The most recent comparison of migrants and nonmigrants finds migrants to have higher median levels of education—10.9 years, compared to 9.4 for the population of Puerto Rico as a whole.[7] This study also found higher proportions of college graduates among the migrant group—10.5% versus 9.4% for nonmigrants (Junta de Planificación de Puerto Rico, 1986: 20 ff.).

Why Did Puerto Ricans Come?

This question has been asked continually in the literature, and has resulted in numerous answers. For example, early theorists such as Chenault (1938) and Handlin (1959: 50 ff.) argued that overpopulation in Puerto Rico was the major factor inducing migration,[8] and that this overpopulation had come about as a result of health and medical improvements made under U.S. policies (Sánchez-Korrol, 1983). Senior and Watkins (1966), Mills et al. (1950), and Perloff (1950), on the other hand, argued that the pull of job opportunities was the major factor motivating migration. More recent researchers have tended to see migration as a response of surplus labor to the economic transformations occurring in Puerto Rico. Influenced by the larger context of economic and political dependence, these transformations have yielded increasingly larger numbers of displaced and surplus workers who were forced to migrate elsewhere for jobs (Reynolds and Gregory, 1965; Maldonado-Denis, 1972; Bonilla and Campos, 1981; Morales, 1986; Uriarte-Gastón, 1987; Padilla, 1987b).

More micro-level analyses have also examined economic push and pull factors (Fleisher, 1961, 1963; Glazer and Moynihan, 1970; Reynolds and Gregory, 1965; Pantoja, 1972; Rodríguez, 1973; Sánchez-Korrol, 1983). It has been found that when U.S. national income goes up and unemployment goes down, Puerto Rican migration increases. Relative wages and unemployment rates in Puerto Rico and the United States have also been found to affect migration to the United States and back to Puerto Rico (Fleisher, 1963; Friedlander, 1965; Maldonado, 1976).[9] Thus, Puerto Ricans migrate when job opportunities look better in the United States and/or when those opportunities appear worse in Puerto Rico. It has also been found that Puerto Ricans do *not* migrate to secure greater welfare benefits (Maldonado, 1976).

Other researchers have emphasized the role of U.S. companies in recruiting Puerto Rican labor to work in the United States (Morales, 1986; Maldonado, 1979; Piore, 1979; Lapp, 1986; Uriarte-Gastón, 1987).[10] Originally, Puerto Ricans were "greatly valued" by their employers because of their citizenship status and their agricultural background; they were seen to be "excellent workers" (Morales, 1986: 87). The low wages paid to these workers also produced "substantial profits" for their employers and enhanced the attractiveness of Puerto Rican laborers (Morales, 1986: 96).

Still other researchers cite the role of government in encouraging migration (Lapp, 1986; Padilla, 1987b; Maldonado, 1979; Senior and Watkins, 1966). Although the official position of the Puerto Rican government was that it did not encourage or discourage migration, Padilla (1987b: 53) maintains that the Puerto Rican government requested that the Federal Aviation Administration set low rates for air transportation between Puerto Rico and the United States. Lapp (1986) argues that the Puerto Rican government's Migration Division Office in New York facilitated migration.

Migration was undoubtedly a combination of all these factors. There were, in addition, other factors that have received less attention. For example, Sánchez-Korrol (1983) points out that the conferring of U.S. citizenship status in 1917, as well as the 1921 legislation restricting immigration, directly and indirectly induced Puerto Ricans to migrate. After the Second World War, there may also have been era-specific factors that contributed to the migration: greater participation by Puerto Ricans in the armed forces; pent-up travel demand; surplus aircraft and pilots, resulting in cheaper and more accessible air travel; and greater opportunities in the United States.

It cannot be denied that economic push factors often affected the decision to migrate—they still do. The most recent analysis of migrants leaving Puerto Rico found that the majority (69%) were *not* employed; this was especially the case for women (Junta de Planificación, 1986).[11] It is also likely that many Puerto Ricans were pulled by the promise (or hope) of a better life, such as the one they perceived Americans to have—a life to which they, as American citizens, were also entitled. They were also undoubtedly pulled by connections to family already in the United States. These connections expanded into networks that became self-reinforcing pulls that grew as the migration continued. Finally, Puerto Ricans were pulled to the United States by an adventurous spirit—a desire to try their luck in a new land, to strive for something better.

The Historical Context

Political Dependence

Perhaps what is most important in understanding the Puerto Rican migration is what is least visible—the historical context from which Puerto Ricans came. In the nineteenth century, Puerto Rico had been a receiving, not an exporting, center of people. Yet, in the 1950s and 1960s it began to experience a concentrated exodus (see Figure 1.1). Although this migration has fluctuated over the years, the flow has continued. In net terms it has been so significant that it has been referred to in the literature as the "Puerto Rican diaspora" (López and Petras, 1974). The net result is that in 1980 over 40% of Puerto Ricans lived outside of Puerto Rico, in the states (Uriarte-Gastón, 1987). The question that persists after all of the analyses and research is this: Why did so many leave a place often called the "isle of enchantment" ("la isla del encanto")?

Throughout Puerto Rico's long and rich history, Puerto Ricans have made concerted efforts to wrest a living from economic and political situations that were not to their advantage. In 1898, as part of its war with Spain, the United States invaded Puerto Rico and took it over. However, for the previous 400 years, Puerto Rico had been a Spanish possession. Columbus, on his second voyage to the new world in 1493, first landed on the island, which was then called *Boriquen* by the Taínos who lived there.[12] After the arrival of the Spanish, Puerto Rico began its existence as a mining center. Gold and silver were exploited, as was the labor of the Taíno Indians. Within a short period the Indians "disappeared," as did the gold and silver.

Spain, interested in retaining the island as a strategic base, encouraged the colonists to pursue more agricultural pursuits. It so "encouraged" the colonists that it forbade, under penalty of death, anyone from leaving the island for the newly discovered gold and silver mines in Mexico and Peru (Morales-Carrión, 1952: 88 ff.; Van Middledyk, 1915: chap. 3). In the seventeenth century, Puerto Rico (which means *rich port*) developed a growing trade in livestock, hides, linen, spices, and slaves. Because of Spain's restrictions on trade, however, much of it was contraband. Thus, early on Puerto Rico began to develop a survival strategy to deal with situations that were not to its advantage.

By the end of the eighteenth century, Spain, having been seriously defeated by England, decided to liberalize its policies in the colonies with regard to trade, immigration, and political rights. Having depleted its treasury, Spain turned to colonial trade as a way of replenishing and improving its economic position. With these more liberalized policies, by the nineteenth century Puerto Rico became a bustling trade center, as well as host to thousands of arriving immigrants. The population grew from 70,250 in 1775 to 330,051 in 1832. By the end of the nineteenth century the population had multiplied more than 13 times (Rodríguez, 1969: 25).

Not only did Puerto Rico grow tremendously during the nineteenth century, it also continued to enhance the diversity of its population. Although the bulk of the nineteenth-century immigrants probably came from Spain and its possessions, there are indications that a great many came from other European countries (Cifre de Loubriel, 1960). The present-day linguistic diversity of common Puerto Rican surnames reflects the varied origins of the migrants of the nineteenth century: Colberg, Wiscovitch, Petrovich, Franqui, Adams, Solivan. Both African slaves legally owned by Puerto Ricans and runaway slaves continued to arrive until 1873, when slavery was officially abolished. Slaves running away from other countries had been admitted to Puerto Rico as free men and had been allowed to earn a wage since 1750. By the time Puerto Rico legally abolished slavery, free Negroes outnumbered slaves on the island.

Puerto Rico's situation with regard to slavery and race relations was unusual. As Eric Williams (1970), distinguished historian and specialist in West Indian politics, points out, "The Puerto Rico situation was unique in the Caribbean, in that not only did the white population outnumber the people of color, but the slaves constituted an infinitesimal part of the total population and free labor predominated during the regime of slavery" (p. 280). Puerto Rico did not have the same need for slave labor as other islands with large plantation economies. With a small farming and diversified economy, it may have been seen as a less profitable, less wealthy colony. But if "Puerto Rico, by the conventional standards of the final quarter of the nineteenth century, ranked as one of the most backward sectors of the Caribbean economy, in intellectual perspective it was head and shoulders above its neighbors" (Williams, 1970: 292). Puerto Rico argued in cogent economic terms for the superiority of free labor over slave labor. This position distinguished it from other colonial possessions.

In the nineteenth century, Puerto Rican political development blossomed. By the end of the century, when the United States invaded the island, it appears that a strong sense of national identity and political articulation was firmly in place (Pico, 1986; Cruz-Monclova, 1958; Vivas, 1960; Lewis, 1963; López and Petras, 1974; Wagenheim and Jiménez de Wagenheim, 1973; Figueroa, 1974; Morales-Carrión, 1952; Zavala and Rodríguez, 1980; Liden, 1981; Dietz, 1986). This basic unity existed despite the political frictions and class divisions also evident then. The Puerto Rican community in New York in the late nineteenth century included many who were working for the independence of Puerto Rico and Cuba. Some of the Puerto Rican *independentistas* (independence advocates) assisted the United States in its invasion of Puerto Rico because they expected that the United States would help to liberate Puerto Rico from its ties with Spain. There was disappointment and disillusionment when it became clear that the United States would not grant greater autonomy or independence (Iglesias, 1980: 119–120; Berbusse, 1966; Lewis, 1963: 86; Dietz, 1986: 82).

Indeed, under the U.S. government there was less political and economic autonomy than Puerto Rico had enjoyed under the Autonomous Charter, which Spain had granted in 1897.[13] Although the Charter was opposed by some in Puerto Rico who felt it did not go far enough, it did give Puerto Rico the right to full representation in the Spanish Cortes (that is, Puerto Ricans could elect *voting* representatives to the Spanish Congress), the right to participate in negotiations between Spain and other countries affecting the commerce of the island, the right to ratify or reject commercial treaties affecting Puerto Rico, and the right to frame tariffs and fix customs on imports and exports. These rights were not retained under U.S. possession.

In many regards, the Autonomous Charter granted greater autonomy than Puerto Rico currently enjoys under the U.S. government (Morales, 1986).[14] At present, Puerto Rico is represented in the U.S. Congress by a resident commissioner who *cannot* vote. Puerto Ricans who are residents of Puerto Rico also cannot vote in national elections. Although they may be party members and may participate in the primaries, they cannot vote for president, nor can they send representatives to the Senate or the House of Representatives. The president and Congress can (and do), nonetheless, send Puerto Rican men to fight in U.S. wars.[15] In addition, Puerto Rico today does not have as much control over its commerce as the Charter had granted in 1897.[16] The construction of the recent Caribbean Basin Initiative, for example, did not give Puerto Rico the right to reject or ratify changes in tariffs or taxes that affect the island.

Economic Dependence

The political relationship between Puerto Rico and the United States made Puerto Rico not just politically dependent, but also economically dependent. The changes experienced by the Puerto Rican economy after the U.S. invasion were dramatic.[17] The economy went from a diversified, subsistence economy around the turn of the century with four basic crops produced for export (tobacco, cattle, coffee, and sugar) to a sugar-crop economy, with 60% of the sugar industry controlled by U.S. absentee owners (Steward, 1965; González, 1966: 21). The decline of the cane-based industry (combined with no reinvestment and continued population growth) in the 1920s resulted in high unemployment, poverty, and desperate conditions in Puerto Rico. These factors propelled the first waves of Puerto Rican migrants in search of a better life. The 1930s saw more migration, as workers sought to deal with the stagnant economic situation of the island.

In the 1940s, the Second World War boosted the flagging economy somewhat. The Puerto Rican government initiated a series of reforms and entered into what has been variously called its "state capitalist development phase" and its "socialist" venture.[18] A series of government-owned enterprises were established and run by the Puerto Rican Development Corporation; these included glass, pulp and paper, shoe leather, and clay products corporations as well as a hotel and a textile mill that were financed but not run by the government. Influenced by the New Deal philosophy, this program stressed both "social justice and economic growth" goals. It was, in these regards, "ahead of its time" (Dietz, 1986: 243).[19] Had this program succeeded, Puerto Rico would have achieved greater economic independence. However, these efforts were frustrated by a combination of technical problems and ideological opposition from Congress, the local press, business interests in both Puerto Rico and the states, and conservative legislators and government bureaucrats (Dietz, 1986; Carr, 1984).

Between 1947 and 1951, there was a changeover from government development of industry to promotion of private investment (Ross, 1976). The new approach was called Operation Bootstrap. A forerunner of the economic development strategies developed throughout the world later, the idea was to industrialize Puerto Rico by luring foreign companies, mainly from the United States, to Puerto Rico with the promise of low wage and tax incentives.[20] The tourism industry was also developed at this time. Puerto Rico began its industrialization thrust and its clear incorporation into an emerging global economy. Much in Puerto Rico improved during this period, including education, housing, and the quality of drinking water, electrification, and sewage systems, and roads and transportation facilities. To the residents of Puerto Rico there was a clear sense of development and progress and, for some, the sense of a more equitable income distribution.

However, the industry attracted to Puerto Rico in this period turned out to be increasingly capital intensive, to have little commitment to the development of the island, and to be integrated into sourcing and distribution networks in the United States or other countries, not in Puerto Rico. As a result, these industries had few indirect employment effects; the industrialization path chosen did not provide sufficient jobs. With increased population growth and displacement from traditional labor pursuits, the result was a growing surplus population that could not be accommodated in Puerto Rico's new industrial order. Much of the surplus labor migrated to the United States (Bonilla and Campos, 1981; Morales, 1986; Uriarte-Gastón, 1987).

What happened in Puerto Rico with Operation Bootstrap fore-shadowed what was to happen in numerous ex-colonies and developing countries—the development of "off-shoring" operations (movement of production to sites with cheap labor) in these countries by foreign capital or multinational corporations. Just as investment, labor, finance, and finished and intermediate products flowed more easily between the United States and Puerto Rico, so the new global economy is one in which all economic factors flow more easily from place to place. But Puerto Rico's economic development not only foreshadowed that of others, it also was part of the same evolution toward a world economy. As Padilla (1987b: 53) states: "The emigration of Puerto Rican workers to the United States took place within the context of an ever-increasing capitalist penetration of the Island and its concomitant absorption into the world capitalist economy."

Thus, perhaps the most important factor driving the Puerto Rican migration is the one least visible to the migrants: the political and economic relationship between Puerto Rico and the United States. But for this tie, U.S. tax breaks would not have been granted to U.S. firms doing business in Puerto Rico; duty-free export and import would not have been allowed between Puerto Rico and the United States; capital could not have flowed without controls; and American factories and American management would not have entered the Puerto Rican economy in such numbers.[21] In addition, without this context, increases in national income or employment in the United States would *not* have provoked emigration as quickly from Puerto Rico; there would not have been open borders, a military experience for Puerto Rican men and women, citizenship status, accessible and frequent air travel, and early communications and educational systems tied to the colonial center.

Although the political and economic context of the Puerto Rican migration has been critical, it has often escaped the consciousness of the migrants themselves. They do not fully see that their jobs have been lost because companies have left the island, or because the labor market demands fewer low-skill workers. Instead, their reasons for deciding to leave their homeland are personalized; they decide to leave because they lost their jobs or were laid off, because they separated from their spouses or wanted a change of scene, or because they were needed by the family in New York. The migrants do not usually see the larger structural forces that create these personal situations. Often they do not see that families break up because husbands are without jobs, or because the pay for men and women is insufficient for supporting their families. Very few migrants see that they are or were part of a surplus labor pool. Fewer see that surplus labor is a by-product of the economic development strategy or of global economic trends. In short, the decision to leave is seldom seen by the migrant in macroeconomic terms.[22]

Colonial Immigrants

Despite the fact that Puerto Rico and the United States came to be joined through an act of conquest, this relationship has often been understated in the literature. This has been particularly true in much of the early literature on Puerto Ricans in the states. Puerto Ricans tended to be seen as the last in the continuum of immigrant groups to the United States (Chenault, 1938; Gordon, 1949; Mills et al., 1950; Handlin, 1959; Rand, 1958; Wakefield, 1959; Glazer and Moynihan, 1970; Senior, 1965; Sexton, 1966; Fitzpatrick, 1971; Sowell, 1981).[23] Although Puerto Ricans were (and to a large extent still are) like previous immigrants in that they were foreign in culture, language, and experience in the United States, this comparison obscured the fact that Puerto Ricans differed from European immigrants to the United States in a number of significant ways. Unlike such groups, Puerto Ricans entered the United States as citizens, served in the U.S. armed forces, had accessible transportation to their country of origin, came from a strategic base of the United States, and had a Caribbean (as opposed to a European) cultural and racial background.[24]

Oppositional Mentalities

What influence has Puerto Rico's colonial history had on the development of its people? People with colonial histories have in common structures of political, economic, and cultural dominance that influence their societies in hegemonic fashion. In some ways, it is a very old story—the story of conquest. Conquest establishes power relations very clearly. The conquered can resist dominance, support it, or ignore it. Generally, in colonial situations all of these reactions occur. The histories of colonized countries are written by those who opposed the colonial power, those who favored greater association or integration, and those who argued for a status quo relationship. These patterns are not surprising. They are dialectical reactions to the structure within which people live. As in other dimensions of life, some people will accept an oppressive situation, others will fight it, and still others will deny its existence.

What is of interest, however, is that it is inherent to the situation of colonialism that forces antithetical to the imposition of foreign domination develop. Indeed, it is these forces that often come to frame the colonial debate. Whether these forces become the dominant ones, as in the case of the American Revolution, or whether they are politically marginalized, as in the case of Puerto Rico, the articulation of resistance, defiance, and struggle against oppression is often part of the *realpolitik* of colonies. Thus, regardless of the political position of Puerto Ricans vis-à-vis status, they are aware of alternative positions and evaluate the soundness of those positions within their own context of logic, practicality, and relevance. This degree of "consciousness" may make those immigrants with a colonial past quite different from those without such a relationship to the host country.

The colonial structure affects both the colonized and the colonizer. Implicit (and sometimes explicit) in the colonial relationship is the psychological fallout of the relationship. Articulated most eloquently by Fanon (1968) and Memmi (1965), and in fictionalized form by Achebe (1959), these psychological outgrowths involve myriad relations between the colonized and the colonizer. To note just a few: the colonizer's view of the colonized as "subjects"; colonial ambivalence about the colonial history; and historically evolved defenses against encroachments on one's culture, sense of dignity, and way of life. Finally, just as colonial settings produce "colonial mentalities" (i.e., the mentalities of those who acquiesce to the dominant power) (Fanon, 1968), they are also inherent breeders of "oppositional mentalities" (i.e., in those who oppose the system in all its representations).[25]

Consequences of a Colonial History

What the consequences of this colonial inheritance are for Puerto Ricans in the United States is still unresolved. There have been some erroneous assumptions and some more recent intriguing observations. On the error side, there is the assumption that Puerto Rico's political dependence has bred a political passivity among its citizenry and that this has been transported to the states. The basic argument is as follows: Because of Puerto Rico's long periods of political dependency, first with Spain and then with the United States, Puerto Ricans are afflicted by political passivity; indeed, they have formed a colonial or welfare mentality with regard to government.[26] Glazer and Moynihan (1970: xx), for example, suggest that low voter participation among Puerto Ricans in the United States is tied to the fact "that attitudes developed toward the paternalistic government of Puerto Rico were easily transferred to the government of New York."[27] Yet voting participation has, for some time, been dramatically higher in Puerto Rico (83%) than in the United States as a whole (46%) (Rodríguez, 1974b: 96; Carr, 1984: 243).

In addition, political activity cannot be measured by voting patterns alone. Nelson (1984) found that Puerto Ricans in New York were, like Hispanics as a whole, weak in voting participation relative to other ethnic groups. However, he found Puerto Ricans to be more active than other groups in protesting, signing petitions, and joining community organizations, and moderately active in contacting public officials.[28] Moreover, if newspaper coverage is an indication of political activity, then it would appear that Puerto Ricans in the states are a highly politically oriented group. A recent computerized search of articles in major newspapers for the period 1976–86 indicated that of the 103 articles mentioning Puerto Ricans in the United States, 35% dealt with terrorist activities and political activity in New York.[29]

Political Interlacing

There are, however, some recent observations in the literature that may be more accurate regarding the consequences of Puerto Ricans' colonial history. First is the persistent political interlacing that exists between Puerto Rican communities in the United States and Puerto Rico, evidence of which is found in a number of areas.[30] The Puerto Rican government's Migration Division in New York made possible the early establishment of a connection between the Puerto Rican government and the Puerto Rican community in New York. Indeed, some argue that this agency has served as the official representative of the Puerto Rican community in New York (Lapp, 1986) and has in this regard thwarted the political recognition of political organizations and leadership from New York (Jennings and Rivera, 1984). The annual Puerto Rican Day parades in different northeastern cities bring the mayors of Puerto Rican towns as honorary guests. Spanish-language newspapers, radio, and TV routinely cover events in Puerto Rico. More specifically, the campaigns of politicians running for office in Puerto Rico and in New York have both included visits to the other place. (Baver, 1984: 45, 49, 51). Most recently, the government of Puerto Rico has sponsored a voter registration drive in New York City.

Finally, there are the fierce debates on "the national question"— whether the Puerto Rican nation is to be defined by its people or by its territory—that have taken place in academic and nonacademic circles (Falcón, 1984b). The question that follows and, to a large extent, fuels the debate is, Where should the allegiance and involvement be—with the island's struggle (for independence) or with the struggles of those in the state *colonias*? The general political interlacing has been so prevalent that it has led one author to refer to it as the problem of "umbilicalism," implying that the umbilical cord to Puerto Rico has not been cut (Jennings, 1984a, 1984b).

Dominance and Success

Some authors have made the telling observation that in general "dominated minorities" do not seem to prosper in their dominant countries (Ogbu, 1978; Cummins, 1984, 1986). At the same time, there is evidence that these same dominated minorities prosper outside of the framework of dominance. This has been found particularly in the area of education. Cummins (1986), for example, cites the experience of Finns in Australia compared with the Finns in Sweden and the Burakumin in Japan compared with the Burakumin in the United States. West Indians in England compared with West Indians in New York and Puerto Ricans in St. Croix compared with Puerto Ricans in New York City could also be added to this list.[31] These contrasting experiences raise the question of why this should be the case and whether there is at work a colonial holdover that impedes the success of immigrants with a colonial history.

Resistance to Cultural and Linguistic Assimilation

Padilla (1987b: 54) makes a very different argument; he says that Puerto Ricans have been resisting American colonial domination since conquest and that this struggle toward liberation continues in different forms on the mainland. One of the historical forms this resistance has taken has been the struggle to "retain their culture and language even during periods of intense repression" (Padilla, 1987b: 54). Contributing to this perspective is the observation that Puerto Ricans have shown a proclivity *not* to abandon their culture, language, and identity. In Puerto Rico, despite over 88 years of American rule and clear, ongoing Americanization of the culture, Puerto Ricans continue to speak Spanish and to use Spanish as the language of instruction.[32] This is in contrast to the experience of the Philippines, which was also acquired by the United States in 1898, but was given its independence.[33] Nor has Puerto Rico evolved a patois, as in other colonies, that combines the colonizer's language with indigenous languages or phrases—although there are clearly many Americanisms in Puerto Rican speech.[34]

Cultural Affirmation

In the literature on Puerto Ricans in the United States there are other findings that appear to be supportive of the Padilla perspective. We find, for example, that "the general hypothesis emerging from studies of Spanish-English bilingualism among Puerto Ricans in New York City is that there exists a broad allegiance to maintenance of Spanish as a marker of cultural, social, and political identity" (Duran, 1983: 27). The 1980 census data also indicate that a very high percentage of Puerto Ricans in New York speak Spanish at home (see Chapters 2 and 3). Moreover, there is continuing evidence that both first and second generations identify as Puerto Rican, use Spanish at home, and view Puerto Rican culture positively (Rogler and Cooney, 1984; Colleran, 1984; Martínez, 1988; Rodríguez, 1975; Díaz, 1984; Ginorio, 1979; Vásquez, 1985; Padilla, 1985, 1987b). As Colleran (1984: 3) states, "It is evident that the young people are retaining their Puerto Rican heritage as a symbol of their identity even when they were not born in Puerto Rico and have little direct connection with the island and its culture."

It is also of interest that many of the most personally successful Puerto Ricans have continued to identify strongly with being Puerto Rican or Hispanic.[35] Apparently, for this group, "making it" does not include severing ties to the community or to ethnic identity. Indeed, Padilla (1987b: 12) observes that in Chicago the emerging Puerto Rican middle class and the Puerto Rican working labor force have developed a "continuous intra-ethnic unity and solidarity," wherein both groups express their class interests in explicitly ethnic terms. He argues that this has occurred

17

because Puerto Ricans have entered an American economic context not suited for the creation of a class-conscious workers' movement on the factory floor. Whatever the exact reasons, Puerto Rican immigrants have maintained a continuing and positive identification as Puerto Ricans, despite a generally harsh and economically difficult experience in the United States.[36]

External Factors

However, the reluctance to leave behind one's cultural roots cannot be seen purely as the result of an internalized colonial experience. Ethnicity is not sustained only internally.[37] The long-lasting quality of Puerto Rican identity is also related to the disadvantaged position of the group as a whole, and to the "continued revitalization of ethnic symbols through the process of labor migration" (Tienda, 1985). Indeed, it has been argued that bilingualism is a necessity for a people, such as the Puerto Ricans, with "circulating migration"; that is, they are involved in constant back-and-forth migration to and from Puerto Rico (Flores et al., 1981; Bonilla, 1974; Bean and Tienda, 1988).[38] Even though not everyone is involved in the circulating migration, for an individual to function in both or either community, in familial networks, and the general community, it is important that he or she be both bilingual and bicultural.[39]

Residential segregation or concentration has also had an impact on the ethnic identification of Puerto Ricans. In turn, the concentration of Hispanic children in particular schools has affected and will continue to affect the future identity of Puerto Ricans and other groups.[40] As long as groups are located in residential ethnic enclaves and in segmented job sectors, ethnicity will persevere. Identity will then be politically articulated via a number of cultural, artistic, and social mediums. The unanswered question, of course, is why the segmentation and segregation occur and persist in the first place. As has been pointed out above, the mode of incorporation into the United States is a factor, but the historical moment of that entry must also be considered (Bean and Tienda, 1988; Padilla, 1987b); this factor will be covered in Chapter 4.

Other Colonial (Im)migrants

Given the historical as well as current significance of the political and economic relationship between the United States and Puerto Rico, perhaps a more propitious avenue for future analysis of the Puerto Rican experience

18

would be to compare it with the experiences of other colonial immigrants, such as Algerians, Tunisians, Moroccans, and West or East Indians, who have immigrated to English, French, and Dutch "fatherlands" over the past two decades. Despite the independence of many of these former colonies, there appear to be broad parallels with Puerto Rico. These former or present colonial immigrants have migrated to the colonial center after the Second World War for reasons similar to those that drove the Puerto Rican migration.[41]

Having migrated from colonial peripheries, these colonial people of color have ended up in similar situations of segregation.[42] They have all come to live in ethnically homogeneous (ghetto) areas, to work in similar jobs or job sectors, to "service" their "own kind," and, finally, to be educated in similar, often inferior, schools. At present these ethnic enclaves give every indication of persisting beyond the second and third generations. In many instances, these communities are also characterized by lower socioeconomic conditions.[43] The racial and ethnic visibility of these communities makes them prominent additions to the working-class areas of the host countries.

It is important to understand how situations of segregation quickly become all-inclusive and circular. Residential segregation determines educational options, particularly in the early grades. Subsequent educational attainments determine labor market power (i.e., technical or professional skills) which, in turn, influences income. Labor market income, in large part, determines housing options. These situations of segregation are further reinforced by the development of ethnic entrepreneurs who cater to their own ethnic communities and/or to other foreign workers. These developments are not all bad. Income generated by such entrepreneurial efforts sometimes stays within the communities. Such communities may also become fountainheads for cultural and artistic developments. To some degree because of racial differences, the second generations in these communities have not lost their visibility or their ethnic-minority status. Indeed, they have evolved new versions of ethnicity and cultural differences. These groups have come from the Third World into the First World to become racial-ethnic minorities.

Notes

1   In his review of legal decisions concerning the political status of Puerto Rico, del Valle (1984: 14) finds that Puerto Rico's current status is that of an unincorporated territory of the United States—pretty much the same status it had when the United States acquired it in 1898.

The status of Puerto Rico as a colony has been debated many times. For the past 11 years, a resolution has been introduced by supporters of Puerto Rican independence to the U.N. Special Committee on Decolonization. The resolution has passed in committee, but the United States has succeeded in keeping it off the agenda of the General Assembly. The resolution has recognized the right of the Puerto Rican people to self-determination and has condemned the repression of the independence movement in Puerto Rico.

For an extensive study by the U.S. government and Puerto Rico of the legal and constitutional aspects of the status issue, see the United States-Puerto Rico Commission on the Status of Puerto Rico (1966: Vol. 1). See Cabranes (1979) for a similarly extensive analysis of the status of Puerto Ricans as citizens.

2   A new and different approach to this is taken by Pedraza-Bailey (1985), whose in-depth analysis of Cuban and Mexican immigrants examines the interactive roles of immigrants' social class of origin, the economic or political push of the migration, and the role of the state in aiding or hindering structural assimilation.

3   A similar issue has preoccupied Puerto Rico. The fear of a Puerto Rico "brain drain" has been a long-standing concern. In the early 1960s, Reynolds and Gregory (1965) concluded that migrants were *not* stripping the island of the cream of its labor force. Their study found that most migrants had fewer skills, were younger and from rural backgrounds, and had jobs prior to leaving the island and lower incomes.

Recently, however, concern has again been expressed over the departure of many professionals from Puerto Rico. There have also been journalistic accounts that depict the most recent migration of Puerto Ricans as a professional migration. This assertion has not been substantiated in the literature. Ortiz (1986), utilizing cohort analysis data for 1960, 1970, and 1980, found there were no significant differences between recent migrants and earlier migrants. Rivera-Batiz (1987a) arrived at similar conclusions, but found agricultural laborers and technical workers overrepresented among 1984 migrants to the states. It may be that what is a significant and real phenomenon may not yet be well captured in the data because U.S.-standardized occupational classifications do not accurately reflect class positions in Puerto Rico.

That the brain drain concern persists is evident in Rivera-Batiz's (1987b) note that there are other indications of a drastic emigration of engineers and of intensive recruitment by U.S. companies of high-level professional personnel. Indeed, he goes so far as to say that "there is a remarkable resistance in the Island's more highly-trained personnel to leaving, in spite of considerable worsening of economic conditions during the time period examined" (p. 2).

4   The very high proportion of urban migrants from large cities in this study is surprising; my own observations and descriptive statements by other authors (López, 1973: 322; Handlin, 1959: 51) would not have led to this conclusion. Since the names of these cities were also the names of *distritos* (districts), it is possible that respondents in answering this question may have been referring to the fact that they lived in the larger area, rather than in the city itself. The distrito would have included rural areas as well as the large city.

5   To a degree, the decreased ratio was to be expected as the general level of education in Puerto Rico increased.

6   These surveys were subsequently discontinued because of methodological questions raised in 1962 about the validity of the ramp survey. Two factors confounded validity: the increased numbers of Puerto Ricans traveling as tourists to and from Puerto Rico, and the farm labor program, which "began to function in an organized fasion," that is, under an agreement between employers and the Puerto Rico Department of Labor, in 1948 (Senior and Watkins, 1966: 715). The islandwide surveys noted in the text were developed as alternate measures.

7   Migrants consisted of a sample of migrants leaving Puerto Rico in the period 1982–83. Data for Puerto Rico as a whole came from the 1980 census. In the migrant group, women had an even higher (11.6) median educational level.

8   See History Task Force (1979: 23 ff.) for a critique of studies of Puerto Ricans that have focused on human capital characteristics. The general points made are that such studies are often politically motivated and that they are not very useful, because the reasons for the failures and frustrations of Puerto Ricans to find a stable means of securing a livelihood are not to be found in the characteristics of the migrants themselves.

9   Santiago (1985) critiques the approach some of these studies take; he argues that they look at aggregate migration flow per unit of time, while the model predictions refer to individual migrant behavior.

10 Of particular interest is an article titled "Labor Recruited," which appeared in a 1944 issue of *Business Week* (April 29: 114). This article noted that three large U.S. firms were recruiting skilled Puerto Rican workers for jobs on the mainland in cooperation with the War Manpower Commission, and that the Commission expected that more workers would be recruited by other firms.

11 However, as the Junta de Planificación (1986) points out, employment was not the decisive factor for all those leaving, because 52% of those with more than 16 years of education had jobs.

12 This is the origin of the term *Boricua*, which today means Puerto Rican and sometimes assumes political or nationalist connotations. *Borinquen* is still used to refer to the island of Puerto Rico, and it is used often in verse, song, and colloquial conversations.

13 The Autonomous Charter established self-government for both Cuba and Puerto Rico (Commonwealth of Puerto Rico Office, 1964). Recently, Carr (1984: 20) has argued that "autonomy came to Puerto Rico on Cuban coattails," that it came as part of a package deal in a last-minute bid to save Cuba for Spain. Regardless of the motivation of Spain in granting this Charter, the fact remains that it would not have granted any Charter to Puerto Rico if there had not been persistent pressure from Puerto Ricans to do so. (For details of the transition of authority to the United States, see Berbusse, 1966.)

14 See note 1.

15 In World War II, Puerto Ricans had the second largest number of wartime casualties (after the Hawaiians) (Falcón, 1984a: 37). More recently, *Caribbean Business* (April 9, 1987: 8) cited figures that indicated that "the participation of Puerto Rican soldiers in combat in Viet Nam was disproportionately high."

16 Bean and Tienda (1988) point out that, in return for lack of political representation, Puerto Ricans are exempt from federal income taxes and excise taxes.

17 There were also changes in class formations. For discussion of class structures in the nineteenth century and after 1898, see Baggs (1962), Brau (1894),

21

Berbusse (1966), Carroll (1899), Cruz-Monclova (1958), Descartes (1943), Figueroa (1974), Goodsell (1965), González (1966), Hanson (1960: 54 ff.), Lewis (1963), Reynolds and Gregory (1965: 10–12), Stahl (1965), Steward (1956), Van Middledyk (1915), and Vivas (1960).

18 For analyses of the New Deal period in Puerto Rico, see Stahl (1965), González (1966), Reynolds and Gregory (1965), Hanson (1960), Baggs (1962), Goodsell (1965), Lewis (1963), Carr (1984), Dietz (1986), and Wells (1969).

19 Dietz (1986) argues that the contradiction of pursuing both these goals in a colonial capitalist economy became too intense once the relative autonomy of the war years was gone.

20 For analyses of the impact of the industrialization program on Puerto Rico, see Reynolds and Gregory (1965), Friedlander (1965), Galbraith and Soto (1953), Bonilla and Campos (1981), Andic (1964), Pantoja (1972), Fleisher (1963), and Maldonado-Denis (1972).

21 The distinctions between colonies and client-states have become less clear-cut in recent years. In today's world economy we may no longer need a colonial framework to find conjunctures of political and economic dependence that induce migration. Economic dependence and political dependence are no longer so clearly distinguishable when it comes to the flow of labor, capital, or goods.

22 A story comes to mind that illustrates how economic circumstances influence the decision to migrate. I have been to Puerto Rico many times and have met very few Puerto Ricans who have never been to the states. On a recent trip, I met such a woman; she and her husband had never gone to the states. I asked why, and she said, "I don't know, I guess we always had to stay and mind the store my husband owned." Since their country store had done quite well, they never had an economic need to leave. Her children, on the other hand, had all been to the states. The only one who hadn't stayed in the states was the one who inherited the store.

23 This European immigrant group model has been referred to as the "assimilationist" model. Portes and Bach (1985: 336 ff.) find that the assimilationist school tends to emphasize an equilibrium-restoring system and the achievement of individual mobility through personal characteristics. They do not find support for this perspective in their longitudinal study of Cuban and Mexican immigrants.

Blauner (1972: 303) also argued earlier that minority groups and European immigrant groups did not follow the same assimilationist model. He maintained that minorities differ from immigrants in that they experience forced entry into larger society, subjection to forms of unfree labor that restrict physical and social mobility and political participation of the group, and cultural policy that constrains, transforms, or destroys their original values, orientations, and ways of life.

24 The military experience accounts for a significant share of migrants leaving Puerto Rico and later returning (Junta de Planificación, 1986).

Ramos and Morales (1985) argue that in general Hispanics differ from previous immigrant groups in the following respects: (1) the absence of choice that initially characterized their participation in the United States (thus, Mexican and Puerto Rican lands were ceded as war booty, Cubans arrived as reluctant exiles, and current Central and Latin Americans come out of political and economic necessity); (2) their proximity to the United States, which has

22

historically facilitated back-and-forth migration; (3) their migration at a time of significant economic shifts in the United States; and (4) the unique political economic context, which, combined with the 1965 immigration law, aided the immigration of Third World Latin American peoples. Díaz (1984: 40) also points out that Mexicans have great accessibility to their homeland because of the increasing movement across the border; this serves as "a cultural reinforcement that did not exist for earlier immigrant groups."

25 Those with colonial mentalities accept as correct and legitimate that those in power are superior in most matters, while the colonized are inferior.

26 Anderson (1965: 2) has said, "Few areas of the world have lived longer in unrelieved dependency."

27 C. Wright Mills also argued that "Puerto Ricans were conditioned not to challenge governmental policies concerning their life chances; instead their island background encouraged them to seek help from friends" (cited in Jennings and Rivera, 1984: 8).

28 See Guzmán (1984) and Fuentes (1984a), who depict the active political involvement of Puerto Ricans in two significant areas: community control in the educational system and delivery of services in the barrios. See also Falcón (1984a; 1984b), Jennings (1984a, 1984b), Rivera (1984), and Baver (1984) for analyses of the Puerto Rican political experience in the states.

29 Other areas of Puerto Rican life received far less attention. Only 10% of the articles looked at the social conditions of Puerto Ricans, and many of these covered tangential issues, such as occasional spotlights on Puerto Rican groups organized to deal with social conditions. While Puerto Rican drama and art were the focus of more of the articles (18%), the Puerto Rican Day parade and the Fiesta de San Juan accounted for only 5% of all the articles. The papers reviewed were the *New York Times*, the *Wall Street Journal*, and the *Christian Science Monitor*.

30 This interlacing of political concerns has been evident since the nineteenth century, when Puerto Rican and Cuban patriots used New York City as a base from which to plan political action in their home countries (Iglesias, 1980). The "century-old presence" of a politically active Puerto Rican community in New York is detailed in Falcón (1984b). Independence party chapters in New York have been a continuing phenomenon, for example, the Nationalist party of the 1950s, the Movimiento Pro Independencia of the 1960s, and the Puerto Rican Socialist Party of the 1970s and 1980s.

31 Sowell (1981) discusses West Indians' success in New York, while Carby (1982) discusses their difficulties in British school systems. Mintz (1972) explores the success of Puerto Ricans in St. Croix in the fields of merchandizing, importing, and retailing.

32 This practice has not been arrived at by accident. For a history of the conflicts over language policy in Puerto Rico, see Rodríguez Bou (1966), Lewis (1963), Rodríguez (1973), and Santiago-Santiago (1987: 1–4).

33 In the Philippines, English was useful in uniting diverse language groups; in Puerto Rico, such diversity did not exist—the population spoke the same language, Spanish.

34 For analyses and discussions of the speech patterns of Puerto Ricans in the United States, see Fishman et al. (1971), Fishman and Keller (1982; especially papers by Lipski, Milán, Pousada, Zentella, and Poplack), Amastae and Olivares (1982; especially Zentella), Varo (1971), and Zentella (1981).

35 One is reminded of the independence-oriented group in Puerto Rico, which is composed of many class backgrounds, with perhaps an overrepresentation of the middle and upper strata. This is a group that continues to reproduce itself, regardless of the level of political repression experienced or the lack of economic gain to such an identification.

36 Some might argue that the more disadvantaged the situation of a group, the greater the tendency toward in-group solidarity and ethnic identification. Nelson and Tienda (1985) found an inverse relationship between Hispanic ethnicity and socioeconomic status.

37 Herbstein (1983) proposes another external factor that maintains ethnicity. She argues that the political structure in New York provided the opportunity for Puerto Ricans in New York to become a politicized ethnic group. She argues that it is the dialectic between official policy and grass-roots adaptations that underlies the emergence of an ethnic group "for itself."

38 The term "circulating migration" was introduced and developed by Bonilla and Campos (1981) and Bonilla (1985). It refers to the need of surplus labor to migrate back and forth between the island and the states in search of economic opportunities. It has recently been used in the journalistic media to explain the lack of progress of Puerto Ricans in the United States. That is, it is suggested that because Puerto Ricans are constantly flying back and forth they do not stay long enough in one place to progress; they also do not develop the commitment they need to endure the hardships necessary to succeed in the United States (*Wall Street Journal*, January 23, 1986: 1; *Los Angeles Times*, March 16, 1986: pt. 4; *New York Times*, June 5, 1987: B1; August 28, 1987: A31). However, there are to date few data to support the contention that a great many Puerto Ricans are involved in this back-and-forth flow, nor do we have clear data on the volume or nature of the flow (Rodríguez, 1987).

39 Zentella (1981: 228) cites the following as important factors contributing to Puerto Rican bilingualism and biculturation: the political status of Puerto Rico; the proximity of the island; the availability of fast, modern travel; and the class background and racial mixture of Puerto Ricans. She also concludes that Puerto Ricans' participation in social and educational movements may alter the usual historical pattern of linguistic assimilation for immigrants to the United States: "Contrary to the experience of other non-English speaking migrations to the U.S., Puerto Ricans will likely maintain their language beyond the second generation."

40 The majority of Hispanic children are in schools that have significant proportions of other Hispanic children. New York State figures indicate that as of 1984, 68% of Hispanic students were in schools that were 30% or more Hispanic. Only 10% of Hispanic children were in schools that had less than 10% Hispanic students (Prieto, 1984). It can be anticipated that this concentration will contribute to a continuing Hispanic presence and identification.

41 The term *center* in this context refers to those developed market economies that control through economic and/or military power the trade, financial, and other economic relationships throughout the world economy. *Periphery* refers to developing countries, whose economies are largely determined by the center.

42 The term *people of color* as used here implies positive acknowledgment of color, as opposed to being defined in terms of not having a "white" color or not

being "white." It is used by those who see themselves as beige, tan, black, yellow, red, or whatever, as opposed to not white or nonwhite. It is possible to be of an equivalent "white" color to "whites" in the United States but still be a "person of color'', or belong to "people of color." The term also implies a unity with other groups who are defined as nonwhite in the United States, but it allows for the unique differences of culture, color, and perspective of each of the groups.

43 It is unclear whether, *ceteris paribus*, the experience of white Australians moving to Britain is different (economically, as well as socially) from that of Australian aborigines, of fair-skinned East Indians, or of Black Jamaicans. Ogbu (1978: 244) maintains that white immigrants to Britain do make greater social and economic progress than "colored" people, regardless of generation.

2

BEYOND THE CENSUS DATA:
A PORTRAIT OF THE COMMUNITY

In this chapter we will examine the perspective from which Puerto Ricans are often viewed: the perspective of the data. Utilizing the best available data, we will look at the Puerto Rican community in terms of the standard indicators used in the literature. The data are first presented, then analyzed and interpreted. In examining the data critically, going beneath and beyond it, we can explore questions the data do not answer, and the methodological limitations of data alone are demonstrated. The purpose of this approach is to provide as full a picture as possible of the Puerto Rican community; the reader must remember that the data alone are not the people.

In general, the socioeconomic data on Puerto Ricans and Blacks paint pictures that are similarly distressing. But in almost all of the tables generated for this chapter, Puerto Ricans have ranked below Blacks. However, this chapter departs from convention in that it downplays comparisons between Puerto Ricans and Blacks, for a number of reasons. First, the issue is not who is more disadvantaged, but that both groups are considerably disadvantaged relative to Whites. Second, the primary purpose of the chapter is not to highlight relative disadvantages, but to examine more closely what can be inferred from the data about the situation of Puerto Ricans.

There appears to be an emerging trend in contemporary public policy analysis to state that Puerto Ricans "have become more similar to blacks over time" (Tienda and Jensen, 1986: 41). While it may be true that, in a narrow data sense, Puerto Ricans and Blacks are similar, in a cultural sense, Puerto Ricans are quite distinct from Blacks. Puerto Ricans speak another language, come from a cultural ambience that is more Latin American than North American, and have migration patterns that are quite distinct from those of Black Americans. A danger of comparing Blacks and Puerto Ricans in this way is that it may lead to similar conclusions and policies for both, when distinct approaches are clearly called for, for instance, in education policy.

26

Advantages and Disadvantages of the Data

The census analysis presented here focuses, in the main, on the Puerto Rican population in New York City, for several reasons. For a number of decades, NYC was the place where the majority of Puerto Ricans in the United States lived. Second, the concentration of Puerto Ricans in NYC is still greater than elsewhere. Third, most of the research on Puerto Ricans has focused on Puerto Ricans in New York.[1] The use of New York City census data also presents certain limitations, however, most important of which is the recurring undercount problem.[2] A second limitation is that the analysis of the decennial census data is, in the main, limited to cross-sectional presentation of data. As such, changes over time are not covered and the time order of the variables is not explored.

On the other hand, these census data *do* give us a fairly accurate picture of the way things are for Puerto Ricans today. The data are relatively recent and are based on the largest counts possible. The data also allow us to see the relative situation of Puerto Ricans vis-à-vis other groups. Thus, we have a reliable picture of where Puerto Ricans stand today relative to other groups measured by the same indicators. Also, with regard to the undercount, were an estimate of the undercount included in this analysis, the already difficult picture evident with these unadjusted figures would in all probability be more accentuated, because those who are *not* counted by the census tend to be marginal to the labor force or to have low incomes.

It should be borne in mind, however, that these are New York City figures and that today there are more Puerto Ricans living outside of New York City than in New York City. A comparison, along selected indicators, of Puerto Ricans in New York City and in the United States as a whole indicates the New York City population is in some regards quite different from the national Puerto Rican population. As Table 2.1 indicates, in 1980 mean household income was considerably lower in New York City and the proportion of female heads of household, and of individuals in poverty, was considerably higher. Differences in unemployment rates were also evident, but these differences may be related to the lower labor force participation rates of Puerto Ricans in New York City. The New York City Puerto Rican population is similar to Puerto Rican populations in all states in that its education, income, labor force status, and poverty rates were generally worse than those of other groups. Nonetheless, there are areas where the Puerto Rican profile is quite different from that in New York—for example, in Florida, Texas, and California—and where Puerto Ricans showed better scores than other minorities.[3]

Table 2.1

Puerto Ricans in New York City and in the United States, Selected Indicators

	New York City	United States
Mean years of education		
(individuals 25 years old and older)	9.4	9.98
Female-headed households (%)	33.4	23.67
Unemployment (%)		
males	7.6	11.12
females	4.2	12.67
Labor force participation rate (%)		
males	65.6	70.24
females	33.7	39.73
Below poverty level (%)	34.9	29.47
Mean household income	$12,896	$14,930
Totals	27,999	62,755

Source: New York City data derived from sample of 1980 Public Use Microdata Sample, 5% A files, New York City boroughs; U.S. data derived from U.S. Bureau of the Census (1985: 2).

The Data Picture

Demography. In 1985 there were 2.562 million Puerto Ricans residing in the United States and another 3.270 million in Puerto Rico. Together, the two groups constituted 28.86% of all the Latinos within U.S. borders (see Figure 2.1).[4] In New York City in 1980, there were 1,036,680 Puerto Ricans, constituting the largest Hispanic group (60.45% of all Latinos).[5] Since Puerto Ricans constitute 12.67% of the total New York City population, one out of every eight New Yorkers is Puerto Rican. The majority of NYC Puerto Ricans live in the Bronx (37%) and in Brooklyn (32%), with smaller numbers in Manhattan (19.71%), Queens (9.50%), and Staten Island (1.29%) (U.S. Department of Commerce, 1980).

Sex. Overall, in the NYC Puerto Rican population, there are about 54 women for every 46 men.[6] If we control for age, we find that the numbers of males and females born are roughly the same. However, at about the age of puberty, males begin to disappear. This continues through the older ages, when women begin to outlive men. Thus, by the time Puerto Ricans reach the age of 30, for every five Puerto Rican women there are four Puerto Rican men (see Figure 2.2).[7]

Age. Puerto Ricans are quite young, on the whole. Their median age of 23.7 is considerably less than the median ages of White women (40) and

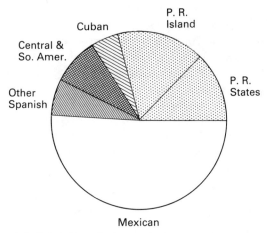

Figure 2.1 Spanish-Origin Population in the United States, 1985
Source: U.S. Bureau of the Census (1985).

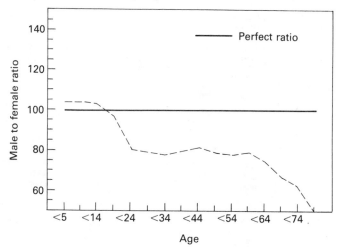

Figure 2.2 Puerto Rican Sex Ratio, New York State, 1980
Source: 1980 Census, New York State.

White men (34.8). It is also less than those of Black women (29.5) and Black men (25.5) in New York State.[8] This, plus high fertility levels for correspondingly younger Puerto Rican women, means that the Puerto Rican population will grow significantly in the next few decades.

Birthplace. In New York City there are now more Puerto Ricans who were born in the United States (49.4%) than were born in Puerto Rico (48.1%). However, the difference in the sample is not large.

29

Language. A very high proportion of Puerto Ricans still speaks *Spanish* at home—91%. This is a higher percentage than for any other Spanish-origin group in New York City (for Cubans and other Spanish, the figure is 90%; it is 64% for Mexicans).[9] At the same time, a higher proportion of Puerto Ricans (compared with other Latino groups) indicate that they speak *English* "well to very well" (see Figure 2.3). As Figure 2.3 indicates, 70% of Puerto Ricans, but only 60% of Cubans, 42% of Mexicans, and 55% of other Spanish place themselves in this category. Correspondingly, proportionately fewer Puerto Ricans indicate that they speak English "not well or not at all"—Puerto Ricans, 21%, compared to Cubans, 29%, Mexicans, 22%, and other Spanish, 34%. (The proportion speaking "only English" at home is only 9% for Puerto Ricans, compared to 10% for Cubans and other Spanish, and 36% for Mexicans.) Thus, Puerto Ricans report greater fluency in both languages than other Latino groups.

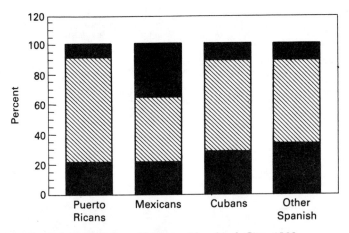

Figure 2.3   English Proficiency of Latinos, New York City, 1980
Source: 1980 Public Use Microdata Sample, 5% Sample, New York City.
    Note: Striped areas represent those who indicated they spoke English "very well" or "well" Top solid areas represent those who spoke only English, and bottom solid areas represent those who said they spoke English "not well" or "not at all."

Education. Skimming over the education data, which will be covered in detail in a subsequent chapter, we see that Hispanics have a median educational attainment of 10.3 grades, compared with 12.3 for Whites and 12.2 for Blacks.[10] Moreover, there is a very high dropout rate for Hispanics. Table 2.2 shows the distribution of educational attainment of Puerto Ricans over 25 years old compared with comparable Whites and Blacks.[11] For this older age group, differences between Puerto Rican men

Table 2.2
Educational Attainment of Puerto Ricans, Whites, and Blacks
in New York City, 1980 (in percentages)

	Puerto Ricans	Whites	Blacks
No school	2.85	1.48	.95
Less than 8 years of school	35.01	17.9	16.9
Some high school	25.87	14.33	22.71
High school graduate	21.91	29.63	32.86
Some college	7.07	12.14	12.29
College graduate plus	2.86	20.54	7.26
Totals[a]	404,800	2,668,680	920,680

Source: 1980 Public Use Microdata Sample, 5% Sample, New York City. Based on persons 25 years or older.

[a] Percentages do not total to 100 because those currently attending school were not included in the table. Those figures are as follows: Puerto Ricans, 4.43%; Whites, 3.97%; Blacks, 7.02%.

and women are minor. So, on the whole, educational levels, relative to Whites and Blacks, are low for Puerto Ricans. However, if we look at the proportion of Puerto Ricans 23 and over who were enrolled in post-secondary education in 1979—that is, the nontraditional students—we find that in the youngest age group, 23–34, there is a stirring of activity, while those over 35 are underrepresented relative to Whites and Blacks. Thus, even though the numbers are small, these data suggest that younger Puerto Ricans may pursue education later in life.

The Economic Dimension

Income. The median annual family income of Puerto Ricans in 1979 was $8,705, compared with $21,515 for Whites and $12,210 for Blacks. Thus Whites had a median family income that was almost 2.5 times that of Puerto Ricans. Mean and household income measures diminish the gap somewhat, but in no case is the gap significantly less; no matter how you slice it, the income of Puerto Ricans is less than half that of Whites.[12]

What is apparent from Figure 2.4 is that the distribution of income for Puerto Ricans is quite different from that for Whites. There is, in the case of Puerto Ricans, a concentration of income at the lower end of the scale, while among Whites the income spread is greater. Puerto Rican and Black income distributions are more similar, except that Blacks have larger proportions in the upper-middle to upper reaches of the income scale.

Work force. Why is income so low for Puerto Ricans as a whole? Who's working and who's not? Table 2.3 compares the labor forces of

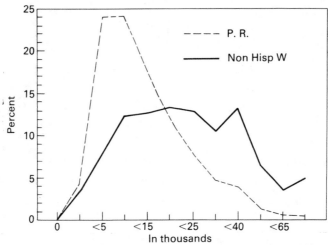

Figure 2.4 Distribution of Household Income, New York City, 1980
Source: 1980 Public Use Microdata Sample, 5% Sample, New York City.

Table 2.3
Male Labor Force Status

	Puerto Ricans		Whites		Blacks	
	Number	%	Number	%	Number	%
Employed civilian	140,020	57.72	950,080	66.37	287,020	56.36
Unemployed	18,460	7.61	54,440	3.80	41,520	8.15
Armed forces	600	.25	3,520	.25	1,340	.26
Not in labor force	83,500	34.42	423,440	29.58	179,400	35.23
Total	242,580	100.00	1,431,480	100.00	509,280	100.00

Source: 1980 Public Use Microdata Sample, 5% Sample, New York City Boroughs. Population over 16.

Puerto Rican, White, and Black males in NYC in 1979. Three things are evident in the Puerto Rican labor force: (1) the *majority* of Puerto Rican males are employed (58%), although this rate is lower than the rate for White males (66%); (2) the *unemployment rate* of Puerto Rican men is two times that of White men; and (3) Puerto Rican men are "out of the labor force" to a greater degree (34%) than White men (30%). The pattern for Blacks is similar to that of Puerto Ricans.

For Puerto Rican women, the most significant fact is their low labor force participation rates—66% of Puerto Rican women are *not* in the labor force, compared to 53% of White women and 49% of Black women. Thus, Puerto Rican women are proportionately less involved in the world of *taxed* work (Table 2.4).

Table 2.4
Female Labor Force Status

	Puerto Ricans		Whites		Blacks	
	Number	%	Number	%	Number	%
Employed civilian	93,520	29.46	748,420	43.93	323,480	46.23
Unemployed	13,200	4.16	45,640	2.68	35,200	5.03
Armed forces	0	0	180	.01	260	.04
Not in labor force	210,680	66.38	909,400	53.38	340,800	48.70
Total	317,400	100.00	1,703,640	100.00	699,740	100.00

Source: 1980 Public Use Microdata Sample, 5% Sample, New York City Boroughs. Population over 16.

Household structure and income. Given the income picture, it comes as no surprise that Puerto Rican families have the highest poverty rates even when one controls for household structure (see Figure 2.5). Regardless of whether Puerto Rican families are headed by women, by men, or by couples, they are still disproportionately represented below the poverty line. This is true whether we compare Puerto Rican families with White, Black, or other Latino families.

Female-headed households. The rise in the number of Puerto Rican households headed by women is often cited as an important variable in the persistently low family income levels of Puerto Ricans. The distribution of families by household structure shows that the highest proportion of female-headed households (FHH) are in the Puerto Rican community

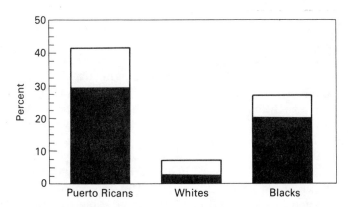

Figure 2.5 Families in Poverty, New York City, 1980
Source: 1980 Public Use Microdata Sample, 5% Sample, New York City.
Note: Striped areas represent female-headed households; solid areas represent couple or male-headed households.

(33% versus 8% for Whites and 30% for Blacks). This pattern is strongly affected by regional factors, as the national pattern indicates that the Black community has the highest proportion of FHH. Nonetheless, it is surprising that, in *absolute numbers*, there are more Puerto Rican female-headed households in poverty than there are White female-headed households in poverty. This is astounding when you consider that there are many more White than Puerto Rican females.

Puerto Rican FHH are less likely to be in the labor force and more likely to depend on public assistance than either White or Black FHH. Only 25% of the heads of female-headed households in the Puerto Rican community are in the labor force, contrasted with 51% of White and 54% of Black FHH. Wages and salaries do not provide the main source of income for any of the three groups—although Black women rely more on this source than either of the other two groups. Because Puerto Rican FHH derive less of their income from other sources (e.g., alimony, private wealth, child support payments), they depend more on public assistance. Thus, while 34% of White and 20% of Black FHH derive their income from other sources or a combination of sources, only 16% of the Puerto Rican FHH do likewise. The majority of the Puerto Rican FHH (57%) rely solely on public assistance to cope with their difficult economic situation; comparable figures for White and Black women who head their own families are 9% and 28%, respectively.

Couple families.   In contrast to Puerto Rican FHH is the fact that the majority of Puerto Rican men in *couple* families rely on salary or wage income to a greater degree than comparable men in the White or Black communities. Some 62% of Puerto Rican men in couple families receive their income solely from salaries and wages, compared with 29% of White men, who can rely on other additional sources of income, such as interest, dividends, and social security. In addition, Puerto Rican men in couple families also participate in the labor force to a higher degree than do White and Black men; respective figures here are 82%, 75%, and 81%. They also participate to a slightly higher degree in the armed forces. Thus, Puerto Rican men in intact families are working or looking for work to a greater degree than others.

Other families.   While the form of Puerto Rican families is changing, the importance of families seems secure. The household structure data show that, even though Puerto Ricans have the highest percentage of female-headed households and the middle position for the traditional "couple head" families, they have the lowest percentage of nonfamily households. Only 23% of Puerto Rican households are single or other

34

"nonfamily," compared with 34% and 42%, respectively, for Blacks and Whites. Conversely, 77% of Puerto Rican households are families (couple, female-headed, or male-headed), compared to 66% for Blacks and 58% for Whites. Thus, proportionately more Puerto Ricans live in households that are families, compared with the other groups. This may be related to the lower labor force participation rate of Puerto Rican women.

Occupations. There are no real surprises when we look at the occupational data. Relative to Whites and Blacks, there are fewer Puerto Rican men and women in the generally higher-paid professions, as managers and officials, as technicians, and as clerical or office workers. Correspondingly, there are proportionately more Puerto Rican men and women working as laborers or factory operatives. Some details are of interest:

(1) very high concentrations of Puerto Rican women, and to a lesser degree of Puerto Rican men, in factory operative occupations, despite the serious decline in New York City over the last 20 years of manufacturing jobs;
(2) an unexpectedly high (relatively speaking) proportion of the Puerto Rican *female* work force found in the crafts/foremen and laborers categories;
(3) a relatively good representation of Puerto Rican men in crafts or as foremen and as clerical workers;
(4) healthy proportions of Puerto Rican men and women in the sales occupations; and
(5) very low proportions of Puerto Rican women in service occupations or in private household work.

Government employment. The pattern of government work is of interest because government has often served as the "employer of last resort" for Blacks. Rodríguez (1979) notes that until 1970, government had not served this role for Puerto Ricans, but since that time, government, particularly local government, has improved its role, employing about 19% of the Puerto Rican work force. Government employs a larger portion of the Black work force (29%) and a smaller portion of the White work force (15%).

Interpretation of the Data

The General Picture

The data picture drawn in this chapter is consistent with that found in other studies.[13] Although there may be some minor deviations, there is a general conclusion to be drawn: by the standard statistical indicators, the "average" Puerto Rican in New York City is not doing very well relative to the White population. This also parallels the national picture found of Puerto Ricans in the United States (Tienda and Jensen, 1986; Tienda and Lii, 1987: 2; Bean and Tienda, 1988). Moreover, recent studies indicate that the economic situation of Puerto Ricans in the United States has worsened with time.[14]

However, the data reviewed here raise a number of questions about the conclusions or inferences that are derived from these data and about the methodological limitations of the data. It is important to discuss these questions for a number of reasons. First, this type of questioning often points the way for future research. Second, the inferences made about data often determine the direction of current policy and research; therefore, those inferences should be examined carefully. Third, many of the issues raised may be known to researchers, but they are all too often initially acknowledged and then abandoned when the research gets under way or when the results are explained. It is important that these issues be raised along with the presentation of research conclusions, because that is often where users of research and policymakers go directly.

In the following section, I will raise questions that are not answered by the data, suggest avenues for further research, and point out methodological limitations of this and similar data sets, all within a policy-relevant context. I will focus first on the findings presented, and then will examine four methodological issues: the need for a wide-angle lens, a shifting population, the underclass, and unmeasured characteristics.

Beyond and Beneath the Data Variables

Sex and disappearing men. The one basic question that must be raised with regard to the unbalanced sex ratio is, Where have all the good Puerto Rican men gone? There are a few explanations. Some may just be absent from the census count. But if so, why are fewer men counted than women as they get older? It is possible that the men die of natural causes or as a result of hazardous conditions to a greater degree than women, or that they disappear into unrecorded street activities. They may also stop identifying themselves as Puerto Rican and thus leave the census data in this way, or they may leave the NYC population. Yet why would either of these latter two possibilities occur more for men than for women? Adding to the mystery of the disappearing males is the fact that recently greater numbers of males are migrating from Puerto Rico (Junta de Planificación, 1986). The answers to these questions must necessarily affect policy research and program planning, especially with regard to FHH.

Age and its future significance. The young age trends and high fertility rates indicate that the Puerto Rican population will grow faster than other groups for several decades. This trend, combined with that of Whites toward smaller families and out-migration, will, in all probability, make Puerto Ricans a more significant part of the future New York City and New York State population. Given the high rate of female-headed households and associated welfare dependency, the city and the state would do well to develop policies to assist this growing sector of the electorate.

Birthplace and assimilation. Can we interpret the larger numbers of Puerto Ricans born in the United States as a sign that Puerto Ricans are on their way to assimilating out of existence? As the data on language proficiencies suggest, and subsequent material will substantiate, this does not appear to be the case.[15] Particularly intriguing in this regard is the fact that there is higher retention—relative to other Latino groups in NYC—of "Spanish at home." (This in a population where *more* people were born in the states than in Puerto Rico.) More important, however, is the policy research point raised by this fact: birthplace is not an absolute determinant of socialization for Puerto Ricans—because of ongoing back-and-forth movements to the island.[16]

Education and success. The relationships among educational attainment, English-language proficiency, and income and occupational attainments have tended to be anomalous for Puerto Ricans. In this data set, we saw that Puerto Rican English proficiency levels are high relative to other Latino groups who fare better in the New York City economy. Nelson and Tienda (1985: 64) similarly found in their *national* sample that "Puerto Ricans combine the highest levels of English proficiency with the lowest levels of socioeconomic achievement"—this compared with Cubans, Mexicans, and other Spanish.[17] Other studies have argued that, even when education is equal, Hispanics/Puerto Ricans earn less than other groups (Díaz, 1986: 31; Hernández, 1983). The most recent and extensive national study found Puerto Ricans to be economically disadvantaged, relative to Mexicans, even though they had slightly higher educational attainments (Tienda and Lii, 1987: 2). These results raise doubts about the easy policy response of some human capital theorists who argue that increasing education and English proficiency are the answer to the "Puerto Rican problem." This also introduces questions about the quality of education received by different groups.

The difference between education and wisdom.   Low educational attainments are apparently not the whole story, nor do these data allow for the generally accepted distinction within the Puerto Rican community between wisdom and knowledge. As most people within minority communities know, there are many "academies of learning" beyond those officially registered with the State Board of Regents. Indeed, it is my experience that these noncredentialed but "street-smart" or wise individuals are common and often successful features of the community. While their knowledge may not be measurable by years of education, wisdom is often seen to have flourished in its place. These unsung heroes and intellectuals do not appear in the data, but they appear in every family, on every street corner, at all social gatherings, and, certainly, in everyone's biography.

Household structure and the destruction of the Puerto Rican family.   On the issue of female-headed households, it is important *not* to conclude that the high proportion of FHH implies the destruction of the Puerto Rican family. We could no more conclude that this represents the destruction of the Puerto Rican family than we could conclude that the very high proportion (42%) of nonfamily households in White communities sounds the death knell of the White family. Nor can we conclude that children in female-headed families necessarily receive less love or attention than those in households headed by couples. Indeed, they may receive more if women are not working, or if the families are part of a familial or fraternal support system, than if the families are isolated, nuclear families. Or, they may receive less.

The point is, we cannot generalize about family life from data based just on family structure. There have always been families headed by women—because of desertion, death, separation, or female choice. There is no historical evidence that sustains any generalization other than that life becomes economically difficult for a woman alone with children. And this is what we see in the data. This is not to deny the difficulties of raising children alone (for men or women); rather, it is an attempt to remove the veil of psychological encumbrances that often obscures the term *female-*

headed household. This term has become somewhat synonymous with insinuations about childhood deprivation, psychological as well as economic. It conveys immediate unmet needs for all concerned. This is not necessarily the case, although one can always find examples to prove the point.[18] The real issue here is poverty, not FHH, and this is what should be addressed.

Female-headed households, Puerto Rican men. It is also important for policymakers to distinguish the economic situation of Puerto Rican female heads of households from that of White female heads of households. It is apparent from the data that there are few sources of support, beyond governmental funds, for Puerto Rican female heads of households. Darity and Myers (1987) conclude that the poorest families, even after the receipt of government transfer payments, were Puerto Rican female-headed households. It is important to see the economic situation of these households in relation to the economic situation of Puerto Rican men. There are apparently no large support payments forthcoming from men who have disappeared, whose income is insufficient to cover their own needs, who don't have jobs or income, or who disclaim responsibility. White female heads of households, on the other hand, rely to a greater degree on other sources or a combination of sources of support.

Sources of support and earning a living. On this point, the data don't tell us why, or how, some groups of people manage (more than others) to acquire income from sources other than salary. It appears that a higher proportion of Puerto Ricans (37%), compared with Whites (29%), derive their income solely from wages. A higher proportion of Whites derive their income from wages plus interest, dividends, social security, or other combinations. Puerto Ricans also rely more on public assistance and report "no income" to a higher degree.

Thus, Puerto Ricans rely to a greater degree on public income that some define as charity; Whites, on income that is not directly gained as a result of their labor. Some savings or investments may have originated as labor income, but other investments or savings may have come from inheritances or other class advantages. Part of the difference in income sources may be due to age and household structure, but another part of the differential may be the result of inherited wealth. (This gives support to the saying that "you have to have money to make money"—at least you have to be able to borrow it.) Whatever the exact reasons for the divergent patterns, the data suggest that Puerto Ricans may not benefit as much as others from booms in the financial sector of the economy.

Income, resources, and the underground economy. The intriguing and unanswered question, of course, is not how Puerto Rican families receive what they receive, but how they survive on what they receive.[19] Puerto Ricans have less income than any other group. In addition, Puerto Rican households need two workers to equal the income of White households with one worker.[20] The question thus is not how many people are on welfare, but how it is possible to subsist without it. There is, of course, the possibility of a strong underground economy, but no one knows how many people participate in it and to what degree. There are also, however, other untold, heroic stories of the Puerto Rican community—how enough for one becomes enough for two; how old curtains become dresses; how restaurant work yields not just a minimum wage but food for the family; how ecologically life is (must be) lived; how friends, family, and community nourish the spirit where elsewhere it is broken; and how all of this is accomplished without injury to dignity. This is all outside the data and should be researched.

Labor force participation and informal economies. The decline in the labor force participation rates of Puerto Rican women is intriguing, because demographic changes between 1960 and 1970 would have predicted an increase in these rates. These changes include greater educational attainment, greater numbers of FHH, greater proportion born in the states, and lower proportion of women with children under 6 years old (Santana-Cooney and Colón-Warren, 1984; Barry-Figueroa, 1988; Meléndez, 1987). In addition, it is unusual that the labor force participation rates of Puerto Rican women would have declined at a time when all women have increased their labor force participation (Santana-Cooney and Colón-Warren, 1984). Sanchez-Korrol (1983), in her study of the pre-World War II Puerto Rican community, found Puerto Rican women were strong contributors to the economy of the household in "less accounted for" ways. They did factory piecework at home, took in boarders, and cared for other people's children, in addition to being the core of the support networks that assisted new migrants in finding housing, jobs, medical services, schools, churches, and so on. In the 1950s, Puerto Rican women had higher labor force participation rates than any other group of women, yet in 1980 their rate was the lowest of all (Rios, 1985).

The decline of manufacturing industries in New York City after 1970 (particularly in the garment sector) reduced the possibilities for doing piecework at home. It may be that Puerto Rican women opted, in light of few and diminishing employment opportunities, to stay home and be traditional mothers and wives. Meléndez's (1987) analysis is suggestive in this regard. He finds that not only were the majority of Puerto Rican women concentrated in manufacturing between 1950 and 1970, but that many did not make the transition to service sector employment—especially those in prime age groups. The presence of children also affects women's decision to work. In New York State only 31% of Hispanic women with children under 6 were labor force participants. As children got older, the participation rates of Hispanic women increased to 45% (i.e., for those with children between 6 and 17). However, this rate was considerably below that of comparable White and Black women, whose rates were 60% and 67%, respectively (Rodríguez, 1984a).

The questions for future research here include whether the initial decline and the still lower labor force participation rates for Puerto Rican women reflect more women working "off the books," taking care of other people's children, selling home-produced goods, and distributing or manufacturing products or services in the informal sector.[21] Another question is whether Puerto Rican women have chosen families over paid work or whether the choice had been made for them. Also, with regard to labor force nonparticipation rates of Puerto Rican men and women, one wonders if the reasons for nonparticipation are the same for all groups. Are, for example, men in all groups marginalized (i.e., discouraged workers) to the same degree? Are they missing from the labor force because they are students, or because they are engaged in underground economies? These are avenues for further investigation.

Occupations and sedimentation. One question left unanswered by the aggregate data is whether there is a settling process within each occupational category that accounts for low incomes. That is, if we were to examine each category, would we find Puerto Ricans concentrated at the lower income end of each disaggregated occupational category? If this is the case, even those Puerto Ricans within the professional category would tend to occupy the lowest ranks of this category. Are Puerto Ricans routinely relegated to the lowest strata within social class subgroups? This question cannot be answered for Puerto Ricans without further disaggregation and analysis of the data. However, there is evidence from other sources that this may be the case.

The National Committee on Pay Equity (1987) took note of occupational settling or sedimentation patterns in its national analysis of 1980 census data. Barrera (1979) found this to be the case for Mexicans and Mexican-Americans in the southwest. Rodríguez (1984a: 6–7) also found that within New York State there was considerable evidence of settling within occupations for Hispanic women. Within the sales occupations, a larger proportion of Hispanic women were employed as cashiers than as supervisors and sales representatives. In the administrative support area, there were proportionately *fewer* Hispanic women as computer operators; and in financial records, fewer were secretaries and typists and proportionately *more* were handling the mail. In the "Operatives" category, Hispanic women still "manned" or "tended" the *nonprecision* machines to a greater degree than White women. Only in the "Managerial and Professional Specialty" occupations was there a small but proportionately significant representation of Hispanic women in traditionally male-dominant occupations. Stafford (1983) has also found that in the major private industries, Blacks and Hispanics held subordinate positions and that there was significant segmentation within the public sector.

Tienda (1985: 73) also notes in her analysis of 1980 national census data that there is a tendency for Puerto Ricans to hold lower-paying jobs within broad occupational groupings: "Besides being unrepresented in executive, management and professional occupations, Puerto Rican men holding such jobs on a full-time, year-round basis in 1980 earned between 6–9000 less than similarly employed white men." She cautions, however, that these data do not take into account job tenure, training, experience, and other human capital characteristics. However, even in lower-skill jobs, Puerto Ricans make less money than comparable White workers.

Government: the steeplechase and the differential impact of cutbacks. The data on government employment are curious. Puerto Ricans and Blacks are more represented in government employment than Whites. Is it possible that, as Higgenbotham (1987) suggests, government employment represents the new dead-end world of work for minorities?[22] Meléndez (1986) argues that minorities are overrepresented in those sectors of government that are declining and more subject to budget cuts. It would be ironic if working conditions in government have begun to decline just at the point where employment has begun to open up to minorities. Does government employment represent the new steeplechase for diminishing jobs?[23]

Methodological Issues

The Need for a Wide-Angle Lens

There is a basic problem with most of the data collected and reported on Puerto Ricans. The data tend to represent—as do the data presented in this chapter—a snapshot of the community at one point in time. This snapshot is very narrowly focused, and it omits significant dimensions of the situation of most Puerto Ricans. Their unique situation requires that Puerto Ricans be viewed through a more "wide-angle lens" than has been generally applied, and that diverse situations of Puerto Ricans in the states be analyzed.

Such a view of Puerto Ricans would incorporate activities in Puerto Rico as well as those in the states. For example, economic measures of Puerto Ricans' income in the states do not generally take into account land and/or houses Puerto Ricans own in Puerto Rico, nor do they consider informal sales of goods in Puerto Rico. Yet, both are quite common, and they influence estimates of income and net worth. Such a view would also examine contrasting situations—those in which Puerto Ricans have been successful, and those in which they have not. For example, a comparison of Puerto Ricans in California—where Puerto Ricans are relatively better off than other Latino groups—with Puerto Ricans in New York will provide greater insight into what the real problems are (see 1980 Census, General Social and Economic Characteristics, California, PC80-1-C6). Clearly, the more usual comparison of Puerto Ricans in New York with those in similarly troubled economies, such as in Chicago, will not yield startling new information.

Shifting Population

Because the data focus on given places and points in time, they do not capture the shifts in population that form a very important factor in the case of Puerto Ricans and other shifting migrations. For example, a longitudinal study that uses decennial census data and compares Puerto Ricans between 1940 and 1980 may find that little progress has been made in this 40-year period. However, it may be that a radically different population is being examined in each decennial period. It may be that the population is constantly being replenished by "newer" Puerto Ricans or "disguised" Puerto Ricans (i.e., illegal immigrants pretending to be Puerto Ricans). These newer immigrants may have less education, fewer skills, and lower English proficiency levels, which would tend to depress the indicators of "progress" (Morales, 1986: 219). It is also possible that more successful Puerto Ricans leave the city.[24] Do they go to other states or back to Puerto Rico?[25] We do not have, at present, a measure of the way in which the population changes because of additions and departures. This is an important consideration in the analysis of data and in the development of policy.

43

The Underclass

It might be inferred from the data reviewed here and elsewhere that Puerto Ricans are increasingly becoming members of an "underclass."[26] This term has had increasing usage in the policy arena, in part because of methodological advances in its definition and consequently in its measurement. In general terms, the underclass is made up of those who are consistently out of the labor force, dependent on welfare, in persisting (often transgenerational) poverty, and somewhat isolated from more mainstream activities. Less precise, more journalistic or pedestrian definitions of the term include a position outside of, or beneath, the regular class structure, a dimension of criminality and attitudinal and behavioral predispositions to not working.

However, despite its increasing use in policy circles, the term has a number of problems: it has been roundly criticized (Morris, in press; McGahey, 1982), and it is difficult to define (Ricketts and Sawhill, 1988) and therefore difficult to determine who is and who is not a member of the underclass. Its behavioral implications have not been substantiated; see Corcoran et al. (1985), who find that the majority of the persistently poor do not fit underclass stereotypes and that it is changes in economic circumstances that lead to changes in psychological attitudes and not vice versa. In addition, it is unclear what proportion of those in designated underclass areas have recently moved there and what proportion have been there for some time. Finally, the underclass concept has spawned "workfare" solutions (programs that require that welfare recipients work in exchange for the assistance received), but these have had mixed results in New York (*New York Times*, March 23, 1987: 1).

If this new buzz word is so inaccurate, why is it still in use? It is used because it places the blame on individuals, thereby diverting attention from more structural problems. It resonates well with the articulation of a "new social contract" that emphasizes increasing self-reliance and reducing dependency. It also responds to the position raised by Charles Murray (1984) in *Losing Ground*, that government intervention has created an underclass. It reinforces concerns raised over "self-defeating patterns of behavior" and allows liberals, who are concerned with the social problems engendered by the shift, to develop policies that provide "opportunities for self-sufficiency."

The problem comes in the implementation. What is the impact of labeling individuals as members of the underclass? Will training accompany jobs? Will jobs have mobility? Should mothers be required—under threat of having their children's allowance taken away—to leave their small children so they can work at welfare wages? Where will these children be left? Will publicly funded, quality day care be provided? It appears that the underclass concept has provided another diversion from the real problems—how to employ all members of the society effectively and how to deal with the long-term joblessness that has become a chronic condition for increasing numbers of people in the economy.

Unmeasured Characteristics

Important methodological questions have been raised about how data in general are conceptualized, organized, and gathered. For example, some would argue that the "progress" of minorities is always measured relative to "the White man's" standards and that this reflects the assimilationism prevalent in research settings. As Bonacich (1986: 12) says:

> The obsessive concern with mobility studies, with examining the distribution of minorities along a given and unquestioned social hierarchy, reflects an assimilationist bias. . . . Minorities will have "made it" when their distribution looks like the white distribution. No questions are raised about the structure of the dominant society that might be a little less than the ideal of human happiness. Obviously, it goes without saying, that all minorities want is to become like the "white man," fit neatly into his world and never raise another peep.

Although we may quibble with whether progress and success are measurable via socioeconomic indicators, the point implicit in Bonacich's statement is that there are other characteristics—such as dignity, pride, warmth, and generosity—that are part of the picture but are not measured. These characteristics are not any less in evidence in the Puerto Rican community than in communities with higher socioeconomic status— indeed, they may be more in evidence. Given the approach taken in many research studies, what should be obvious is in fact often ignored. This is that the dignity and value of the people represented in the data are often missed; the data are not the people.

Notes

1   Also, New York City is the area with which I am most familiar, as a second-generation Puerto Rican born and raised in the South Bronx; therefore personal insights will give greater depth and direct resonance to the analysis.

2   In August 1980, New York State, New York City, and other plaintiffs filed suit against the U.S. Bureau of the Census, claiming that the Bureau had undercounted the city and state populations. As of 1984, this litigation was still active.

3   In Texas, for example, Puerto Ricans have a higher labor force participation rate (73.52%) than Mexicans (61.93%), Cubans (71.4%), other Spanish (63.9%), Blacks (63.9%), and even Whites (64.9%). In addition, in the percentages with four or more years of college, working as professionals, and in per capita income, they are exceeded only by Whites and Cubans (1980 Census, General Social and Economic Characteristics, Texas, PC80-1-C45).

4   The figure for Puerto Rico is based on Current Population Reports, "Local Population Estimates" (U.S. Census, July 1984). The figure for Puerto Ricans in the states comes from Current Population Reports, "Population Characteristics" (Series P-20, No. 403, issued December 1985, based on the March 1985 current population survey).

    Unless otherwise indicated, the other data cited are derived from the Public Use Microdata Sample (PUMS) from the 1980 5% census sample. It will be referred to throughout this volume as 1980 PUMS. Totals in the tables differ from published census data because they are based on sample data.

5   The terms *Hispanic* and *Latino/a* will be used interchangeably in this text. See Hayes-Bautista and Chapa (1987) and Treviño (1987), who take opposing positions on which term should be preferred.

6   Interestingly enough, the same imbalance does not exist in Puerto Rico, where there are 49 men for every 51 women. *Census of Population and Housing, 1980, Puerto Rico,* indicates there were 1,556,727 males (or 48.7%) to 1,639,793 females (51.3%) in 1979. The NYC Puerto Rican ratio is the lowest of all groups except Blacks.

7   The sex ratios are derived from U.S. Department of Commerce, Bureau of the Census, 1980 Census of Population, General Social and Economic Characteristics, New York.

8   The figures on median age are derived from U.S. Department of Commerce, Bureau of the Census, 1980 Census of Population, General Social and Economic Characteristics, New York.

9   Grenier's (1981) data also show high Spanish retention for Puerto Ricans, but Cubans in his national sample showed even higher retention rates than the NYC data.

10 The figures on median education are derived from U.S. Department of Commerce, Bureau of the Census, 1980 Census of Population, General Social and Economic Characteristics, New York.

11 The classificatory schema of Puerto Ricans, Whites, and Blacks is problematic, for it mixes racial and ethnic categorizations. More preferable might be terms that highlight the stronger cultural (as opposed to racial) distinction between Puerto Ricans and other groups—for example, terms such as Euro-Americans and Afro-Americans. However, such terms also are problematic because they convey different meanings to different people, for instance, some might understand the terms above to refer only to second-generation Europeans or Africans. This issue will be discussed in Chapter 3.

12 Rodríguez (1984a) found that the income gap between Hispanics and Whites in New York State narrowed somewhat with increasing age; however, during the prime earning years of 45–54, Puerto Rican income was still only 52.73% of

what Whites earned during those years. Díaz (1984: 24) found that the income gap between Hispanics and Whites at the national level fluctuated between 1972 and 1982 but had not improved. In 1982 Hispanics in the United States earned 66% as much as Whites. More recently, Tienda and Jensen (1986) found that the income gap between Puerto Ricans and non-Hispanic Whites grew between 1970 and 1980.

13   See, for example, New York City Department of City Planning (1982), Díaz (1986), Wagenheim (1975), and Mann and Salvo (1984).

14   Tienda and Jensen (1986), in their analysis of the 5% decennial census data (1960–80), found Puerto Ricans in the states to be the *only* group to experience a drop in real family income between 1970 and 1980 and to show a steadily increasing concentration in the lowest income quartile (other groups compared were Blacks, Mexicans, other Hispanics, and Native Americans) (see also Tienda and Lii, 1987: 2). Bean and Tienda (1988) also find Puerto Ricans to have declining economic well-being, as measured by falling labor force participation, high unemployment, poverty, and declines in real family income.

15   Chapter 3 shows that the majority of Puerto Ricans born in the states still speak Spanish at home and identify strongly as "Spanish." All other Latino groups in New York City had lower proportions born in the states, except for Mexicans, 60% of whom were born in the states.

16   One particular family comes to mind that has had three generations born in the states, but none of these generations has ever been raised or socialized primarily in the states.

17   Tienda (1983a) finds that for Hispanics, in general, English skills are necessary but not sufficient to bring about earnings parity with the majority White population (see also Grenier, 1981; Tienda and Neidert, 1984).

18   Pelto et al. (1982) find in their study of 153 Puerto Rican households in New Hartford, Connecticut, that single-parent households were no more or less effective than dual-parent households in coping with the stresses of urban life. Indeed, dual-parent, unemployed households evidenced the highest levels of psychiatric problems. Capello's (1986) recent study in New York also revealed patterns of successful as well as unsuccessful coping styles for Puerto Rican female-headed households.

19   See Valentine (1978) for an excellent discussion of how different families, with distinct household structures, in a low-income Afro-American community devise ways of coping with limited incomes.

20   Rodríguez (1984a: Table 3) shows that in New York State Hispanic families must have *two* workers to equal the income of White families with *one* worker.

21   See also Santana-Cooney and Colón-Warren (1984) and Ríos (1985); for an analysis of women in Puerto Rico's informal economy, see Petrovich and Laureano (1986).

22   Of interest in this regard are Higgenbotham's (1987) findings on public to private sector shifts. She examines Black and White professional women in standard metropolitan statistical areas throughout the country and finds that although there has been a strong shift between 1970 and 1980 from public sector to private sector jobs, the rate of shift has been much faster for White than for Black women.

23   The "steeplechase for jobs" refers to an oft-quoted *New York Times* article (March 31, 1981: 1) on the movement of southern Blacks to northern cities. It

argues that in the early part of the century, most Blacks lived on the farms and in the cities of the South, which were then severely depressed economically. After World War II, they migrated in great numbers to northern cities, just as the unskilled jobs there, which had been the basis for assimilating other members of poor minority groups, were giving out. In the 1970s Blacks increased their relative numbers in the troubled old cities and the declining industrial areas of the North, while many Whites were moving to the South and West to take jobs and to retire. Questions that are raised within this analogy include the following: Will there be the same perceptions about government that developed about urban areas? Will certain sectors in government be perceived as declining in efficiency because of the large numbers of Blacks and Hispanics working in these government areas?

24 However, the question of whether the successful leave the pool or are successful *because* they leave the pool cannot be answered definitively without better migration histories and age controls.

25 Indeed, there is some inferential evidence that this is the case. According to the 1980 census of Puerto Rico, it appears that those born in the states and living in Puerto Rico are making more money, are better educated, have less poverty, and have higher proportions of managerial, professional, and executive jobs, compared with those born in Puerto Rico. However, a slightly higher proportion of those born in the states are unemployed.

26 Tienda and Jensen (1986: 41) have said that "Puerto Ricans have become the Hispanic underclass during the past two decades and in many ways have become more similar to blacks over time." Rosenberg (1987: 25) also finds that "Puerto Ricans appear to be at the bottom of the City's class structure."

3

THE RAINBOW PEOPLE

The racial context that Puerto Ricans encountered when they entered the United States was at once contradictory and ironic. Puerto Ricans entered a heterogeneous society that articulated an assimilationist, melting-pot ideology, but that, in fact, had evolved a racial order of dual ethnic queues, one White and one not-White.[1] It was a society that denied that difference should exist, while at the same time it tolerated, and sometimes supported, separate schools, jobs, and housing for those who were racially and/or ethnically "different." This race order was quickly and clearly perceived by Puerto Ricans. The irony was that Puerto Ricans represented the ideal of the American melting-pot ideology—a culturally unified, racially integrated people. However, this presented a problem to their acceptance in the United States. The dilemma that Puerto Ricans faced early on was essentially the need for them to regress to a more racist society (Robert Schwartz, professor of sociology, SUNY—Stonybrook, 1986, personal correspondence).

Historical Antecedents

Puerto Ricans had had their own earlier experiences with racism; they did not enter the United States race order as total innocents. First, there was Puerto Rico's interaction with the United States that came about as a result of the political relationship that preceded the Puerto Rican migration to the states. Although this interaction may have been more intense for those who had direct dealings with the North Americans, racial distinctions were not strictly an American import. There was a similar emphasis on the racial superiority of White Europeans during Spain's colonization period, a feature inherent in Spain's legacy to Latin America. The centuries of Moorish occupation in Spain and other parts of Europe and the enslavement of Africans and Indians undoubtedly contributed to the concern with European White dominance. However, it was in the United States that Puerto Ricans would confront an adamant biracial order that dominated all aspects of society.

49

The Racial Order

In the United States a racial order based upon a White/not-White classification system evolved in colonial days. This system of classification provided a racist but utilitarian method of ordering society.[2] It was utilitarian because it was a broad, two-category system that, to a large degree, was congruent with, reflected, and helped order the reality of life in the United States (dual labor markets, inner-city and suburban school systems, primary and secondary job sectors, dual housing markets, and so on). It was racist because it was based purely on racial distinctions. The point of reference was the "White race"; one was or was not "White."[3]

Ethnicity: The Worst-Kept Secret

Ethnicity (and its close cousin, culture) has generally been less clearly dichotomized,[4] yet it has also been important in the formation of this country. U.S. history has recorded many incidents that have reflected strong "fears of difference." Beginning with the persecution of religious sects in early colonial days, through lynchings, the evolution of the Know-Nothing party and other nativist organizations in the nineteenth century, to the protectionist immigration laws of the early twentieth century, the fear of "difference" has been a central, recurring phenomenon. Although these and other events surfaced at different times in U.S. history, they have generally been viewed as aberrations. They have not been seen as themes, trends, or even part of the America we are today. They have been treated as isolated incidents that after a while disappeared—although on occasion they might make reappearances, as in the case of the Ku Klux Klan.[5]

In short, there has been a general reluctance to address U.S. history as ethnic history. It is a paradox: despite the fact that this is "a nation of immigrants," ethnicity has been suppressed. Most Americans (White and not-White) have been socialized to downplay group differences. It is almost as if group differences are an embarrassment that should not be discussed. Indeed, the combination of embarrassment and lack of discussion has often led to (silent or active) condemnation, or avoidance, of group differences. This has been the unwritten ideology.

Despite the social changes of the 1960s, ethnicity is still not given much attention in the research area. It is sometimes the main or independent variable, as when "special" studies are done on Koreans, the Chippewa, or Puerto Ricans. However, it is seldom viewed as a dependent variable, that is, a variable that might predict the independent variable. This is particularly true for post-second-generation Euro-Americans. We learn of the effect of class, gender, and race on SAT scores, for example, but we know little of the effect of ethnicity on SAT scores. Indeed, we generally don't even collect data on ethnicity, almost as if to do so would be in bad taste.[6] The assumption is that ethnic differences should no longer exist after the immigrant generation.

The ethnic order was subsumed into the race order. European ethnics were White, Africans and Asians were not-White. Hispanics straddled the queues or were not-White. These racial and ethnic patterns were clear to arriving Puerto Ricans—as it was also clear that these categorizations were real in their consequences.

Puerto Ricans: An Enigma

Puerto Ricans presented an enigma to Americans because (from the North American perspective) Puerto Ricans were both an ethnic group and more than one racial group. Within the U.S. perspective, Puerto Ricans, racially speaking, belonged to both groups; however, ethnically, they belonged to neither. Thus placed, Puerto Ricans soon found themselves caught between two polarities and dialectically at a distance from both. Puerto Ricans were White and Black; Puerto Ricans were neither White nor Black. From the Puerto Rican perspective, Puerto Ricans were more than White or Black. This apparent contradiction can best be understood through an examination of the contrasting racial ambiences and histories of the United States and Puerto Rico at the time of the "great migration."

Race in Puerto Rico

First, it is necessary to appreciate the degree to which racial heterogeneity was an integral factor of Puerto Rican life when Puerto Ricans first migrated in large numbers to the United States. It was not, as in the United States, a matter of Black and White families living within a community. It was often a matter of a Negro-appearing brother and his Anglo-appearing sister attending the same school.[7] The variety of racial types in the Puerto Rican community is the biological result of a relatively unexamined history of racial mixing and of diverse migratory flows. Although a number of works have touched upon the issue of racial mixing in Puerto Rico, they have achieved no real consensus. Puerto Rican and American researchers have assumed or found Puerto Rico to be everything

51

from a mulatto country to a predominantly White country with small subgroups of Blacks and mulattos. Nevertheless, the process of racial mixing has continued and the existence of significant racial heterogeneity continues.[8]

Puerto Rico's history also yielded a unique set of social attitudes that contributed to a racial ambience quite different from that which existed in the United States when Puerto Ricans arrived. Understanding this Puerto Rican racial ambience is vital to an understanding of the Puerto Rican experience in the United States. A few points of contrast will shed light on the racial attitudes that accompanied racially heterogeneous Puerto Ricans to the United States.

Cultural over Racial Identification

Perhaps the primary point of contrast was that, in Puerto Rico, racial identification was subordinate to cultural identification, while in the United States, racial identification, to a large extent, determined cultural identification.[9] Thus, Puerto Ricans were first Puerto Rican, then blanco/a (white), moreno/a (dark), and so on, while Americans were first White or Black, then Italian, Irish, West Indian, or whatever. This is not to say that Puerto Ricans did not have a racial identification, but rather that cultural identification superseded it. The system of racial classification in Puerto Rico was based more on phenotypic and social definitions of what a person was than on genotypic knowledge about a person. In other words, physical and social appearance were the measures used to classify, rather than the biological-descent classification (i.e., "one drop of Negro blood makes you Negro") used in the United States.[10] Thus, in the United States the White-appearing offspring of an interracial couple was classified "Negro." In Puerto Rico, the child would probably have been called White. Alternatively, an obviously dark or "colored" person in the United States would have been seen (perceived) as dark in Puerto Rico, but not Black, especially if there were other mitigating circumstances—class, for example.[11] Many other examples of the contrasting racial classification criteria could be cited, but these serve to point up the main differences.

There is no doubt that because of Puerto Rico's unique racial history, it has evolved a unique racial ambience. However, a number of authors argue that, in general, the Latin American conception of race is quite different from that of North Americans. Ginorio (1986: 20), for example, says:

As a result of all the extensive racial mixture and the fluidity of racial definitions, the conception of race in Latin America is one of a continuum with no clear demarcation between categories. In contrast to this racial system, in the U.S. race is seen as a dichotomous variable of white or black. Not only does the U.S. racial system differ from the Latin American one in recognizing discrete as opposed to continuous groups, it also limits racial distinctions to a very small number of categories—four or perhaps five, if in addition to white, black and yellow, red and "brown" are seen as distinct racial categories. The basis for such distinctions in the U.S. is genealogical. If an arbitrary set amount of black blood can be determined to exist, the individual is classified as black. Thus, an individual is racially defined at birth and can change that identity only by "passing."

Wade (1985) also argues that what exists in Latin America is a "black-white continuum." Puerto Ricans share more with the Latin American conception of race than with the North American.

Not Just Color Based

Another point of contrast between the U.S. racial ambience and that in Puerto Rico is that racial categories in Puerto Rico are based on color, class, facial features, and texture of hair. This is quite in contrast to the mainly color-based, White/non-White, or white, black, yellow, red, and brown coloring classifications of the United States.[12] A whole spectrum of racial types is thus found in Puerto Rico: *blancos*, the equivalent of Whites in this country;[13] *indios*, similar to the U.S. conception of (Asian) Indians, that is, dark skinned and straight haired; *morenos*, dark skinned and with a variety of Negroid or Caucasian features; and *negros*, equivalent to very dark-skinned Black people in the United States.

(As an aside, it is interesting that the term *negro*, literally Spanish for black, is used as a term of endearment, at which time it bears no connotation of color whatsoever and can be used to refer to an individual of any racial type. It can also, however, be used, depending on the tone, as a derogatory term, like *nigger*.) Finally, there is the *trigueño*, a name applied to what would be considered brunettes in this country or to Blacks or *negros* who have high social status. Despite the term's lack of congruity with physical characteristics, it is considered a term of racial classification.[14]

The fact that this term can be used both ways is indicative of the attitudes that Puerto Ricans brought toward class and race. A "Black" or "Negro" person became "White" by achieving high economic status or one's friendship. It was an obvious form of "passing" without, however, the connotations given to that term in the United States. In the United States, a person who passed had become outwardly White, leaving one group to become a member of another, separate, group. Some would argue that the physical appearance and cultural ways of such a person were

"White," that is, that he or she had become, in 1960s parlance, an "Oreo." In Puerto Rico, a *negro* who moved up the status ladder had not altered his or her physical appearance (that is, did *not* necessarily look White) and had not necessarily experienced a cultural change, but would be classified *trigueño*.

A Culturally Homogeneous, Racially Integrated Society versus a Multiethnic, Biracial Society

Although not without strong class differences, the society in Puerto Rico is basically culturally homogeneous and racially integrated (Giles et al., 1979).[15] This contrasts with the more biracial, multiethnic society that has historically existed in the United States. While in the United States ethnic-racial minorities have traditionally been segregated, in Puerto Rico, Blacks were not a distinguishable ethnic group. This is not to say Blacks were evenly distributed throughout the social structure, for there is still debate on this issue. Nor is it to say that Blacks in Puerto Rico were treated in all regards exactly as Whites. But in terms of housing, institutional treatment, political rights, government policy, and cultural identification, it appears that Black, White, and tan Puerto Ricans were not treated differently. Perhaps the clearest testament to this difference was the lack of response of dark Puerto Ricans on the island to the Black power movement of the 1960s, in contrast to the high degree of involvement in the Black movement evidenced by Puerto Ricans of all colors in New York, Chicago, and other cities.[16]

Another reflection of the more integrated society that existed in Puerto Rico was that intermarriage between White and Black was not taboo, as it was in the United States. Puerto Ricans have intermarried in the past and continue to intermarry with a fair amount of frequency. The strong emphasis on close family ties among Puerto Ricans tended to make the world of most Puerto Rican children one that was inhabited by people of many colors. These colors were not associated with different ranks, as was (and is) the case in many middle-class American homes—where only the "help" were of a different color. This racially intermingled world was *not* generally known to the majority of children growing up in the suburbs and inner cities of the United States. It was this diversity of color and mix that led to the depiction of Puerto Ricans as a "rainbow people."

Two-Way versus One-Way Integration

This leads us to another area of contrast: two-way integration as opposed to one-way integration. In the United States, one-way integration had generally been the norm. Blacks were usually sent to White schools and integrated White residential areas and job sites, but not vice versa. Blacks integrated into White America; Whites did not integrate into Black America. In the United States, there is a very low probability that a Black couple or Black head of household would raise or adopt a White child. (Admittedly, the limited number—relative to demand—of White babies available for adoption and the limited income of many Blacks tends to discourage such actions.)

In Puerto Rico, however, it was a fairly common occurrence to rear other people's children as one's own. These *hijos de crianza* came in all colors. Thus, a "dark" couple might rear the lighter, orphaned children of a relative or a neighbor and a "White couple" could rear their own or another's "dark" child. There was no segregation and thus no need for integration. There were no distinct groups, so how could there be "integration"? It is perhaps propitious for Puerto Ricans that the year of peak Puerto Rican migration to the United States (1952) was only two years before the Supreme Court declared "separate but equal" school systems to be unconstitutional.[17]

In addition, it has been a common complaint that the contributions of Blacks to U.S. culture have often been "whitewashed" and lost. For example, the argument has been made that Black cultural contributions to U.S. music have been "lost," "stolen," "denegrified." Black artists have "crossed over" to white markets and in the process have altered (lightened? Whitened?) their images. In Puerto Rico, the traditional island music was a synthesis of Indian, African, and Spanish elements, but it was always perceived as "Puerto Rican" by all. This synthesizing of diverse elements continues in today's island music, with added elements of American rock, rhythm and blues, and jazz.

A similar type of synthesis evolved (and continues to evolve) in the U.S. Puerto Rican communities. The new Latin sound incorporated Afro-Cuban, White rock, Black soul, and the Latin rhythms. In New York, all Puerto Ricans—of all colors—danced to this new *salsa* music in the same way. This was quite different from the situation that had traditionally existed in the United States, where Blacks and Whites not only danced differently, but danced to different music. Thus, while jazz in the United States split into White and Black styles, Puerto Rican music development in the United States and in Puerto Rico was unifying.[18]

Prejudice in Puerto Rico

These descriptions of differing racial ambiences in New York and Puerto Rico should not be taken to mean that Puerto Rico is the ideal racial environment. Indeed, some authors argue that "Puerto Ricans seem to have developed a Creole ethos tolerant of the mulatto group . . . but scornful of the black sector" (Duany, 1985: 30; see also Zenon Cruz, 1975; Longres, 1974: 68 ff.).[19] Betances (1972) argues that the general lack of concern with racial issues on the island constitutes for some "the prejudice of no prejudice." He argues that claiming that there is no prejudice may in itself be a prejudicial act.[20] But, "if racism can be seen in terms of degree, then obviously there is much less racism in Puerto Rico than in the United States" (Longres, 1974: 68). This was the situation from which Puerto Ricans came.

The Puerto Rican Racial Experience in the United States

Given the experiences Puerto Ricans brought with them, and given the U.S. racial context they entered, there was bound to be a clash as the North American system was superimposed on the rainbow people. As Puerto Ricans entered into "the American dilemma" (Myrdal, 1944) two facts about the racial order were quite clear. One was that the context into which Puerto Ricans stepped offered only two paths—one to the White world and one to the not-White world. Choice of path was dependent on racial classification according to U.S. standards. Use of these standards divided the group, negated the cultural existence of Puerto Ricans, and ignored their expectations that they be treated, irrespective of race, as a culturally intact group.[21] The other quite obvious fact about the race order was that those Americans who were White were socioeconomically better off.

A Theme in the Literature of the Migration

The early literature of the Puerto Rican migration reflects these facts and the consequences of these facts for Puerto Ricans. Jesús Colón was a socialist writer who had migrated to New York as an adult. In one chapter of his book, *A Puerto Rican in New York and Other Sketches* (1982), he tells of being on a train and seeing a White woman with a child and bulky packages get off at the same stop as he. The station was fairly abandoned. He wanted to assist her with her load, but he was fearful that she would be frightened and create a scene when approached by the "Negro man." He watched helplessly. He would not have hesitated to help in Puerto Rico.

Colón also tells of a light-skinned woman who loves her mother dearly but sees her only in restaurants because her mother is dark and the young woman works for people who do not like the "colored." He recounts the trip of a friend to visit a patriotic uncle who lived in the capital of democracy, Washington, D.C. Here the visitors learn (to the uncle's great embarrassment) that there are restaurants that will serve those Puerto Ricans who are white, but not those who are "colored." When Colón sent in his resume for a job as a writer, he received a return letter saying he was hired. Yet when he showed up for work, he was told he could not have the job; his would-be employer explained, "We thought you were white." Finally, he tells of a child he saw in a cafeteria, who he heard say to her mother that she didn't want to sit next to that "colored" man (Colón).

In Colón's reminiscences it is evident that he has a clear-eyed awareness that, to the American eye, *he* is colored. Yet, he entitles his book *A Puerto Rican in New York*. He is also aware of the fact that for Americans, some Puerto Ricans are colored and others are not.

Colón also wrote stories in which the Puerto Rican is not a Puerto Rican, that is, he or she is just "colored"—Negro or Black. Ethnicity is ignored by the White North Americans in his stories. Being Puerto Rican is part of the story only for the author; the non-Puerto Ricans in the stories have minimal, if any, awareness of this dimension. These stories, these experiences, are reflective of the time within which Jesús Colón wrote— the 1950s. The race order was abstractly imposed: You were White or you were "colored." Ethnicity was subdued or unacknowledged; you were not yet clearly a White or a Black Puerto Rican. (Being "Spanish" was, for some, a way of coping with the division—a way of avoiding the imposition of the race order.)

The imposition of the U.S. racial classification system is also evident in Piri Thomas's book, *Down These Mean Streets* (1967). This is perhaps the major, most widely read work of the second generation of Puerto Ricans in the United States, who were "coming of age" at the time. The book is set in the late 1950s, perhaps the early 1960s. The narrator is a second-generation Puerto Rican, raised in East Harlem. He gets involved with drugs, then crime, and ends up in prison in Lexington, Kentucky. It is here that he has his "awakening." He is in line, waiting for chow, with a fellow Puerto Rican. The line divides into two, the Negro line and the White line. The main character is engrossed in conversation and not really aware of the division, or of the basis for the division. He follows his Puerto

Rican friend in the line. Suddenly a guard stops him and asks, "Where do you think you're going?" He is pushed into the Negro line and separated from his Puerto Rican "brother."

Both Thomas's and Colón's accounts reflect the imposition of the race order and identification by race and not by culture. But in Piri Thomas's novel, there is none of the quiet anger or resolute acceptance of the situation that is shown in the Colón stories. The Colón stories seem to say, "I don't like it but that is the way it is." Colón will fight for "the cause" (and against his personal discrimination) on a larger, more political, basis. Piri Thomas's character questions: Is this the way the world really is? Is this what I am? Then I am not what I've always thought I was. Anger and rage result from the denial of his identity, as he perceives it. A purely racial identity is imposed and this leads to perceptual dissonance.

The response of many second-generation Puerto Ricans in the United States to racial division was anger and resistance—anger at the imposition, anger at being divided, anger at the injustice of it all. For others, there was and still is confusion. In a somewhat later book, Edward Rivera's *Family Installments: Memories of Growing Up Hispanic* (1983), we see the confusion expressed.[22] Rivera's central character, Santos, is a Puerto Rican who is not perceived, nor does he perceive himself, as Black. Santos was raised in the Washington Heights section of Manhattan, going to Catholic schools, in the early to mid-1960s. Like the character in the Thomas novel, he perceives himself strongly as growing up "Hispanic."

Rivera devotes one chapter to the race experience. Santos's experience with racism involves a friend he has always thought of as Puerto Rican but who has Black features. (Both Santos and the "Black" friend, it seems, attach negative connotations and images to Blackness.) The two are playing in an out-of-turf park when his friend trips him and Santos responds with a racially disparaging remark. His friend takes strong offense. Santos is very surprised at how upset and angry his friend is over the remark, and he apologizes. Soon after, they are accosted by a gang of Black youths who want their money. The gang lets Santos's friend go, but not Santos. Nothing too serious happens, but Santos is confused. They were close friends; the friendship cools after that.

In this story, we see again the separation and the differing treatment given to each "race." Santos assumed, like Piri Thomas's character, that he and his friend were both in the same boat. Despite physical differences, both characters assumed that they had the same identity. In essence, until Santos's reference to race and the park incident, both characters proceeded as if cultural identification were more important than racial identification. In their U.S. environment, however, both were mistaken. From the characters' perspectives, they were stunned by the racial identification.

These incidents were not returned to in either Thomas's or Colón's stories, but they were incidents that undoubtedly changed their characters' lives in a particularly decisive way.

It can be argued that these books represent a denigration of Blackness—in Santos's epithet toward his friend, in the anger displayed at being seen as "colored." This may be true and it may reflect the historically evolved denigration of Blackness in Puerto Rico and in the United States. However, the more powerful force at work is the imposition of the bifurcated race order. Being identified racially not only denied these Puerto Ricans their personal identities, but also encumbered them with low social status. If the group on the bottom of the New York City socioeconomic structure had been Native Americans instead of Blacks, and if the Puerto Ricans had been called "Indians," there would still have been the same anger and confusion. Therefore, the issue is not so much Blackness as it is the denial of personal identity and the receipt of discriminatory treatment. Puerto Ricans who are perceived to be "White" are similarly deprived of their personal identity.

This theme of being perceived (by non-Hispanics) as something other than one's Hispanic self is echoed in everyday experiences. Nearly every Puerto Rican has heard, at least once in his or her life, "You don't look Puerto Rican." The implication is that there is a Puerto Rican "look"—although, given the racial diversity of Puerto Ricans, it is hard to tell what this would be. A more recent version of this remark is, "Are you 100% Puerto Rican?" The same implication exists.[23]

In summary, a recurrent theme in the literature describing the Puerto Rican experience in the United States, and a fact of life for all Puerto Ricans, is the dilemma of being treated racially instead of culturally. This usually involves Americans mistaking Puerto Ricans for Black Americans or for White Americans, or being unable to accept "known" Puerto Ricans (of all colors) as Puerto Rican. One consequence of the imposition of the race order, as illustrated by the works of fiction discussed here, has been a separation of some Puerto Ricans from Puerto Rican friends. This has yielded anger, resistance, and confusion over the divisive racial perceptions of Americans.

Research Literature on Race

Perceptual Dissonance

The imposition of the U.S. race order has meant the dominance of racial over cultural classification, that is, the division of Puerto Ricans and other Latinos into Whites and non-Whites. Research in this area has found evidence of the strains this imposition has produced. The major findings in this area reflect the *realization* of the competing racial classification systems (perceptual dissonance), *resistance* to the U.S. system (intermediate classifications), and *acceptance* or compromise with the U.S. system (the "browning tendency"). These findings are reviewed below, and the influence of important temporal and regional effects is analyzed.

Findings from a 1972 study of 52 first- and second-generation Puerto Ricans in New York indicate that Puerto Ricans see themselves as racially different from the way they are seen by others (Rodríguez, 1974a). Respondents were asked to classify themselves in terms of color; meanwhile, the interviewer also classified respondents in terms of color, using U.S. racial classifications. These classifications were based on whether or not the person would be considered "White" by White Americans in a White setting—in other words, standing at a bus stop in Minneapolis, Minnesota, would the respondent be seen as White or not-White? Four U.S. categories resulted: White, Black, and two intermediate categories—"possibly White" and "not White, not Black." These two categories can be thought of as an intermediate "tan" group.

The major finding to emerge from this study was that a substantial proportion of respondents did not see themselves as the interviewer saw them. Objective perceptions—how they were seen—did not correspond with subjective perceptions—how they saw themselves. There was persistent perceptual dissonance with regard to racial classification.[24] Although some respondents classified themselves as lighter than they were perceived, a large number of respondents of both generations tended to classify themselves as darker than they were perceived by the interviewer (this was referred to as the "browning tendency").

A subsequent study by Martínez (1988) of second-generation Puerto Rican college students in New York found similar results. The students were asked how they thought North Americans saw them and how they saw themselves. Table 3.1 illustrates the findings. When asked what color they were (White, Black, or tan), the majority of the students (60%) said "tan," a third (33%) "White," and a small minority (7%) "Black." When asked, however, how they felt North Americans saw them, 58% said "White" and 42% said "Black." Clearly, many recognized a difference in how they saw themselves and how they were seen. Thus, the first study showed there was a difference, and the second that there was awareness of the difference on the part of Puerto Ricans sampled.[25]

Table 3.1
Racial Perceptions

	White	Tan	Black	Total
Self-perception				
Number	119	214	25	358
%	33.24	59.78	6.98	100.00
North American Perception				
Number	202		145	347
%	58.21	0.00	41.79	100.00

Source: Martínez (1988).

Intermediate Classifications

What is perhaps most interesting in the results of these studies is the tendency of many respondents to place themselves in racially intermediate positions in the United States, that is, between Black and White. Whether the term *tan* or Spanish-language terms such as *trigueño* are used, the point is that more respondents opted *not* to choose the clear White or Black designation. This response parallels the 1980 census results, which will be discussed below.

The Browning Tendency

Also of interest in the studies is the "browning tendency" noted in Rodríguez (1974a), Ginorio (1979), and Martínez (1988). This is the name given to the phenomenon of some respondents tending to see themselves as darker than they were seen by others. In the Martínez study, when respondents were asked how they thought North Americans perceived them, the percentage who said "Black" increased from (a racial self-perception of) 7% to 42%. The percentage who said "White" went from 33% (self-perception) to 58% (other perception). This indicates that many thought that North Americans would see them as "Black" even though only a small percentage saw themselves this way. It also indicates that many who thought North Americans would see them as "White" actually saw themselves as tan or Black (see Table 3.1). Thus, self-placement within the North American bifurcated system "browned" some respondents while it "blanched" others.

The whitening process is consistent with what has been normally assumed to underlie the racial-formation process among Latin Americans. Latin American racial terms and classification systems have tended to

61

"lighten" individuals. This is implicit in what Wade (1985: 243) has called the "blanqueamiento" (bleaching or whitening) tendency in Latin America and what Rodríguez (1973, 1974a) has referred to as "the preference for white" in Puerto Rico. (The studies do not explain why some respondents shifted from a darker self-perception to a lighter other perception within the North American racial classification system.) What is unexpected is the browning tendency; this contrasts strongly with the previous tradition of blanqueamiento. Why is the U.S. "melting pot" browning Puerto Ricans? Izcoa (1985: 126) finds that Puerto Ricans in the United States appear to be adopting the North American conception of race for their own racial self-definition.

There are a number of factors that may be influencing this process. Regional setting can influence browning. The studies mentioned above took place in New York City, where juxtaposition of the term *Black-and-Puerto Rican* with *White* is common and induces the conception of Puerto Ricans as a third, non-White race. (It is reflective of the times that in recent years the more common term has become *Blacks-and-Hispanics*.) This conception of a third race has usually translated into something lighter than Black and darker than White—that is, brown or tan.

The browning may also represent a political identification with "people of color."[26] Browning may reflect an ongoing struggle for racial redefinition. This struggle results from the clash of Puerto Ricans (perhaps of Latinos in general) with the U.S. race order. Although Puerto Ricans entered an essentially biracial society where integration was only one-way and where ethnicity or cultural differences were generally suppressed, the second generation came of age during intense Black power struggles. This younger group and subsequent Puerto Rican migrants encountered a society that was more intensely aware of its basic racial divisions and that was undergoing a racial transformation (Omi and Winant, 1983a, 1983b). This period of ferment crystallized the bipolar White/Black distinctions in the system. In so doing, it may have forced the choice—to be White or Black—for some Puerto Ricans, or it may have made them aware of the fact that the choice would be forced. In either case, the browning process would reflect an accommodation to, or compromise with, the U.S. race order. In a broader sense, it reflects the ongoing struggle for racial definition.

Another ramification of this struggle (and, perhaps, another result of the Black movement of the 1960s) may be seen in the large numbers who chose the intermediate racial classifications. The Black movement, in reconceptualizing the meaning of *Black*, also altered the meaning of *White* (Omi and Winant, 1983a: 45). The greatest triumph of the civil rights and Black power movements was their ability to redefine *racial identity* and consequently *race* itself (Omi and Winant, 1983b: 35). They placed on the agenda the politics of difference.

62

The second generation of Puerto Ricans encountered a society that was undergoing a comprehensive reevaluation. These basic reevaluations and redefinitions undoubtedly had an impact on a group that was already (because of its unique political status, racial makeup, and economic position) at the crossroads of the basic issues contested: race, class, and gender. The intermediate racial classifications may have represented as much an evolution of Puerto Rican intermediate racial categories as an alternate cultural-racial option to White and Black.

Racial Classification and the Census

That the United States has had difficulty coming to grips with the racial heterogeneity of Puerto Ricans and other Hispanics is reflected in the continuing debate over how to count Hispanics.[27] In 1930, Hispanics/Latinos were included in the census as a racial category. In 1950 and 1960 they surfaced as "Persons of Spanish Mother Tongue." In 1970 they were "Persons of Both Spanish Surname and Spanish Mother Tongue" (Omi and Winant, 1983a: 56). By 1980, Hispanics had lobbied for the introduction of a new item on the 100% count of the decennial census. This item asked specifically whether the person was "Hispanic" or of Spanish origin or descent and allowed individuals to specify whether they were Mexican, Puerto Rican, Cuban, or Other Spanish/Hispanic. For the 1990 census there was a proposal to abandon the 1980 format and again there were new proposals on how to count Hispanics (see U.S. Bureau of the Census, 1984).

How Puerto Ricans and other Hispanics have been counted racially also illustrates the enigma that Latinos represent within the U.S. race context.[28] In the decennial censuses of 1950, 1960, and 1970, Puerto Ricans were overwhelmingly classified as "White"—the proportion classified as Black or Negro was always less than 10%. (In reality, it is likely that more than 10% of Puerto Ricans were viewed, and treated, as non-White.) In 1980 the special Hispanic identifier noted above was introduced. The 1980 census also included the usual race question, which asked "Is this person . . ." and provided check-off categories for White, Black or Negro, Japanese, Chinese, Filipino, Korean, Vietnamese, Indian (Amer.), Asian Indian, Hawaiian, Guamanian, Samoan, Eskimo, Aleut, and Other—Specify.[29] The Other category provided for a write-in response to race. (It is this last category that yielded the groups referred to subsequently as "Other" and/or "Spanish.")

Thus, there were two questions asked, one to ascertain Spanish origin and the other to ascertain race. An analysis of these two questions for Puerto Ricans in New York yielded some provocative results.[30] Less than 4% of Puerto Ricans in New York City identified as Black, only 44% as White, and the remainder (48%) responded as "Other" and wrote in a Spanish descriptor—Puerto Rican, Boricua, Hispanic, or the like (see Table 3.2).[31] These results seem to go against earlier social scientists' predictions.[32] It was thought that Puerto Ricans who were Black would assimilate into the Black community, while those who were (or could pass for) White would assimilate into White, middle-class, suburban America, and that a few would be left as ceremonial standard bearers of the Puerto Rican community (Mills et al., 1950: 133 ff.; Herberg, 1955: 56 ff.). It

Table 3.2
Racial Self-Identification by Sex

	Male	Female	Total
White	5,459	6,920	12,379
	44.1	55.9	44.2
	45	43.6	
	19.5	24.7	
Black	513	582	1,095
	46.8	53.2	3.9
	4.2	3.7	
	1.8	2.1	
American Indian-Asian	20	17	37
	54.1	45.9	0.1
	0.2	0.1	
	0.1	0.1	
Spanish-write	5,597	7,718	13,315
	42.0	58.0	47.6
	46.1	48.6	
	20.0	27.6	
Other	540	633	1,173
	46.0	54.0	4.2
	4.5	4.0	
	1.9	2.3	
Column total	12,129	15,870	27,999
	43.3	56.7	100

Chi-square	D.F.	significance	min E.F.	Cells w/
22.82328	4	0.0001	16.028	E.F.<5
				0

Source: 1980 Public Use Microdata Sample, 5% Sample, New York City Boroughs.
Note: For each category, first row indicates number, second row indicates column percentage, third row indicates row percentage and fourth row represents the cell's percentage, of the total.

appears, on the face of it, that the few ceremonial standard bearers left—those who identified as "Other, Spanish"—constitute the largest proportion of Puerto Ricans in New York City.

On the National Level

The tendency to identify as "Other" was also seen on the national level for all Hispanics. Fully 40% of all Hispanics in the country indicated their race as "Other."[33] The proportion classifying themselves "Black" on the national level was about the same (under 4%) in 1980 as in 1970, while the proportion of "White" Hispanics fell from 93.3% to 55.6%.[34] Thus, this is not just a Puerto Rican phenomenon. A substantial proportion of all Hispanics opted for the "Other" category. Approximately 60% of the nation's Hispanic population is of Mexican origin. There are undoubtedly different racial identification patterns for different Spanish-origin groups.[35]

Hispanic Racial Classification by State

The distribution of Hispanic racial self-classification also varied by state. The proportion identifying as "other" varied from a low of 6% in West Virginia to a high of 48.5% in Kansas. Moreover, a multiple regression analysis of Hispanic racial identification by state indicated that the percentage of Hispanics identifying as "other" was positively related to the density of Hispanics in a state and negatively related to the proportion of Blacks in a state.[36] (It was not related to the proportion of Whites in a state.) Thus, the larger the number of Hispanics in the state, the *greater* the probability that Hispanics identified as "Other"; the greater the number of Blacks in the state, the *lower* the probability that Hispanics identified as "Other."[37] Assuming there is no racial selectivity in migration to different states, the data indicate that Hispanic racial identification as "other" increases with relative Hispanic density and decreases with the proportion of Blacks. It may be that the greater the proportion of Blacks—that is, the more salient the biracial structure—the more likely Hispanics are to accept biracial classifications for themselves, as White or Black. Conversely, the greater the number of Hispanics, the greater the tendency to identify as "Other, Spanish."

However, these results focus on only one variable, proportional representation of Hispanics, Whites, and Blacks within states. It is possible that the different patterns of Hispanic racial identification within these states may be due to other demographic, economic, and/or political differences among states. Moreover, since they are state-level data, they do not capture the finer details and influences of residence and socio-economic status. Nonetheless, the data do point up two important facts: (1) the prevalent, but varying, pattern of Hispanic identification as "other"; and (2) the need to research this apparent variability. It may be that racial definitions and perceptions are structurally defined, just as class and gender are. In other words, race and racial self-perceptions may reflect the economic and political context within which social relations evolve.

Hispanic and U.S. Racial Classification Patterns

The pattern of Hispanic racial identification is drastically different from that of non-Hispanics in the United States. In 1980, the proportion of non-Hispanics identifying themselves as "Other" was less than 2% in all the states, except Hawaii, where it was 2.9% (U.S. Bureau of the Census, 1982). What does this mean? Why did 40% of the nation's Hispanics, and 48% of New York City's Puerto Ricans, answer they were "Other" and explain they were "Spanish" (in some way) when asked to indicate their race? Some maintain they misunderstood the question. However, it seems unlikely that more than 7.5 million Hispanics would all "misunderstand" the question. Others might argue that these results indicate that these Hispanics considered themselves to be of "another" race. However, many Latinos would object to this interpretation.[38]

Latin American Race

On a social level, what is more probable is that Hispanics have a different conception of race, one that is as much cultural or "social" as it is racial. Vazconcelos's (1966) early book, *La Raza Cósmica*, seems to suggest that in Mexico there was an amalgamation of cultures and peoples that produced a new, stronger "race." Indeed, this concept has been a strong theme in Latin American literature and political thought (Muñoz, 1982). The common use of the term *la raza* by and for Mexicans and Chicanos and the reference to Columbus Day in Puerto Rico as El Día de La Raza (Race Day) seem to imply that there is among Hispanics a conception of "race" that differs from that prevalent in the United States. This conception may have had antecedents in Spain, may have been redefined in the colonial context, and may now be again in the process of redefinition in the United States.

Pitt-Rivers (1975: 90) has argued that in Latin America the concept of "race" is equivalent to a concept of "social race" (see also Wagley, 1965). He says that although the concept of race in Latin America is unclear, as a minimal definition it "refers to a group of people who are felt to be somehow similar in their essential nature." He argues that the word "owes little to physical anthropology but refers . . . to the ways in which people are classified in daily life. What are called race relations are, in fact, always questions of social structure." This may shed light on why Hispanics answered they were "Other" and wrote in a Spanish descriptor.

Mind-Sets Underlying Responses

On an individual level, we can logically derive a few reasons for Hispanics in the United States choosing to be "Other, Spanish." For example, some may have answered "Other" because they saw themselves as racially "other"—as being tan, beige, or brown. Others may have been "Other" by default—not White, not Black, not either of these two colors, but another color or race. This is what the census item was intended to elicit, a racial response. But others may have responded culturally. They were "Puerto Rican," "Mexican," and so on. This did not necessarily imply a racial designation or classification. The presence on the census form of separate categories for Koreans, Japanese, and other cultural categories of Asians may have increased the probability of a Hispanic cultural response (Tienda and Ortiz, 1984; Lowry, 1982).

Also possibly underlying the responses is a particular political mind-set. This is related to the cultural mind-set, but it represents a more conscious resistance to the Black/White racial classification system of the United States. Here, there is a conscious choice to reject Black-White racial classifications. In this case, the Spanish write-in classification represented not just a cultural response, but a political one as well.

Finally, there is the mind-set of the person who answered the race item from the perspective of "this is how others see me." Although how others see you should influence how you see yourself, in racial situations, where opposing perceptions are always at work, this congruence may not always be present (see the earlier discussion of perceptual dissonance).

These different response modes and mind-sets are not necessarily mutually exclusive, although one may predominate most of the time. The mind-sets may also change with length of residence in the United States, perhaps with greater exposure to non-Hispanic settings and with increasing levels of education. It is possible that the longer the time in the United States, the less the cultural response and the more individuals move toward the racial response, the cultural-political response, or the "as others see me" response. But which response mode predominated in the data, and why, we cannot say.

We can speculate, but we cannot know definitively why Hispanics chose the "Other" option to the extent that they did. What is evident, however, is that many Hispanics bypassed the "White" or "Black" options, deciding they were neither of these. It seems very probable, then, that in declaring they were "Other" and in writing in a Spanish descriptor they were declaring a cultural-racial sense of identity that had not previously been picked up in census counts. It is possible that the 1980 census captured (unwittingly) the tendency of Puerto Ricans (and other Hispanics) to identify themselves first culturally and then, perhaps, racially. This possibility requires further investigation. However, what the results indicate very clearly is that there is a substantial group of Hispanics who do *not* identify in traditional U.S. racial terms.

Race and Class:
An Analysis of Census Data

Given the traditional relationships between race and class in the United States, the question that occurs, of course, is how these "race" groups are faring economically. For example, are "White" Puerto Ricans faring better economically than "Black" Puerto Ricans? The larger question under which this is subsumed is whether the race order in the United States has affected the Puerto Rican community so as to produce different economic consequences for Puerto Ricans of different color. Do these "race" groups represent different classes?[39] These questions were investigated using the 1980 Public Use Microdata Sample census data. The results were intriguing.

Statistical analyses of this large sample indicate that racial classification is a significant stratifying variable within the New York City Puerto Rican community.[40] How Puerto Ricans classified themselves *is* significantly related to the socioeconomic position they occupy in New York City. However, the relationships found between race and economic status were somewhat unexpected.[41] Puerto Ricans identifying as "Black" or "White" fared about the same, while those identifying as "Other" (and writing in that they were Spanish) lagged far behind the first two groups.

For example, regardless of the income measure used (household income, family income, income from wages and salary, self-employment income, welfare, or income from all sources), the pattern was consistent: White Puerto Ricans were the most well-off, followed by Black Puerto Ricans, while the Other, Spanish group had a distant third place. This is illustrated by the mean household incomes of the three groups, which were $14,444, $13,396, and $11,539, respectively. The "race" groups also differed significantly with regard to education, jobs, government employment, occupations, labor force participation, hours and weeks worked, and poverty levels, and the pattern noted above generally held.[42] Thus, those who identify as "Spanish" are, as a group, more disadvantaged than those who identify as White or Black. They are less employed in the government sector, have fewer upper-level occupations, less college education, more unemployment, greater poverty, work fewer hours and weeks, and are more concentrated in declining manufacturing areas.[43]

The Assimilation Hypothesis

It might be reasoned that the "Spanish" group was less successful because they were less assimilated, that perhaps their very classification as "Other, Spanish" indicated a less assimilated stance.[44] Less assimilated they would be at a greater disadvantage in the society. However, further analysis using birthplace, English proficiency, speaking Spanish at home, fertility rates, and age as measures of assimilation did not substantiate this hypothesis. The "Spanish" and the White groups appeared to be quite similar to each other, while both these groups were significantly different from the Black group, which had higher proportions born in the states and speaking "only English" at home.[45]

Puerto Ricans Born in the United States

Traditional theories of assimilation would lead to the expectation that Puerto Ricans born in the states would tend to be more assimilated. Being more assimilated, they would therefore identify more as either White or Black, and choose the "Spanish" write-in classification least often. (This assumes, of course, that those born in the states were to a large degree raised in the states.) But the pattern of racial self-classification of those born in the states did not differ radically from that of Puerto Ricans born in Puerto Rico but living in New York.[46] The proportion identifying as "Other, Spanish" was 48% in both cases. Being born in the states seems to increase identification as Black and to decrease identification as White. This provides some support for the browning tendency noted earlier.[47] It is of interest that (1) the overwhelming majority (85%) of those born in the states still speak Spanish at home and (2) the youth (ages 16–24) identify as "Spanish" to a greater degree than the population as a whole. (This may, to some extent, be affected by the fact that parents may have filled out the census information for youth.)

Racial Identity Is in the Language

What may be more important than birthplace is where people have been socialized and for how long. Thus, we would expect to find that older U.S.-born Puerto Ricans would identify less as "Spanish" and more as "White" or "Black." We would also expect the older group to speak less Spanish at home. This appears to be the case. Up to the age of 39, the majority of Puerto Ricans born in the states speak Spanish at home and identify as Spanish. Those 40 and over, on the other hand, increasingly identify as White or Black. For Puerto Ricans born in Puerto Rico but living in New York City, there is the same tendency to take on White and Black racial classifications as age increases.[48]

The language spoken at home also appears to play an important role in racial identification. Given that English-only groups—regardless of age—tend to identify more as White or Black and less as Other, Spanish,[49] speaking English at home seems to increase the likelihood that Puerto Ricans will identify as White or Black, regardless of age. Thus, the hypothesis that Puerto Ricans born in the states would be more assimilated and, hence, identify less as Spanish and more as either White or Black held only for those who were older or for those who spoke only English at home. (Both these latter groups were relatively small in number.) This suggests that racial identity is to some extent carried or reflected in the language.

If we were to use these findings to predict the racial self-classification of those born in the states, then we would say the following: If Puerto Ricans speak only English at home, they will tend to classify themselves as White or Black, regardless of their age. If, on the other hand, they speak Spanish at home, then age is a factor, with those over 40 identifying more as White or Black and those 39 or younger classifying themselves as Spanish, as often or more often than the Puerto Rican group as a whole, and than those born in Puerto Rico but living in New York.

Gender, Race, and Class

Before proceeding to a discussion of the implications of these findings and of current trends, it is important to address the question of how gender has intersected with race and class for Puerto Ricans in the United States.[50] The distribution of Puerto Rican women's racial classification was similar to that of men.[51] In addition, among the group born in the United States, there was the same tendency to identify as Black. However, a significant theme in the data results was the significance of gender within race groups. That is, within the segmentation outlined above, there is often a further division—that of gender. Thus, within each "race" group women often tended to be worse off than their respective men. They had higher rates of poverty and were less often employed by government or in higher-paying occupations. (However, more women were employed in the professional services area.) The differences between women tended to parallel those between men. Although the numbers are not large, there is some indication that Puerto Rican women who identified as Black were exceptional in a number of ways: they were more often represented in the professional services and went to college to a higher degree than the men in their group; indeed, their college attendance exceeded that of Puerto Rican men in all groups.

Discussion and Implications

Assimilation or Biculturation?

It may be that the assimilation measures used here (and generally elsewhere) are better measures of exposure and adaptation to the United States than of acceptance and assimilation. Thus, it may be that among the most "assimilated"—by these measures—we also have the most bicultural. That is to say, among those most assimilated (i.e., those older individuals, most proficient in English, born in the states, speaking the least Spanish at home, and with the fewest children) there may also be many who are interested in retaining their ethnic culture and identity. These individuals may have dual cultural identities; they are, in essence, bicultural. For these individuals, taking on the characteristics mentioned above does not necessarily mean accepting or endorsing the host country's norms and mores and rejecting those of their home country, as the term *assimilation* implies.

71

As Portes and Bach (1985) have found in their study of Cuban immigrants, the acquisition of characteristics generally associated with assimilation in the United States need not mean that ethnic ties are weakened (see also Carillo et al., n.d.). Similarly, birthplace, by itself, is not indicative of greater assimilation for Puerto Ricans because of the strong migration and visiting flows back and forth between the states and the island. Moreover, the retention of cultural traits is not necessarily indicative of less assimilation and consequently less economic success. For example, the retention of Spanish at home has *not* been found (by itself) to have a negative impact on economic status (Tienda and Neidert, 1984). Rosenthal et al. (1983) have found that speaking Spanish at home does *not* necessarily lead to lower attainment in math and reading among children in school; instead, they find there are differential effects.

The Future

It is apparent that age and language are factors in racial identification, but it is unclear what role these factors will play in the future of Puerto Ricans in the United States. It can be argued that as those born in the states age, they will "settle" into an acceptance of the race order, that is, of the "race over culture" racial classification system. If it is a question of "settling" (with age) into traditional U.S. racial classifications, then the future of the Puerto Rican community is fairly clearly laid out. As Grenier (1981) argues, the language shift to English as usual language is completed by the age of 35, and this is indicative of Anglicization. After the age of 35, little language shift is to be expected because people have settled into the labor market, gotten married, and been more exposed to the language spoken outside of the early childhood family. In this case, as the large population of Puerto Ricans who migrated in the 1950s and 1960s ages, the community will become increasingly Black and White.

However, it can also be argued that when these data were collected these post-40 Puerto Ricans, who were born in the states and who identified more strongly as White or Black, had been less involved in the upheaval of the 1960s, when cultural and racial identification became more closely linked (Mohr, 1986). If identity is a question of socialization during the 1960s, then the future is less clear—for we do not know what impact this experience has had and will continue to have on the current and future generations of Puerto Ricans. The "settling" and the "1960s socialization" hypotheses are not mutually exclusive. However, they both require further sensitive investigation with more qualitative data.[52]

72

Emerging Trends

Race is a social category.[53] In the same way that gender has come to be separated from biological sex, so too can biological race be distinguished from social definitions of race. Since race is to a large extent socially constructed, racial definitions can change from society to society. This is evident in Wagley's (1965) example of the man who, traveling from Puerto Rico to Mexico to the United States, changes his race from White to mulatto to Negro. It is also evident in South Africa's designation of the Japanese as "honorary" Whites in their country, in Nazi Germany's designation of Jews as a race, and in the designation of East Indians, Pakistanis, and South Americans as Blacks in Great Britain. (In the United States, where race has been more biologically defined, the social or cultural dimensions of race have been less evident—although they have, nonetheless, existed.) Race as a social category also changes over time. Five trends are evident now in the Puerto Rican community as the clash between biological and social concepts of race continues: the use of *White* and *Black* as cultural terms, the concept of being non-White by default, the use of contextual racial definitions, the use of deflected racial classification, and the emergence of racial "chameleons." Each of these is discussed in turn below.

White and Black as cultural terms. Some of the trends emerging in the intense, but quiet, struggle over racial definition, that is, the race versus cultural criterion, have yet to show up in the literature or to be measured.[54] One such trend is the increasingly common use, by Puerto Ricans (and by other Hispanics), of the term *White* as a cultural designator. Earlier groups of Puerto Ricans referred to White Americans as *americanos* and Black Americans as *morenos* or *negros*; cultural subdivisions were also used when appropriate—*italianos, judios, haitianos*, and so on. In effect, and quite consistent with tradition, groups were perceived culturally—not as White or non-White.

Today the term *White* is commonly used as a cultural and not as a racial term. This is especially common among second- and third-generation Puerto Ricans as well as many other second-generation Latinos in urban areas. Thus, in speaking of speech, dress norms, attitudes, and other important criteria of status or friendship definition, Puerto Ricans and other Latinos will say quite often "He [or she] is White," or "But that's so White." Whites have become a cultural group. In the same way that ethnics are (culturally) identified by Americans (or non-Hispanics) as "the Puerto Rican boy" or "the Spanish woman," so now Americans are referred to as "the White guy," "the White woman," or, for purposes of identification, "You know, the White one." Such classifications immediately distinguish the person within a group of similarly "White-looking" Hispanics or first-generation Italians.

This cultural use of the word *White* is used by Latinos of all colorations and racial self-perceptions. The significance and depth of this change was evident when recently a Puerto Rican college professor described, in passing, a Black-looking Hispanic as "culturally Black." Thus, to be "Black" is not just to be a member of a race, for Latinos can be racially Black but culturally Spanish. It is to be a member or representative of a culture. Similarly, Latinos can be seen to be racially "White," but not be "White." Indeed, some have used the term *Spanish-White* as opposed to *White-White*.

This dimension is not so much new as it is more openly acknowledged or more acceptable today than it was in the past. What is new today is the prevalence with which the term *White* is used and how culturally specific it is, as it is used for assimilated White Americans. In the past, the term *American* would have been used in its stead. In essence, what appears to be happening is that Puerto Ricans (and perhaps other Latinos) are using U.S. racial terms as cultural terms. However, the racial terms have apparently not totally lost their original significance or their connotations of dominance or power.[55] *White*, as a cultural term, is used only indirectly to refer to a person or a group—it is generally not openly used in the company of Whites, for there is the expectation that they would be offended.

It appears there has been both some change and some continuity with regard to racial definitions. Originally, Puerto Ricans perceived, within each of the two categories—White and non-White—spectrums of color, of facial features, of hair texture, of bodily form, and of cultural predisposition that determined what kind of *non-White* or, for that matter, what kind of *White* you were. Thus, Puerto Ricans perceived different groups of people in a basically cultural way that, nonetheless, also took account of racial difference. Increasingly today, Puerto Ricans appear to be perceiving racial categories culturally. Culture continues to be foremost, but change is evident in the fact that North American race has become culture. This change is a result of the clash between the racial order in the United States and Puerto Rican/Latino racial attitudes and perceptions.

Non-White by default. Another curious result of the interaction of Puerto Ricans with the race order in the United States is the default designation of Puerto Ricans and Latinos as non-White. (This has occurred somewhat in tandem with the use of *White* as a cultural term.) To the unreflecting Americanized mind, if Latinos are not White, they must be non-White.

At the research level, excruciating mental steps are taken to be precise about racial designations and yet not offend anyone. The result is often a fairly cumbersome, almost unintelligible system of categorization. For example, academics have often used the following racially precise but convoluted categories: Non-White, Non-Hispanic, Non-Hispanic White, and any combinations thereof. These are attempts to come to terms with the fact that two categories are based on race and one on culture. The new labels may be correct, but they are somewhat removed from the reality of life for each group, which is that usually they live as Whites, Blacks, or Hispanics.

The search for multiple categories, however, reflects the difficulty of imposing the U.S. racial order on Puerto Ricans and other Latinos. It may be that the perpetuation of racism demands an either/or logic, otherwise the system would crumble. If classified racially, Latinos would subdivide into a continuum of racial categories. If they are not all White, they are non-White. Thus, in the popular lexicon Latinos are often classified as non-White, by default.

Contextual racial definition. To a certain extent, race is always contextually defined. Exemplifying this point is the classic story of the survey researcher who is unaware that he is interviewing two-thirds of an interracial family—the White father and his White-appearing son. When the Black mother returns from shopping, the researcher is seen to quietly but quickly erase his previous racial classification of the child, changing it from White to Black. The child's race changes because the context within which the child is viewed has changed.

For Puerto Ricans, and other Latinos, there are similar contextual cues that define their "Hispanicity."[56] Those who can control the contextual cues to their ethnicity often do so. Some of the most common contextual cues are surname, accent, residence, friendship network, religion, schools attended, music preferences, and, sometimes, political views (e.g., sympathy for civil rights, bilingual education, minority issues). The manipulation of these cues or symbols becomes for many the way in which they cope with the varying receptions they are given as a result of their being Hispanic. Many Hispanics unconsciously control contextual cues as a way of "testing the waters" before revealing they are Hispanic. Thus, in business, particularly in sales, last names are not initially mentioned, while in social situations or at times when the seller and buyer are both Latino, last names are stressed. This manipulation of contextual cues is not novel. All immigrants to the United States have participated in this game. What makes the Latino situation different is that this manipulation of cues can lead to more than one racial classification, and the definition of a person as Latino connotes, for some, a subtle (although often undefined and ambiguous) racial difference.[57]

Deflected race. In a society as racially diverse as that of Puerto Rico, and with the legacies of slavery, colonialism, and the Spanish Inquisition, there has probably always been a concern with being classified as non-White or less White. It is very likely that the presence of darker members in the family has always been downplayed, that they have been relegated to the background while those who were lighter or more European-looking have been advanced as the family's representative claim to the White race. In Puerto Rico, where racial classification often follows appearance, this has been possible. But in the United States, where racial classification follows ancestry, this has been more difficult to control. Consequently, in the United States, Latino families are more determinant of individual classification. If a member of the family is deviant from the European White physical type, this is enough to send the whole family to another race. Given the diversity of Latino families in the United States and their large size (which increases the probability of within-family diversity), many Latinos in the United States experience deflected racial classification.

The use of children to determine the racial identity of parents is an example of deflected racial classification, as is the use of sibling(s) to determine another sibling's race. Deflected race categorization can also be seen as an extension of contextual definitions of race. It is the opposite of the census example given above, where the child of a mixed marriage is automatically classified as Black regardless of his phenotypic appearance. In the case of deflected race categorization, if Latino children appear to be a little "colored," then their parents (regardless of their phenotypic appearance) are also designated as Black or "colored." This does not happen to "White" parents, who are presumed to have adopted the children, or to have participated in an interracial union. With the Latino family, it is not assumed that the child is adopted, but rather that the family is not White. Deflected racial classification is increasingly a part of Latino living in the United States.

Chameleons. "Perceptual dissonance" sounds like the name of a social disease. The reality, while neither infectious nor disabling, is no less painful for being "merely" a state of mind. The experience of being seen in a way different from the way you see yourself, particularly as it pertains to race, is clearly an unsettling process. Indeed, it has often been maintained that for the migrating Puerto Rican, the experience of racial reclassification, and its attendant racism, "frequently undermines the sense of autonomy and initiative . . . and leaves a residue of self-doubt and inadequacy" (Longres, 1974: 67). Longres (1974) argues that this initial shock and its result persist as a psychological dilemma even among the seemingly assimilated.

However, there is another, perhaps more positive but unresearched, side to perceptual dissonance: the chameleonlike quality that many second-generation Puerto Ricans have developed that allows them to adjust to the separate White, Black, and Hispanic worlds within which they travel.[58] This may be rooted in the ability to see oneself in a variety of ways. Not everyone is capable of making these transitions completely, but many Puerto Ricans exhibit more flexibility and adaptability in these shifts than others who are more monocultural. Many Puerto Ricans become bi- and tricultural in addition to having language versatility.[59] These abilities to adapt and to be flexible are generally not assessed in standardized tests of achievement or intelligence, nor are they usually discussed in the literature. Nonetheless, such abilities and talents are important, and should be recognized by the educational system and the wider society.

Conclusion

The material in this chapter raises many important questions. What is the significance of the trends cited? What role does the economic structure have in influencing racial self-classification? Are those who identify as White or Black more successful because they identify as White or as Black? Are they more successful because they are *identified* as White or as Black? Does success lead them to identify as White or as Black? Why do so few identify as Black? We cannot yet provide definitive conclusions. What cannot be denied, however, is that we are witnessing the strongest challenge ever to the U.S. bifurcation of race.[60]

Notes

1 The term *dual queues* refers to the hierarchical ordering of ethnic-racial groups that has historically characterized the United States. These dual job and mobility queues are the result of successive waves of immigrants into a White/ not-White racial order (see Rodríguez, 1973).
2 It is important to point out that, despite the dominant White emphasis within this system, racism is not an exclusively White domain. Not all Whites are racist, and racism can pervade *all* groups of people. Racism is always destructive, regardless of who practices it.

3 Chang (1985: 40) expresses the same idea somewhat differently: "To put it in the language of the unity of opposites, Whiteness and Blackness are coterminous social determinations—White because someone else is determined by it to be Black and Black because someone else is determined by it to be White." Chang views the Black/White distinction as an effort to render what is essentially a continuum into a set of discretes.

4 A number of works have explored the social and economic differences between ethnic groups in the United States. See, for example, Baltzell (1964), Bertoff (1968), Blau and Duncan (1964), Carpenter (1920), Domhoff (1967), Duncan and Duncan (1968), Duncan and Lieberson (1959), Featherman (1971), Fortney (1972), Gockel (1969), Greeley (1971), Griffen (1972), Herberg (1955), Hutchinson (1956), Katzman (1971), Lenski (1963), Lieberson (1963), Nam (1954), Rosen (1959), Sibley (1942), Sowell (1981), Taeuber and Taeuber (1967), U.S. Immigration Commission (1911), Warner and Srole (1960), Warren (1970a, 1970b), and Weller (1960).

5 For views of early ethnic America, see Anderson (1970), Andrews (1919), Beard (1968), Bennet (1963), Channing (1966), Degler (1959), Faulkner (1957), Higham (1956), Hudson (1965), Jones (1960), Keller (1971), and Miller Solomon (1956). For discussions of ethnicity as a neglected dimension of American history, see Anderson (1938), Cinel (1969), and Veccoli (1970).

6 A recent paper argues that the World War II experience tended to inhibit research on Jews as a cultural or ethnic group in the United States (see Kirshenblatt-Gimblett, 1986).

7 The recent autobiography of Mexican-American and Scottish folksinger Joan Baez (1987) conveys a similar sense of striking heterogeneity within one family and differential treatment as a result of this heterogeneity. She recalls being called "nigger" by her White Anglo schoolmates because of her skin color, while her own sister, who was lighter skinned, took to avoiding her in public.

8 See the following for discussions of race relations in Puerto Rico: Betances (1972), Blanco (1942), Celso Barbosa (1937), Díaz Soler (1953), Flores (1984), Giles et al. (1979), Goldsen (1966), González (1980), Gordon (1949), Hollister (1969), La Ruffa (1971), Lewis (1963), Maldonado-Denis (1972), Mathews (1968), Mills et al. (1950), Moviemiento Pro Independencia (1963), National Drug Abuse Center (1979), Pico de Hernández (1975), Seda Bonilla (1970, 1977), Sereno (1945), Rogler (1972), Tumin and Feldman (1961), and Williams (1945). For a discussion of Puerto Rican racial semantics, see Vigo (1976, 1978).

9 Zenón Cruz (1975: 131) argues that for Black Puerto Ricans racial identification is more salient than cultural identification, but that because Black Puerto Ricans deprecate their negritude, cultural identification is used. Following this mode of thought, it is possible that in Puerto Rico, the degree of race consciousness may be positively related to the degree of visibility. Thus, there may be a gradient in which the lighter or less visible one is, the less the perception and experience of discrimination and prejudice in Puerto Rico. Similarly, the greater the visibility, the greater the experience.

10 According to Chang (1985: 37), within the restrictive theories of biological descent used in the United States, one drop of Black blood "contaminates" the pure race and makes a person Black.

11 This does not mean that Black Americans will be perceived as "Whiter" in Puerto Rico; most likely these Americans will be perceived within their own cultural context, that is, as Black Americans. It is of interest, in this regard,

that the term used in Spanish to refer to North American Blacks is *morenos*. This is a term that does not have negative connotations, nor is it the term used for those with darkest pigmentation. It may have first been used because it covers a wide variety of people.

12   Harris (1970) concludes that color categories in Brazil (which are similar to those used in Puerto Rico) cannot be seen in American terms.

13   There would probably be disagreement between Puerto Ricans and Americans on whether some Puerto Rican blancos are the equivalent of Whites in the United States.

14   Ginorio and Berry (1972) provide some interesting empirical findings on the issue of racial perceptions in Puerto Rico. They found that the 201 seniors they tested in two public high schools in San Juan did not agree on where the boundary between Black and White racial classification should be drawn. This provides evidence for the notion of a changing (perhaps ambiguous) continuum of racial types.

15   Whether the arrival, during the 1980s, of significant numbers of Cubans, Dominicans, and other groups will alter the apparent cultural homogeneity of the past remains to be seen.

16   A photo essay of the members of the Young Lords Party—an offshoot of the Black power struggles of the 1960s—provides visual evidence of the involvement of Puerto Ricans of all colors (see Young Lords Party and Abramson, 1971). For an analysis of the party by its former minister of information, see Guzman (1984).

17   Longres (1974) cites an interesting anecdote in relation to the decision on segregation in education. In 1954 the Commonwealth Office in New York was contacted and asked to make a decision regarding the racial designations to be used for Puerto Rican children. The question was, How were the children to be classified, Negro or Caucasian? "The staff of the migration department decided not to use racial categories to describe Puerto Rican children but simply to list Puerto Rican children as Puerto Rican. The staff was fully aware of the invidious divisions that would have been created in Puerto Rican families if the racial categories of the United States had been accepted and imposed on Puerto Rico" (p. 73). However, there were some Puerto Ricans who disagreed with this decision because they felt it made Puerto Rican appear to be a race. Thus, Puerto Ricans were being asked to divide their children, and when they refused to do so, it appeared (to some) that the only category left within the United States was that of a third race.

18   A recent dispute over Latin music in Puerto Rico involves the question of which *synthesis* is the most reflective of the present Puerto Rican culture, the "rockeros" (the rockers') music or "salsa."

19   Wade (1985), in his study of Unguia, Colombia, also found evidence of negative attitudes expressed toward blackness. He concludes that ambiguous race relations do *not* mean that discrimination and prejudice are absent in Latin America.

20   There are some important (but still not definitively answered) questions in the debate over whether or not racial prejudice exists in Puerto Rico; for example, Have Indian and African elements been destroyed or integrated into society? Is the race issue in Puerto Rico simply ignored, or is it really not an issue? Is it necessary for harmonious "race" relations that all Puerto Ricans have some African ancestry? Are there specific prejudices against Africanisms in Puerto

Rico? Are any existing prejudices an American import? Is there an unrecognized color gradient as one moves up the income scale? If so, is this due to Puerto Rican preferential policies for light Puerto Ricans, discriminatory policies against Blacks, inequalities inherited from slavery days, or the result of American imperialism? Is the whole debate over whether there is prejudice in Puerto Rico the result of a colonialized mentality?

21 I first remember being acutely conscious of this situation when I ran into a Puerto Rican friend who asked me to join her for lunch. I scanned the school cafeteria and approached the table I thought my friend had pointed out as our meeting place. When I asked a student who was already seated there if there was a girl seated at this same table, the student asked, "Is she Negro?" As I started to answer, "No, she's Puerto Rican," I realized that to this non-Hispanic, White student, my friend was, indeed, Negro.

22 This book is also currently widely read and used in many courses dealing with Hispanics and Puerto Ricans.

23 The difficulty of correctly grasping the multiracial nature of Puerto Ricans is also reflected in the texts designed for school use. Nieto's (1987) study of children's books found that the racial depiction of the "Puerto Rican" children in the books was stereotypical and missed the diversity of racial types within the Puerto Rican community.

24 Tumin and Feldman (1961: 228) also note that in Puerto Rico, there was a difference between how Puerto Ricans were classified by Puerto Rican interviewers and how they classified themselves.

25 It should be noted that although the studies cited here had substantial numbers, they were purposive, judgment, or exploratory samples, not probability samples. Thus, generalizability of the findings to all Puerto Ricans or Hispanics in New York is limited.

26 For example, in the Rodríguez (1974a) study there were a number of respondents who would have been perceived as White by North Americans but who nonetheless responded that they were "brown" because they identified with the political movements of American Blacks and/or the oppressed in the Third World.

27 A considerable amount of organized community activity and struggle has always accompanied census changes. See Omi and Winant (1983b) and Tienda and Ortiz (1984).

28 The enigmatic situation that Puerto Ricans present was evident in the debates over the 1970 census count of Puerto Ricans. Puerto Rican groups demanded that third-generation Puerto Ricans should be included in the count, pointing out that Blacks are counted as Blacks regardless of generation. The Census Bureau considered Puerto Ricans as it had previous European immigrant groups. However, as one community leader stated: "We are considered Puerto Ricans no matter how long we are here" (New York Times, July 3, 1972).

29 The census used the same question in 1970 that it used in 1980; the only difference was that in 1980 it added the following to the listing of groups: Vietnamese, Asian Indians, Guamanians, Samoans, Eskimos, and Aleuts (Lowry, 1982).

30 The 5% Public Use Microdata Sample from the 1980 census was the basis of this analysis. Only those over 16 years old were included in the sample, which initially consisted of 27,999 Puerto Ricans residing in the five New York City boroughs. With the exclusion of Puerto Ricans who classified themselves

Asian, American Indian, and Other, unspecified, 26,806 remained in the sample. (Puerto Ricans responding that they were Asian or American Indian were omitted because of the small sizes of these categories. The "Other, unspecified" group was also eliminated from the analysis because preliminary runs indicated the group did not follow a consistent pattern.) Chi-square and analysis of variance tests were used to determine whether racial classification was a significant stratifying variable within the New York City Puerto Rican community. For additional research in this area, see Rodríguez (1989).

31 Another 4% responded they were "Other," but did not write in a Spanish descriptor; about 1% responded they were Asian or Native American Indian (1980 PUMS).

32 These are the results of the 1980 census. It is unknown whether or not this represents a significant departure from previous censuses. In the past, Puerto Ricans who might have checked off "Other" and written in that they were Puerto Rican, Spanish, or another Hispanic descriptor were counted as White. Thus, direct comparisons with previous censuses are not possible. Direct comparisons with Puerto Ricans in Puerto Rico are also impossible, because the decennial census form of 1980 did not collect or publish data on the racial classification of Puerto Ricans.

33 About 95% of all the 1980 census questionnaires were self-administered, therefore the data reflect self-classification.

34 In 1970, of the 9.1 million Hispanics in the United States, 87,930 Spanish-origin persons classified themselves as "Other," making for less than 1% in that category. Data on racial classification in 1970 were derived from the 1970 Census of Population, Subject Report Series, Persons of Spanish Origin, PC(2)-1C, Table 2.

35 Nielsen and Fernández (1981: 12) provide some evidence of different racial identification patterns for different Spanish-origin groups. Their study of high school students found that 59% of Puerto Rican high school seniors in the United States said they were "Other," compared with 52% of Mexican, 9% of Cuban, and 21% of other Latin American seniors.

36 For analyses of the role of Hispanic density in economic outcomes, see Tienda and Lii (1987) and Bonilla (1985: 161).

37 The relationship between proportion of the state population that is White and the proportion of Hispanics identifying as "other" was not statistically significant. Beta coefficients for the other two variables were statistically significant at the .001 level of significance, $F(3, 47) = 6.995$. The equation used was as follows: $y(i) = B + m_1 x_1(i) + m_2 x_2(i) + m_3 x_3(i)$, where $y(i)$ = Hispanics identifying as "Other" as a proportion of total Hispanics within each state; x_1 = White population as a proportion of total population within each state; x_2 = Black population as a proportion of total population within each state; x_3 = a dummy variable for Hispanic density, coded 1 for states where Hispanic population exceeded 100,000. (Reimers, 1984b, and Tienda, 1983b: 257, both find a strong relationship between the concentration of Hispanics and lower income for Hispanics.)

  More detailed information on the regression analysis is available from the author upon request. The data are derived from the 1980 Census of Population, Persons of Spanish Origin by State: 1980, Supplementary Report, PC80-S1-7, Tables 4 and 5 (Issued August 1982).

38 This interpretation was, in some ways, tested. In light of the Hispanic

responses to race, the census recently proposed to count Hispanics as a race. The proposal was so strongly opposed "through the most aggressive campaign ever seen by the bureau" that agency officials decided to abandon the proposal, fearing it would cause a withdrawal of needed community support (quote from McKenney, director of the U.S. Bureau of the Census, cited in *Hispanic Link Weekly Report*, May 26, 1986). It was clear from the opposition encountered that Hispanics did not perceive themselves to be a race. This stands to reason, for Puerto Rican and other Hispanic are not races, they are cultures. There are distinct ways of viewing races as well as different mixes of races within these cultures.

39 An earlier study using 1950 data tested a similar question—how race and culture influenced economic outcomes. Although results between Black and White Puerto Ricans were inconclusive, Katzman (1968) found Black Puerto Ricans to be "more successful in obtaining white collar jobs," but less remunerated for their jobs and also more subject to unemployment than Black Anglos.

40 See note 30 for a description of the sample.

41 On the assumption that the greater the coloration of Puerto Ricans (self-perceived), the greater the socioeconomic disadvantage, it was hypothesized that Puerto Ricans who identified as "White" would do best on standard socioeconomic indicators, those who identified as "Other, Spanish" would do second best, and those who identified as "Black" would do worst. Differences between groups were statistically significant with regard to all of the economic variables at the .05 level and below.

42 There was some indication that the group identifying as Black was rather heterogeneous in composition. Despite high mean incomes and an advantaged position on a variety of variables, this group also registered higher proportions of individuals suffering long-term unemployment and looking for work. Thus, the picture that emerged was one where the white and black groups fared better (economically and educationally) than the "Spanish" group, but where the relatively higher means and proportions of the Black group may have been skewed by a small subgroup of advantaged individuals.

43 There were only slight deviations from this pattern. One was the income derived from self-employment: the "Spanish" group derives slightly more income from self-employment than Blacks. Another was that "Spanish" males participate in the labor force, work as many weeks and more hours, and are "looking for a job" as much as Black males. Finally, Black men and women suffer most from long-term unemployment.

44 In many respects, to give a cultural response to a racial question is to speak from the primacy of a cultural framework, while to choose classification as "White" or "Black" implies that racial context is primary. (Although classification as "White" or "Black" need not necessarily imply endorsement of the racial system, to a degree it implies acceptance of the racial terms.)

45 It is possible that, even though those in the Other, Spanish, group were just as much born in the states as the White group, they have spent less total time in the United States. If this were the case, they may have been less exposed to assimilating forces. (The fact that the Spanish group is younger may be indicative of less time in the United States.) However, since the census does not contain "date of entry" information for Puerto Ricans, this question could not be addressed directly.

46 The pattern for women born in the states deviated slightly from the general pattern of racial classification for all Puerto Ricans. A slightly higher proportion of women born in the United States identified as White and as Black, while a lower proportion identified as "Spanish." The differences, however, were very small. Men born in the states identified more as Black and less as White, while the "Spanish" classification remained virtually the same.

47 Generalizations here are hazardous, however, because of the relatively small numbers in the Black cells.

48 However, the group born in Puerto Rico identifies more strongly as Spanish in the younger age groups and less strongly as White or Black in the older age group.

49 There is still a significant subgroup that identifies as "Other, Spanish," but it is less than 25% in all age groups.

50 The question of which of these variables (race, class, or gender) has the greatest weight in women's lives has been the subject of much debate. See, for example, Hooks (1981, 1984), Joseph (1981), Jorge (1983), Baca Zinn (1986), Nash and Fernández-Kelly (1983), Higgenbotham (1985), Rodríguez (1981, 1988), and Ginorio (1979).

51 As Table 3.2 shows, there were some interesting, but not major, differences by gender—for instance, more women saw themselves as "Other" and more men saw themselves as "White" or "Black." But, as an analysis of variance on a smaller sample of 1,395 indicated, these gender differences were not statistically significant.

52 The census is the only source with a sufficiently large number of observations to allow a broad overview of the Latino race phenomenon. Although the census data yield an analysis of considerable breadth, by their very nature they lack depth. These data also raise questions that can be answered only through more qualitative analysis, involving in-depth interviews with a large number of individuals in their family and social contexts. Preferably, these would be part of a series of longitudinal studies. Only in this way would it be possible to capture the complex and subtle dynamics as people move from one society to the other. These dynamics are extraordinarily difficult to measure, both on individual and aggregate levels. Such a study is properly the subject of its own book. It would reveal a wealth of critical information about America's race consciousness and about racial formation that, at present, does not exist.

53 Thompson (1975), Cox (1948), and Hirschman (1986) employ this perspective in their work, but Duany (1985) provides the most relevant discussion of how the economic structures that developed in Puerto Rico and Cuba have influenced the particular racial attitudes, perceptions, and relations in each country.

54 I am indebted to my students and family for heightening my own awareness of these trends.

55 The same question can be raised with regard to the racial terms used in Puerto Rico: To what extent have they lost their original connotations of power or lack of power?

56 For an excellent discussion of the determinants of "Hispanicity" among Puerto Ricans and Mexicans in Chicago, see Padilla (1985).

57 The results of a class survey by Jose Hernández at Hunter College, CUNY, are intriguing in this regard. Students in a Puerto Rican community class were asked whether or not *Latino* was a purely ethnic term (the way people act) or

a racial term (the way people look). The great majority (83%) said racial and ethnic, while only 14% said ethnic; only 1 person said neither. This indicates that the term *Latino* may be taking on racial connotations in the United States that it did not have in Latin America.

58 A similar concept is discussed briefly by de Anda (1984), who describes the cognitive styles of bicultural individuals and the degree to which their styles mesh with the majority culture. Implicit in the meshing is a repertoire of styles and switching ability for bicultural individuals.

Attinasi (1985) also finds the same switching ability in his study of East Harlem residents. He finds that residents switch from Black English to various types of Spanish to various levels of English. This, he argues, represents a diverse array of linguistic and communicative skills that suggests a variety of writing and reading abilities (see also Torruellas, 1986).

59 The question can be raised whether this chameleonlike quality will prevent Puerto Ricans from assimilating—that is, whether they are adopting bicultural skills without assimilating in the usual sense.

60 It might be argued that for multiracial groups, such as Puerto Ricans, there is bound to be a redefinition in the "fatherland" of not just ethnicity (Blauner, 1972; Nelson and Tienda, 1985; Yetman and Steele, 1975) but also of individual racial identity. We would expect ethnicity and race to be redefined according to social psychological experiences, as well as according to placement in the labor market.

4

THE POLITICAL-ECONOMIC CONTEXT

The "Puerto Rican Problem"

Public concern over the "Puerto Rican problem" surfaced with the arrival of large numbers of Puerto Ricans to concentrated areas in New York City (Pérez and Tirado, 1986: 141; Jorge, 1983). The concern began in the post-World War II period and intensified as the numbers arriving increased (see Chapter 1 for a discussion of the factors fueling the migration). Prior to this, Puerto Ricans had had a long, but quiet, history in the United States since the nineteenth century (U.S. Commission on Civil Rights, 1976; Iglesias, 1980; Uriarte-Gastón, 1987; Sánchez-Korrol, 1983). By the 1920s, there was already an identifiable "community ethos" (Jennings and Rivera, 1984: 9). Thus, the pre-World War II Puerto Rican community was a struggling community, but it was an intact, highly organized community that was making progress[1] (Sánchez-Korrol, 1983; Federal Writers Project Guide to 1930s New York, 1982; Iglesias, 1980).

The Context into which Puerto Ricans Stepped

It was the arrival of many Puerto Ricans at a time of disappearing opportunities in the port of entry that contributed to the "problem."[2] The density of the migration did not by itself create the perception of a "Puerto Rican problem." As mentioned in Chapter 1, the historical moment of a group's insertion into the host country significantly affects the experience of that group. Wolff (1982: 362) argues the same point, but from a more contextual and social perspective, when he says that "what is significant for the migrant is the position he is placed in, in relation to other groups, on arrival. That placement determines which of his prior resources he can apply and which new ones he must acquire."

In this chapter I will detail the structural forces within the economy that influenced Puerto Ricans' positioning. In the first section I will discuss a series of structural demand-side changes that embodied New York City's shift from a major manufacturing center to a postindustrial economy based on service industries. The second section takes note of how the racial order and government in the United States mediated the labor experience and positioning of Puerto Ricans.[3] The last section reviews new demand-side features that came to mark the New York City economy in the 1980s, and also influenced the position of Puerto Ricans.

Shift to a Post-Industrial, Service-Based Economy

In moving from a manufacturing to a service-based economy, New York City underwent four fundamental changes that had significant impact on the Puerto Rican work force: (1) sectoral shifts, with significant declines in manufacturing; (2) changes in the forces of production (technological changes), such as automation, robotization, and computerization; (3) changes in the location of productive firms; and (4) blue-collar structural unemployment.

Sectoral shifts. As Puerto Ricans entered the United States in the 1950s and 1960s, the U.S. economy was being transformed from an industrial to a postindustrial, service-based economy with accompanying significant declines in manufacturing (Bluestone and Harrison, 1982; *Business Week*, March 3, 1986; June 30, 1986; Center for Popular Economics, 1986: 32; Bowles and Gintis, 1986; Stevenson, 1986). This restructuring was particularly evident in New York City (Stafford, 1985: 30; U.S. Department of Labor, 1986). In the late 1950s and early 1960s, technological change and plant relocation combined to cause declines in city manufacturing and employment. The rate and volume of this sectoral decline intensified in the 1970s and 1980s, while the financial and business service sectors increased.

The sector that declined the most was manufacturing, the area in which most Puerto Ricans were employed. In 1960, manufacturing accounted for 60% of the Puerto Rican work force. In the decade that followed (1960–70), manufacturing jobs in the city decreased by 173,000 (U.S. Department of Labor, 1972), and in 1970–80, New York City lost 268,000 manufacturing jobs (Stafford, 1985: 31). Manufacturing accounted for half of the total decline of jobs in New York City between 1977 and 1984 (U.S.

Department of Labor, 1986). At the time, this loss was not offset by an increase in low-level service jobs, the other major area of Puerto Rican work-force concentration at the time. Thus, as would be expected and as the staff report of the U.S. Commission on Civil Rights (1972) found, sectoral decline became an important contributory cause of high unemployment among Puerto Ricans.

Despite the continuous decline in manufacturing jobs, this area continued to hold significant proportions of the Puerto Rican labor force. In 1968–69, Puerto Ricans in poor neighborhoods were found to be in overwhelming numbers in manufacturing, which generally paid less than was required to sustain a decent minimum standard of living as determined by the Bureau of Labor Statistics.[4] Manufacturing declines during the 1980s were even sharper than those of the 1950s and 1960s (U.S. Department of Labor, 1986). See Table 4.1, which shows that the labor force of Puerto Ricans still has a disproportionate number in manufacturing— 28% versus 16% of Whites and 13% of Blacks. In 1980, the durable and nondurable manufacturing sectors, combined, accounted for a greater share of Puerto Rican employment than any other sector. This was not true for either Whites or Blacks in New York.

Table 4.1
Location of Jobs by Industry (in percentages)

	Puerto Ricans	Whites	Blacks
Agriculture/forestry/fishing	.24	.24	.13
Mining	.01	.08	.04
Construction	2.34	3.3	2.48
Nondurable manufacturing	16.97	10.78	7.69
Durable manufacturing	11.47	4.98	5.75
Transportation/communications/ utilities	6.85	9.56	11.53
Wholesale trade	4.29	5.32	2.93
Retail trade	15.13	14.67	10.89
Finance, insurance, and real estate	9.722	12.26	9.68
Business services	5.39	6.99	6.9
Personal/hotel/recreational services	4.56	5.1	7.15
Professional services	18.29	22.07	27.88
Public administration and government	4.73	4.67	6.94
Totals	99.992	100.02	99.99
Population totals	320,780	2,151,880	815,640
Durable and nondurable manufacturing	28.44	15.76	13.44

Source: 1980 Public Use Microdata Sample, 5% Sample, New York City Boroughs.

Thus, even in 1980, Puerto Ricans were overrepresented in the most vulnerable (i.e., declining) work sectors, while their representation in growth sectors, such as business and related professional services, finance and insurance, and real estate, was disproportionately low (U.S. Department of Labor, 1986; Tables 20, 14). This situation was even more accentuated for Puerto Rican women. As Tables 4.2 and 4.3 illustrate, fully 32% of the Puerto Rican female work force was engaged in the manufacturing sector in 1980, compared with 16% of Whites and 11% of Blacks. Puerto Rican women were also more concentrated in nondurable manufacturing.[5]

Table 4.2
Male Jobs by Industry (in percentages)

	Puerto Ricans	Whites	Blacks
Agriculture/forestry/fishing	.3	.3	.21
Mining	.02	.09	.05
Construction	3.86	5.52	4.94
Nondurable manufacturing	12.93	9.42	7.95
Durable manufacturing	12.66	6.09	7.98
Transportation/communications/ utilities	9.76	13.29	17.22
Wholesale trade	5.08	6.08	4.19
Retail trade	16.57	14.69	11.93
Finance, insurance, and real estate	9.99	10.92	8.61
Business services	6.86	7.06	8.7
Personal/hotel/recreational services	4.5	5	4.25
Professional services	13.06	15.96	17.2
Public administration and government	4.42	5.59	6.78
Total	100.01	100.01	100.01
Population totals	178,840	1,156,700	378,420
Durable and nondurable manufacturing	25.59	15.51	15.93

Source: 1980 Public Use Microdata Sample, 5% Sample, New York City Boroughs.

Changes in the forces of production. Paralleling the changeover from an industrial, manufacturing-based economy to a service-based, international economy were changes in production technologies. Innovations included automation, computerization, and, to a more limited extent, robotization, all of which resulted in the elimination of some jobs and changes in skill requirements for others.[6] Originally, the effects of these technological changes were felt dramatically in the blue-collar work

Table 4.3
Female Jobs by Industry (in percentages)

	Puerto Ricans	Whites	Blacks
Agriculture/forestry/fishing	.15	.17	.07
Mining	0	.08	.04
Construction	.44	.73	.35
Nondurable manufacturing	22.07	12.37	7.47
Durable manufacturing	9.98	3.68	3.83
Transportation/communications/ utilities	3.18	5.22	6.61
Wholesale trade	3.3	4.43	1.83
Retail trade	13.3	14.65	9.99
Finance, insurance, and real estate	9.38	13.82	10.6
Business services	3.54	6.92	5.34
Personal/hotel/recreational services	4.65	5.23	9.65
Professional services	24.88	29.17	37.13
Public administration and government	5.13	3.53	7.09
Total	100	100	100
Population totals	141,940	995,180	4,372,220
Durable and nondurable manufacturing	32.05	16.05	11.3

Source: 1980 Public Use Microdata Sample, 5% Sample, New York City Boroughs.

force. Since Puerto Ricans had a high proportion of blue-collar laborers in New York City, they were severely affected by these structural changes.[7]

Changes in the location of firms. Coincident with technological change was the trend toward plant relocation. Some firms left, ostensibly to implement new technologies, such as lateral assembly-line operations in the suburbs. In this sense, changes in the forces of production affected the location of productive firms. Plant relocation placed many blue-collar and low-skill service jobs out of reach of Puerto Ricans—first in the suburbs, then in the South, and then in other countries.[8] If Puerto Ricans came to know about suburban job openings, transportation to the jobs, if present, was costly in terms of both money and time, adding one or two hours to each workday.[9] In addition, industries in the suburbs already had substantial pools of labor among the suburbanites who had moved nearby or soon would. Suburbanization of the Puerto Rican work force was difficult because of high housing costs and exclusionary practices. Thus, jobs in the suburbs were fairly unattainable for Puerto Ricans, while the attainable jobs in the city were few and diminishing.[10] The low-skill jobs that in the past had been open to immigrants and migrants were now functionally unavailable to Puerto Ricans.

The growth of government-subsidized highways during the post-World War II period facilitated suburbanization of industry and people. The lack of corresponding growth in mass transit made these suburban jobs and residences inaccessible to urban residents who were poor and/or non-White. Suburban jobs were known and accessible to those with more money, and to those who were White.[11] (See Caro, 1974, for an in-depth description of how and why mass transit construction and development were replaced by highways during this time. See also Sawyers, 1975, who argues that the growth of highways was a direct result of the interests of monopoly capital in collusion with government.) Racism and ethnic exclusion, as manifested in real estate practices, zoning, restrictive government covenants, and social psychological pressures, generally kept non-Whites and minority ethnic groups out of the suburbs. The present urban demographic pattern of White suburbs and increasing concentrations of non-Whites in the inner cities was being solidified. The change in the location of firms, in combination with the exclusionary practices cited above, perpetuated the class-racial divisions that had evolved in the United States.

The effect that suburbanization of industry and people had on Puerto Ricans was not limited to employment. Suburbanization also depleted the tax base of the cities. With a shrinking middle class, revenues proved insufficient to cover the services usually provided. At the same time, the city, with its younger, poorer population, had greater demands put on its services. Thus, while Puerto Ricans had greater needs, the city had less money at its disposal. Recently, with gentrification occurring in many areas, tax revenues have increased but city services (with the exception of the Police Department) have not returned to their precrisis levels (*New York Times*, April 10, 1985).

Blue-collar structural unemployment. By 1972, it was clear that sectoral declines were combining with insufficient educational opportunities to produce what was then termed "blue-collar structural unemployment"—what is today referred to as the "skills mismatch" problem. In simplest terms, the problem was an excess of blue-collar workers for blue-collar jobs and a scarcity of white-collar workers for white-collar jobs. This was viewed (in 1972) as having been an almost chronic condition of the economy for a decade. The Regional Plan Association (1972) found it to be one of the main problems of the regional economy. Because of this feature of the New York economy, the job market faced by the predominantly blue-collar Puerto Rican labor force was one of

90

diminishing opportunities and growing competition with other dislocated (now surplus) blue-collar workers.[12]

The school system played a role in contributing to the problem of skills mismatch. As will be noted in a subsequent chapter, the school system did not prepare Puerto Ricans for "good jobs." In 1972, when the mismatch between white-collar jobs and blue-collar skills became quite evident, the Regional Plan Association (1972: 3) concluded that "it appears that public schools in the regions' older cities and manpower training programs tend to channel Blacks and Puerto Ricans into blue collar work"—this despite decreasing jobs in these areas. This awareness notwithstanding, little was done and the situation worsened. The question has subsequently been raised of whether tracking of students, discriminatory admissions, and unequal treatment and physical facilities constitute "premarket discriminatory practices" in schools (Borjas and Tienda, 1985) and whether these "premarket discriminatory practices" inhibit the labor-market success of Puerto Ricans.[13]

Mediating Forces

The Racial Order

In addition to these structural changes in the economy, which came to affect all Americans, there were (and are) for Puerto Ricans and other "people of color" structural forces that stem from the racial order in the United States.[14] These forces mediated, in a negative and fairly institutionalized fashion, the labor experience of Puerto Ricans. For example, always pervading the worlds of work (housing and schools) was direct, indirect, and/or institutionalized racial and ethnic prejudice.[15] These forces have not disappeared with the shift to a postindustrial society. Indeed, segmented labor markets, which have been strongly associated with racial-ethnic divisions, have typified both industrial and post-industrial economies.[16]

Thus, discrimination based on race or ethnicity was a structural part of the labor market that affected and continues to affect the situation of Puerto Ricans. The structural nature of discrimination based on race, ethnicity, or gender in labor markets has received increasing attention in the past ten years. For many, discrimination is no longer understood to be just a question of people carrying around prejudicial attitudes in their heads. Rather, it is seen to be an institutionalized variable and an important mechanism that has contributed historically to the creation of segmented labor markets (Gilkes, 1980; Treiman and Hartmann, 1981: 62; National Council of Churches of Christ, 1984).[17]

Institutionalized discriminatory actions are often triggered by visibility, so that as a matter of course darker or foreign-looking individuals often elicit differential treatment—even though such treatment may be unconscious on the part of the discriminators. Visibility can be ethnic, racial, or both, and discrimination can be based on either or both. A surname or an accent can trigger discrimination just as quickly as dark skin.

Clearly, racial and ethnic visibility have influenced the labor market experience of Puerto Ricans. Although classified by the census in 1970 as 90% White and 9% Negro, in actuality a much larger proportion of Puerto Ricans appear racially "non-White" to both White and Black Americans and are thus subject to racial discrimination. In addition, Puerto Ricans have had to contend with hostility toward ethnic differences, which were in some cases intensified because Puerto Ricans identified culturally and not racially. Thus, some Puerto Ricans were discriminated against because they were racially not White and because they were culturally not Black (see Chapter 3).

Racial and ethnic discrimination collided sharply with Puerto Rican expectations, because Puerto Ricans entered the United States with a sense of entitlement; in fact and in attitude, they were citizens. The discrimination and racism they met came as a double shock. This was especially difficult for a people unfamiliar with the sharp-edged discrimination of the United States—discrimination that actually limited life chances. What Puerto Ricans found in the labor market was different from what earlier European immigrant groups had found.

Restrictive Union Policies and Practices

Trade unions, formerly an important vehicle for ethnic and minority mobility, came to function (during the great migration) so as to keep the newest or the darker minorities out. Father-son clauses that gave preference to family members for union membership, limited-access apprenticeship programs, informal, unadvertised, often ethnically bounded job recruitment and placement methods, seniority rules, and exclusionary racial practices all contributed to the exclusion of Puerto Ricans from union membership. With the exception of low-level jobs in garment factories and food services, where Puerto Ricans made up a large proportion of the work force, most unions were closed to Puerto Ricans.[18] This was especially true of the skilled and craft unions.

There was an irony in this exclusion, for Puerto Ricans in New York had a strong interest in and a solid tradition of labor activism (González and Gray, 1984: 120 ff.; Galíndez, 1969; Falcón, 1984a). Yet, despite this background and the presence of a (still) predominantly working-class labor force, union activity was not encouraged. González and Gray (1984) conclude that most of the powerful unions excluded Puerto Rican members from important decision-making processes, that civil service unions were used to prevent Puerto Ricans from realizing socioeconomic mobility, and that organized labor reacted adversely to Puerto Rican political mobilization. Thus, despite the interest and prior involvement in union activity on the part of Puerto Ricans, unions did not facilitate the economic integration of Puerto Ricans as they had for other groups.

Restrictive union policies had two major effects. One was that Puerto Rican pay rates and benefits were (and are) inferior to those of other workers doing the same jobs. This has been particularly true in the crafts area, where union blockages resulted in the growth of free-lance, nonunionized, and therefore lower-paid, Puerto Rican plumbers, painters, plasterers, electricians, and so on. (The data in Chapter 2 show Puerto Rican males to be well represented in these areas.) The other major effect was the reproduction of the racial order by unions through rewarding seniority and giving preference to the children or friends of union members.[19]

Government

After World War II, government assumed an increasingly larger role as an employer of Blacks. Indeed, government is often referred to in the literature as "the employer of last resort." It is argued that, because of this, Black unemployment has been kept from increasing too dramatically (Wilhelm, 1971). Government, however, has not hired Puerto Ricans to the same degree as Blacks—despite the fact that Puerto Ricans are also citizens. In 1973, after an extensive survey of New York City municipal government employees revealed a gross underrepresentation of Puerto Ricans, the New York City Commission on Human Rights (1973) specifically recommended that "utmost priority should be given by the Department of Personnel and all agencies to recruiting members of the Puerto Rican community." This recommendation was not made for any other ethnic group. Still, today, even after the implementation of affirmative action programs, there is concern over the lack of adequate representation of Puerto Ricans in government (New York City Commission on Hispanic Concerns, 1986: 77–95; Institute for Puerto Rican Policy, 1982, 1985).[20]

More recently, government has played another role affecting the positioning of Puerto Ricans through its policies of retrenchment. After a period of considerable expansion of social programs in the 1960s and 1970s, government pulled back. In New York City, local government retrenchment began immediately after the fiscal crises of 1975. The 1980s have seen a further dismantling of federally funded training programs, less public sector employment growth, and less attention to, and enforcement of, affirmative action programs. These programs were replaced by an appeal for private sector initiatives to take over these responsibilities, an approach referred to as "privatization." The impact of this governmental shift on the Puerto Rican community has yet to be fully documented, but early indications are that it has left the nonprofit sector in serious straits and has reversed some earlier gains (Borrero, 1983; Meléndez, 1986).

De Facto Discrimination

Government has *not* cut back "across the board"—some areas, such as defense, have had increased spending.[21] Meléndez (1986) argues that the reduction in government employment (and the shift in spending priorities) is a de facto assault on the economic status of people of color. He argues that because most of the social programs being cut are based on financial need, the reduction in government employment and the shift in spending priorities have a disproportionate impact on these groups. In addition, because of the concentration of people of color as employees in the human services divisions, spending cuts in these areas have lowered job opportunities for them.[22] Regardless of whether this is intentional, an oversight, or a de facto assault, the fact remains that current government policy does not appear to be helping the Puerto Rican community. Indeed, it appears to be reproducing the social order within which Puerto Ricans occupy a disadvantaged position.

Subsequent Economic Developments

Continuation of Trends

The context into which Puerto Ricans stepped in the 1950s and 1960s was dominated by demand-side trends, which were to continue in the 1970s and 1980s. As before, manufacturing continued to lose jobs—125,000 jobs in the 1980s alone, and Puerto Ricans continued to be overrepresented in this sector (U.S. Department of Labor, 1987). The structural shifts of the regional economy that had earlier affected Puerto Ricans were now national and international phenomena. New labels, born in the 1980s, reflected the continuing shifts—"plant closings," "runaway plants," "footloose industries," "rust belt," "displaced workers." Changes in the location of productive firms and in the forces of production increased in pace. Computerization spread rapidly to all levels of the business and financial service sector, as well as to nonprofit and social service sectors. Skill requirements continued to shift, and the skills mismatch problems became more acute. Thus, the structural features of the economy that were adversely affecting Puerto Ricans in the 1960s intensified in this decade.

The Fiscal Crisis

The retrenchment policy instituted as a result of the New York City fiscal crisis had severe consequences for Puerto Rican employment (U.S. Department of Labor, 1987). There were no new hires, and many were let go. Those last hired became those first fired and, to the extent that Puerto Ricans were in local government, they tended to be among those last hired. The fiscal crisis (along with other factors and a more conservative national political context) also promoted a change in the attitude of government toward social programs. Puerto Rican community programs, which had often served as informal training grounds for new Puerto Rican leaders (Rivera, 1984), were severely hurt. Although comprehensive data are lacking, anecdotal evidence indicates that many programs with formal employment training components were particularly hurt.

Globalization of the NYC Economy

While the shifts noted above continued in the 1970s and 1980s, a new set of events and trends were to arise that did not substantially improve the positioning of Puerto Ricans. One very important trend was the globalization of the world and New York City economies. Global systems theorists have noted that, more than ever before, capital and labor move within worldwide systems rather than within national borders (Sassen-Koob, 1988; Portes and Walton, 1981; Nash and Fernandez-Kelly, 1983). Contributing to the convergence toward a world economy have been cheaper transportation, advances in telecommunications, and the lowering of trade barriers. The development of a global economy has resulted in more unskilled people from all over the world being drawn into this global system. This has created a situation in which international migrants compete with domestic workers in nearly every developed country, while at the same time jobs are being moved to developing countries in search of cheap labor.

The trend toward a global economy has had other effects as well. American capitalists, in order to produce competitively priced goods, have become involved not just in the search for low-wage sectors, but also in the global search for foreign markets. Capitalists in older, industrial countries have also been involved in this search. It was this constant search and movement of capital that led to the introduction of the expression "hypermobility of capital" (Bowles and Gintis, 1986; Stevenson, 1986; Bluestone and Harrison, 1982). Thus, the issue of disappearing jobs for Puerto Ricans is ensconced in an international matrix of forces that weave their way back to determine the fates of regional economies.

These patterns, as well as the labor market's widening split into two tiers, were evident as New York City consolidated its national and international positions as a global city. The city's move to become an international financial center, for example, provided more jobs, but the bulk of the job growth occurred in the higher-paying, higher-status occupations—managerial, professional specialty, and technical fields. Indeed, for the entire resident population, managerial, professional, and technical workers accounted for three-fourths of all net employment growth between 1977 and 1987 (U.S. Department of Labor, 1987). In addition, global competitive pressures accentuated the propensity of businesses to hire nontraditional (i.e., immigrant) labor with lower labor costs.[23] These features of the international economy in New York hastened the continuing disappearance of jobs traditionally held by Puerto Ricans.

New Immigrants and the Informal Sector

Another significant trend of the past two decades has been the growth of the informal sector—that sector often referred to as "hidden" or "off the books," including not just small-scale home operations but larger economic activities such as unregistered sweatshops.[24] The informal sector is increasingly viewed as a permanent structural feature of the process of capital accumulation on a global scale. Thus, those in the formal economy depend on those in the informal economy to provide low-cost goods and services that they no longer produce or provide. Class relations are reproduced through these informal sector activities, and there is an expansion in the low-wage work force to service high-income tastes and needs. Thus, labor-intensive occupations and services, such as specialty boutiques, customized production, and hired maintenance staff, quickly become integral parts of gentrifying areas. These informal sector activities are seen to be crucial to the city's formal economy and to the larger global economy (Sassen-Koob, 1986).

Many of the new immigrants who arrived during the 1970s and 1980s were accommodated within this informal sector (Waldinger, 1985; Sassen-Koob, 1989). It is unlikely that Puerto Ricans have been, or will be, employed to the same degree by these informal sector firms. As Sassen-Koob (1983: 198) has noted, the greater politicization of women and more traditional minorities with regard to unions, wages, and workers' rights may make these workers less preferable, more costly workers in the informal sector.

The Puerto Rican work force has become accustomed in the formal sector to minimal job standards—minimum or union wages and benefits, overtime rates, social security and unemployment compensation, and 35–40-hour workweeks. In addition, as citizens, Puerto Ricans cannot be forced into compliance by threats of deportation.[25] Thus, Puerto Ricans may be seen as less desirable workers than new immigrants. They may also apply for these jobs less often.

These effects may be transitory, however, for new trends are emerging that will affect both groups: projected labor shortages, the reemergence of crafts in NYC, the greater specialization of manufacturing jobs (with consequent greater retention of higher-skill blue-collar jobs), and the decline of wages in the human services. Also, new waves of immigrants with lower labor costs may replace today's new immigrants, prompting their early withdrawal from the labor force. It is not clear at present how these trends will affect Puerto Rican employment; they are mentioned here to emphasize the vulnerability of labor to the economic shifts in the city.

Credentialism

Credentialism, another more recent feature of economic restructuring, has two dimensions: one is the *emphasis* on credentialism (i.e., the definition of jobs according to credentials), and the other is the surplus of credentialed individuals who compete with noncredentialed individuals for lower-level jobs.[26] To take the latter first, more college graduates have entered the NYC labor market in the last 10 years than in the prior decade (U.S. Department of Labor, 1986). Because of the vanishing number of middle-level jobs (Ehrenreich, 1986; Wessel, 1986), more and more college graduates are "settling" for jobs below their skill levels until something else comes along, or in the hopes that they can move up from there. (These jobs are referred to by some as "nonsupervisory" jobs; see, for example, Stafford, 1985.) A college degree has become a screening device for many of these jobs.

Thus, college graduates become secretaries and may move quickly to administrative assistant positions; or they work, and are paid as, secretaries but are called administrative assistants; or they sell insurance, handle adjustment or credit claims; or they take jobs waitressing until they get their lucky break. They will be hired over high school graduates or those with even less education, who in past might have gotten these jobs. Thus, the labor market that most Puerto Ricans face today has (in addition to displaced manufacturing workers) proliferating numbers of technically or college-trained youth who are competing for the same jobs. Moreover, by applying for these jobs, these more "credentialed" individuals are placing them out of the reach of those with only high school diplomas. They are, in a sense, "credentialing" the jobs by filling them. In other words, they are making new credentials permanent requirements of these jobs.

In addition, jobs within the growth sectors are also requiring credentials that were not necessary in the past. In terms of the tasks to be done, the step from a 7th Avenue garment district secretary to a Wall Street financial district secretary is very short, but it often requires a big credential. Credentials are usually thought of as educational degrees or specific skills training, but they often involve more subjective or class-related characteristics, such as family connections, ethnic group ties, socioeconomic and residential background, prestige of the schools attended, current residence, manner of dress and style of clothing, religion, speech, contacts, travel experience, club memberships, and life-style. The transferability of "skills" or "credentials" is sometimes more problematic if workers are older.

Mobility is now also difficult without credentials. As Thomas R. Bailey, an economist at the Conservation of Human Resources Institute at Columbia University, recently put it: "You can no longer start in the mail room and become a line supervisor or a secretary" (New York Times, December 4, 1986: B16).

Two-Tiered Society

We are also beginning to see the relative contraction of jobs at the middle level (Ehrenreich, 1986; New York Times, September 27, 1988: A22). At the same time, job shares are increasing at the polar extremes.

The fastest-growing service industries have been characterized by larger-than-average concentrations of low- and high-paid jobs as middle-income jobs have been upgraded and downgraded (Sassen-Koob, 1986; Falcón-Rodríguez, 1987: 82, 111). The vague outlines of a future two-tiered society are beginning to emerge. At the top of this society are the new high-level service jobs in the financial, real estate, and business services industries. Those in these jobs service the new corporate clientele from abroad and within the United States; they populate the suburbs and the gentrifying areas of the city. At the very bottom are the homeless and the hungry. Within this emerging class context, the attainment of American middle-class dreams appears to be dimming for Puerto Ricans and others not at the upper end of the scale.

The Positive Side

Economic Dividends to New York City

Despite the economically difficult position in which Puerto Ricans found themselves in New York, they were crucial to the proper functioning of the New York economy. Puerto Ricans enabled New York City to sustain a threshold level of low-wage labor. Without this source of cheap labor, many more firms would have left the city, and those that stayed would have been confronted with more difficult economic conditions. (For example, they might have had to cut back on output or suffer lower profit margins.) This has been particularly true for the hotel and restaurant industry, where Puerto Ricans have made up a large percentage of employees (Economic Equal Opportunities Commission, 1966).[27] It was also true at one time for the textile industry, where Puerto Ricans played a crucial role in an industry vital to New York's economy (this role is played today by the newer immigrants).

In a sense, New York's claim to be the garment capital of the world rested upon Puerto Rican shoulders.[28] In 1970, New York accounted for 70% of all dollar sales of clothing in the United States at the wholesale level. Garment manufacturers produced and sold more than $7 billion in apparel each year. Although the total number of garment firms has declined over the years, the total dollar volume of business has remained high.[29] As late as 1973, the garment industry employed more people than any other type of manufacturing, providing a total annual payroll of $1.5 billion (*New York Times*, November 26, 1972: 1). Despite the continuing and subsequent declines in the number of jobs in garment manufacturing, it is still a major employer in New York City (U.S. Department of Labor, 1986; Waldinger, 1985: 329 ff.). Some scholars contend that but for the Puerto Rican migration, New York City would not have been able to hold on to this very important industry (Senior and Watkins, 1966; Vernon, 1960; *New York Times*, June 27, 1954: 52).

A Note on the Successes

It should be borne in mind that some Puerto Ricans have coped successfully with the structural forces that have tended to have an adverse influence on the economic integration of the group. It is evident from NYC census data that there has been movement to growth sectors within the NYC economy and to other areas of the country. Some groups of Puerto Ricans in New York are doing quite well. For example, mainland-born Puerto Ricans in New York are better educated and have a more favorable occupational distribution than those born on the island; mainland women participate in the labor force at rates as high as or higher than those for non-Hispanic Whites; Puerto Ricans with a college education are employed as often as non-Hispanic Whites, and, at the highest levels of education, approximate the characteristics of non-Hispanic Whites (Falcón-Rodríguez, 1987).

There have also been improvements, for instance, increases in semiprofessional and technical occupations, regardless of gender or nativity (i.e., whether island or mainland born), and an increase in the labor force participation rates of women in the last decade (Falcón-Rodríguez, 1987). In addition, there are indications that Puerto Ricans have fared better in communities outside of New York. As was pointed out in Chapter 2, there are also questions about the data used to measure Puerto Rican progress—for example, whether the continually depressed levels are the result of a continually changing population of people that may include many who are not Puerto Rican. What the successes essentially show is that Puerto Ricans *can* do it. Whether or not more Puerto Ricans will succeed will depend greatly on the future context of opportunities and the position that Puerto Ricans are placed in in relation to other groups.

Summary: The Structural Nature of It All

Despite the important role played by Puerto Ricans in the city's economy and the successes of many, the general experience and context of the migration have been difficult. Puerto Ricans arrived in largest numbers during the city's transition from a major manufacturing center to a postindustrial economy based on corporate and cultural service industries. The Puerto Rican work force was concentrated in the most vulnerable of the manufacturing areas, durable goods and the garment sector. Thus, Puerto Ricans became unknowingly enmeshed in the economic and social dislocations inherent in the city's transition. In essence, low-skill and blue-collar jobs were being eliminated by technological change while others were protected by unions or moving away to the suburbs, the South, and low-wage sectors in other countries.

Fewer jobs meant more unemployed people and greater competition for remaining jobs. Since these trends occurred more rapidly than outmigration or the retraining of blue-collar workers to fill white-collar jobs, a severe problem of blue-collar structural unemployment arose in the region. Puerto Ricans bore the brunt of these shifts because the Puerto Rican work force was so heavily concentrated in manufacturing. Puerto Ricans also had to contend with a societal order than included racial prejudice and ethnic hostility, which were reproduced through restrictive union policies and practices, an educational system that did not prepare Puerto Ricans for "good jobs," and the relative exclusion of Puerto Ricans from government employment.

The 1970s and 1980s saw a continuation of these economic trends, a fiscal crisis, New York City's move to become a national and international financial center, a new emphasis on credentials (along with the proliferation of credentialed workers), the entrance of new immigrants working at lower wages, often in the informal sector, and diminishing middle-level jobs. These new trends and events did not improve the job possibilities of Puerto Ricans. Finally, the government's nonpreferential role in employment vis-à-vis Puerto Ricans, then its reduction of training programs, affirmative action, and social spending in the 1980s, exacerbated the troubled context into which Puerto Ricans stepped.[30]

Notes

1   For a partial listing of newspapers and magazines begun during the early period of the Puerto Rican community in New York, see Perez and Tirado (1986: 165).

2   The role of ethnic group density in the accommodation of groups into regional economies has not received a great deal of attention, but Lieberson (1980) found that, in the case of Blacks and Asians in California, it was the number of increasing Black migrants (plus the more negative attitudes toward Blacks) that contributed to their lack of success vis-à-vis Asians. Tienda and Lii (1987) also found that Hispanic density makes a difference and that it is an important reception factor for Puerto Ricans in different states.

3   As noted in Chapter 2 (note 1), there are other contexts in the states where Puerto Ricans have entered and been able to make better use of the resources they brought. Thus, while in New York, Puerto Ricans were found to be disadvantaged relative to "other Hispanics" in the city (Mann and Salvo, 1984), in Florida and California Puerto Ricans fare quite well relative to other Latinos. Whether this is the result of selective migration to these states or some other factor is unclear.

Also unresearched is the question of whether the more successful leave New York City or Puerto Rico for places where they will be more successful. There is some indication that mobility between states yields higher labor force participation rates for mainland-born Puerto Ricans (Tienda, 1985: 69) and that Puerto Ricans who lived outside of New York in 1970 had larger proportions in the labor force (Jaffe et al., 1980: 236).

4   According to the U.S. Bureau of Labor Statistics, in 1970, 60% of manufacturing jobs paid less than was required to sustain a decent minimum standard of living (New York Times, November 5, 1972: 43). See also U.S. Commission on Civil Rights (1972) for information on the numbers of Puerto Ricans in manufacturing during the 1960s.

5   Although the Bureau of Labor Statistics no longer issues data just for Puerto Ricans, it recently found that Hispanics as a whole continued to be overrepresented in the declining manufacturing sector, while they were underrepresented in new growth areas (U.S. Department of Labor, 1987).

6   As changes in the forces of production have continued, there has arisen a debate on the effect of these changes. It is unclear at this point whether these changes have resulted, in the main, in the deskilling of the bulk of the labor force or whether they have resulted in greater polarization of the work force.

7   See Rodríguez (1973, 1979: 203–204), who shows that between 1950 and 1970, Puerto Ricans consistently had the highest proportion of blue-collar workers. It should also be noted that not only did blue-collar factory jobs decline as a result of the change in the forces of production, but also declining were the "entry-level, paper-pushing posts that in the past absorbed thousands of young people with high school diplomas or less." These were the jobs into which many of the second generation would have moved (New York Times, December 4, 1986: B1, B16).

8   In some cases, plant relocation has come full circle as firms have seen the economic wisdom of establishing firms in the informal sectors of large cities. In essence, why travel to China or Korea when such firms can be established at competitive costs in Chinatown?

9   The American Transit Authority estimated that the nationwide average cost for an inner-city resident to travel to the suburbs for his or her job was $15 per month in 1968. In New York the estimate for transportation from Harlem to Farmingdale, Long Island, was $40 per month in the same year (Will and Vatter, 1970). These estimates did not take into account waiting time or the fact that schedules were usually geared to facilitate the mass of suburbanites coming into the city for work and not vice versa. (It is of interest that in the last decade most of the new jobs in New York City have gone to suburban commuters.)

10 The question of why Puerto Ricans were unable to move to the suburbs for these jobs is perhaps best answered by Barry (1986): "Like new housing in general, the new suburban housing was not available to the least well off or, to a great extent, to minorities. Unlike earlier times, the poor were physically and politically barred from the areas containing the new housing because of jurisdictional fragmentation and exclusionary zoning." Highways and recreational sites were also planned so as to exclude inner-city minorities from suburban sites (Caro, 1974).

11 Even if Puerto Ricans secured jobs in the suburbs, the transportation difficulties were such that the jobs were usually short-lived. As Rosenberg (1974: 204–205) points out: "If Puerto Ricans living in central cities do obtain such jobs, our data suggested that the difficulties of transportation involved in the 'reverse commuting' from their residence areas to the suburban employment centers may be too much of a burden."

12 See Rodríguez (1973) for data on the Puerto Rican work force composition between 1950 and 1970; see also Torres (1987).

13 Tienda (1983a: 69) also raises this question in part and in relation to all Latinos.

14 There is considerable debate about the relative importance of the race order and the economic order in determining class position. Meléndez (1986: 49), for example, argues that not only have people of color had to contend with the forces of institutionalized racial and ethnic prejudice, but they have also served as a buffer between the full effects of downward cycles and other segments of workers. Although this debate will continue, it is clear that the racial order and the economic order reinforce each other and that they are often inextricably intertwined. (See Chapter 3 for an analysis of the relationship of Puerto Rican race and gender to class.)

15 In 1975, I found that first- and second-generation Puerto Ricans in New York City perceived discrimination to be a common occurrence in the workplace and in other areas. Other studies have found that labor market conditions and discrimination have contributed to the disadvantaged status of Puerto Ricans. See Tienda (1985: 63), who states that the "total effect of discrimination has probably been understated." Borjas (1983) finds that it is the "structural" factors (i.e., the interaction of individual characteristics and the probability of employment) and not Puerto Ricans' observable characteristics that lead to lower employment rates. See also Hernandez (1983).

16 Other researchers have argued similarly; for example, Colón-Warren (1984) points out that transformations of the economic system continue to reproduce competition and inequality. In a similar vein, Stafford (1985: 145) discusses how each segmented market has evolved separate criteria for entry and rules for mobility: "These markets have been shaped by historical forces, including immigration and migration patterns, educational requirements, hiring

practices, and the role of unions. These markets are also being shaped by industrial and job reorganization caused by technological changes, the weakening of affirmative action programs, new union agreements that protect present workers but penalize new employees, and the disbanding of publicly funded training programs." It appears that the forces shaping entry and mobility rules for these markets will continue to reinforce the current race order.

17 There are others who argue that discrimination, although it may exist, is not and was not a structural part of the labor market. This recently (re)developed school of thought has been used in analyses concerning the evident stratification of racial-ethnic groups in the United States (Sowell, 1981). Riding on the ideological wave of entrepreneurship, proponents of this point of view argue that the differences between racial/ethnic groups are due to entrepreneurial ability, or the ability of groups to take advantage of the free market. According to this perspective, this is what has given some groups a better place in this society, that is, a greater cultural capital edge: some groups have fared better than others because there have been differing "individual" efforts on the part of these groups. (For a critique of this perspective, see Rodríguez, 1984b).

18 Tabb (1972) presents data (limited to referral unions) that bear out the contention that Puerto Ricans were vastly underrepresented in certain unions, especially the craft unions. See also Stafford (1985: 143, 145), who found that even in the 1980s, union practices have kept Blacks and Latinos from achieving upper-level positions in the crafts area.

19 The construction boom in New York City provides a more recent example of union exclusion. The hiring of out-of-town workers led to new complaints that the unions were denying jobs to minority workers even in a time of full employment and labor scarcity (New York Times, March 30, 1986: sec. 8, p. 1).

20 A recent article pointed up the continuing discontent within the Puerto Rican community over this situation (New York Times, October 31, 1982: 60). See also Institute for Puerto Rican Policy (1982), which documents the under-representation of Latinos in state government, and Rodríguez (1984a), who takes note of this situation with regard to Latinas in New York State.

21 Changes in the shares of gross national product by various categories of federal spending show that three areas have increased between 1981 and 1985: defense expenditures (by 1.1% of total GNP share), interest payments (by 1.0%), and Medicare and social security (by 0.4%). All other areas have declined, including social spending, which declined by -0.8%. These figures are based on Office of Management and Budget, Historical Tables, Fiscal Year 1986, Tables 1.2, 2.1, 2.2, 3.2, cited in Center for Popular Economics, 1986: 152).

22 See Falcón-Rodríguez (1987: 95, 110) for data substantiating the growth of Puerto Ricans in the human services areas in New York between 1970 and 1980.

23 Colón-Warren (1984: 415) points out that capitalists hire workers who are discriminated against because they allow lower labor costs. This, however, does not mean that capitalists are color, sex, or nationality blind, for there are other occasions when discrimination is used as a means of maintaining a larger industrial reserve army and low earnings.

24 A more precise definition of the informal sector is given by Portes and Sassen-Koob (1987: 31): "the sum total of income-earning activities with the exclusion of those that involve contractual and legally regulated employment."

25 An interesting example of such displacement occurred recently when a long-time Puerto Rican worker in the garment industry asked to be paid for overtime work. The boss, not knowing the employee was Puerto Rican, said the time didn't count because the additional hours had not been fully completed each day. When the woman insisted on being paid proportionately, the boss indicated he didn't like troublemakers and would "report her" (the implication being that he would contact the immigration authorities). The woman fought for her rights and did get her overtime, although she lost her job and has been unemployed ever since.

26 Between 1970 and 1980, there was a decline of island-born men in service employment within the food services sector in New York, while mainland-born and non-Hispanic White men registered an increase in these areas (Falcón-Rodríguez, 1987: 110). This would seem to indicate there is some "yuppification" of restaurant jobs going on in New York. The recent refurbishing of the famous 21 Club in New York City also resulted in the ouster of long-time employees who were predominantly Latinos and older workers. A lawsuit was brought by the fired employees (*Newsday*, May 14, 1987, p. 6; *New York Daily News*, May 15, 1987, p. 20).

27 To some extent, the growing numbers of Puerto Ricans (and Blacks) in the health and hospital services might be seen as a forthcoming parallel phenomenon. In this case, however, government subsidy is the larger determining factor in whether or not this industry stays in New York. These services are equivalent to utilities—they do not have the option of leaving the city; their only alternatives are to grow or deteriorate.

28 The Harvard study of the New York metropolitan region took note of this role in the 1950s: "The rate of Puerto Rican migration to New York is one of the factors that determine how long and how successfully the New York metropolitan region will retain industries which are under competitive pressure from other areas. To the extent that some of these industries have hung on in the area, they have depended on recently arrived Puerto Rican workers, who have entered the job market of the New York area at the rate of about 13,000 each year" (Vernon, 1960).

29 In 1972, the *New York Times* (November 26: sec. 3, p. 1) pointed out that although the number of garment firms declined in the 1960s, the remaining firms were larger and financially stronger. Sassen-Koob (1983: 191–192) has more recently argued that it was the larger shops with standardized production that moved, while the less mechanized branches, as well as the industry's marketing and design operations, remained in New York. (See also Waldinger, 1985, who maintains that NYC still competes successfully in the production of unstandardized goods.) In either case, the industry is still a very viable part of New York City.

30 See Stafford (1985: 6–11 ff.), who says that the 1980s have seen a dismantling of training programs, less public sector employment, and less attention to and enforcement of affirmative action programs (see also Center for Popular Economics, 1986).

5

HOUSING AND THE SOUTH BRONX

This chapter focuses on one of the most critical, yet neglected, dimensions of the Puerto Rican experience: housing. A basic need of all peoples, and often the basis for the creation of communities, it is a contextual issue that deserves special mention. The thesis of this chapter is that urban decay and urban renewal have destroyed certain Puerto Rican communities, the major one being that in the South Bronx. This, in turn, has affected both community and family ties. In developing this thesis, I will advance four major ideas: (1) that the degree of residential mobility and housing decline experienced by Puerto Ricans appears to have been greater than for others in New York City; (2) that, to a large degree, this has been due to the forces of urban change—housing abandonment and decline, urban renewal, and gentrification; (3) that the Puerto Rican communities have made, and are making, considerable efforts to reconstruct their communities and survive against great odds; and (4) that, in at least the case of the largest Puerto Rican community—the South Bronx— the response of the city has been inadequate in relation to the size of the problem. Before discussing the responses of the city and the Puerto Rican community to the devastation found in the South Bronx, the first section will examine more generally the issues of geographic mobility and housing within Puerto Rican areas.

Geographic Mobility

The latest journalistic rationale for the "lack of progress" of Puerto Ricans is alleged to be their back-and-forth movement between Puerto Rico and the United States—the "*va y ven*" phenomenon. This, it is argued, prevents Puerto Ricans from making the commitment or the sacrifices necessary for success in the United States.[1] However, there are no solid data on the extent to which Puerto Ricans uproot themselves and their families to settle in the United States and then move back again to Puerto Rico. There is, of course, constant travel back and forth, but the percentage of the Puerto Rican community in the United States that is involved in the back-and-forth trek for employment or settlement is not known. Indeed, the 1980 New York City census figures indicate that less than 5% of Puerto Ricans then in New York had been living in Puerto Rico five years earlier. This does not indicate a great volume of back-and-forth flow. Furthermore, as the current thesis has been articulated, it implies that lack of progress is due to factors that are presumably within the control of the individual, such as the decision to return to the island. It also implies that individuals leave jobs in the states to return to the island; it does not consider that return may have been prompted by the fact that the jobs have left the individuals.[2]

At the same time, there is little mention in these journalistic accounts of the forced movement Puerto Ricans have experienced within the United States because of housing decline, gentrification, and urban renewal. It would seem this has had an impact equal to, if not greater than, back-and-forth movements between the island and the states. Census figures provide some indication of Puerto Rican residential mobility. In 1980 in New York City, almost half of long-term Puerto Rican residents—and more than half of *all* Puerto Rican residents—had lived in different houses five years earlier (Table 5.1). In fact, the proportion of Puerto Ricans whose residences had not changed from 1975 to 1980 was the lowest of all groups: 51%, compared with 74% of Whites and 63% of Blacks. When almost half of a population experiences residential change, there is more going on than changes in tastes, income, or even untabulated upward mobility. The high proportions of Puerto Ricans who moved in the Bronx and Brooklyn are indicative of the housing destruction and abandonment in these areas (see Table 5.1).

The extent to which housing decline and urban devastation have been recent features of the Puerto Rican community is brought home by the following. The Bronx and Brooklyn, the two boroughs where the *majority* of Puerto Ricans live, have also been major areas of housing devastation.[3] Between 1970 and 1980, these two boroughs accounted for more than 80% of the net loss of housing units in the *entire country* (Yong and Devaney, 1982). The recent "Report of the Mayor's Commission on Hispanic Affairs" (December 10, 1986) shows that Puerto Ricans use a larger portion of their income for rent than other groups and are less likely to be homeowners. In addition, in 1981 and again in 1984, compared with Whites, Blacks, other Hispanics, and others, a higher proportion of Puerto Ricans occupied dilapidated units, lived in units with three or more maintenance

Table 5.1
Residence and Mobility

	Puerto Ricans	Whites	Blacks
All residents			
Same house percentage[a]	42.16	63.47	54.15
Long-term residents,			
percentage who had moved since 1975			
Bronx	18.42	3.06	7.84
Brooklyn	17.31	9.64	16.79
Manhattan	9.37	4.98	6.33
Queens	3.05	7.00	5.17
Staten Island	.38	1.67	.41
Same house	51.45	73.65	63.47
Total	99.98	100	100.01
Population base	705,003	3,194,154	1,448,448

Source: 1980 Public Use Microdata Sample, 5% Sample, New York City Boroughs. Population over 15.

[a] The proportion of people who resided in the same house at the time of the census (1979) and in 1975.

deficiencies, and lived in areas with boarded-up buildings on their blocks (pp. 56–57). Yet, the impact of this housing devastation on the Puerto Rican community has received scant attention. This has been especially true in the area of greatest Puerto Rican concentration—the South Bronx.

The South Bronx

While the impact of urban devastation on the Puerto Rican community had not received much attention, the South Bronx has received national and international attention. It has earned an international reputation as an ignominious and distressing victim of urban decline. The South Bronx has suffered such extensive devastation that its name is synonymous with urban blight. It has been called, among other things, the "international symbol of urban decay and devastation," "the nation's most publicized wasteland," "symbol of urban decline, devastation and destruction," "home of the poorest of the poor," "a disaster area," and, finally, "like the bombed-out cities of Europe after World War II."

Although the point of this chapter is the impact of urban decay on the Puerto Rican community, it will undoubtedly occur to readers to ask why this devastation has occurred. There are a number of factors often cited to explain why the southern part of the Bronx became the South Bronx—for example, the failure of local government policy; rent control; drug traffic and other crime; the prevalence of poorly planned housing projects; the gutting of neighborhoods by the construction of the Cross Bronx Expressway; the construction of Co-Op City; the postwar policies of the federal government, which emphasized highway building and suburban residential development and ignored inner-city development (Barry, 1986); and banking policies (Meyerson, 1986). All of these played a role in depleting the South Bronx of people, jobs, and housing. However, the question is still relatively unresearched.

Housing and Population Change

The extent of change in the South Bronx can be seen in the following figures. In 1970, Puerto Ricans were the largest group in the South Bronx; Whites constituted 20.2%, Blacks, 33.9%, and Hispanics, 35.1%. In 1980, 91% of the South Bronx population was Black and Hispanic, with Puerto Ricans constituting the larger share. Thus, in this period, approximately 87% of the White population left.[4] In the same ten-year period, the South Bronx lost 27,763 units of housing. This amounted to a net loss of 10.5% of its housing stock.

As significant as this figure is, it understates the extent and impact of housing loss, because it does not include buildings that had roofs but were abandoned and not inhabited.[5] (It must be borne in mind that over 50% of all the housing units in the Bronx of the 1970s were in the South Bronx.) Every district in the South Bronx, except one, lost housing in this period.[6] To comprehend the impact of this housing loss, one must appreciate the way in which housing loss occurred and the impact it had on the neighborhoods and networks that made up the areas.

It wasn't that every tenth unit disappeared evenly across the South Bronx; rather, certain neighborhoods were swept with devastation, leaving local landscapes where one or two buildings were the lone survivors of an unabated process of destruction. The urban landscape became for some residents an unbroken picture of rubble and brick extending to the horizon. The famous Charlotte Street area lost over 12,000 units of housing in the 1970–80 decade—over 7,000 units in one year alone. Population loss accompanied housing loss. In one district (Community District [CD] 3) there were almost 150,000 people in 1970; by 1980, there were almost 100,000 fewer. The district had lost 65% of its population in one decade.[7] In an adjoining district (CD 2), 63% of the population (or 60,852 people) had been lost. And in the southernmost district (CD 1), 43%, or 59,786 people, were no longer living there in 1980.

109

But even these figures gloss over the residents' everyday reality. People do not live in districts, they live in neighborhoods. Puerto Rican families and support networks were neighborhood based. It is at the neighborhood level that the extent and impact of devastation and destruction can be appreciated. In one census tract that consisted of a nine-block area, for example, 84% of the population was lost.[8] In other words, of 2,954 residents there during the 1970 census, only 478 were counted ten years later. In another six-block area, 76% of 2,520 people "disappeared." In a third area, 74%, or 3,847 people, had left by 1980. And finally, the neighborhood, which lost "only" 60% of its population, had 7,500 fewer people in it in 1980 than it had in 1970.

The Impact of Change

What was the impact of this change on the Puerto Rican population, particularly on those who remained?[9] It is difficult to convey the psychic despair that is felt by people who experience the daily loss of people and places that make up their world. One day there was a supermarket to shop at, the next day it is closed. Last week you had friends or relatives up the street, today they too are leaving. Your own home edges closer to the brink of decay as the buildings on the block empty. The continual reminders of surrounding decay multiply with each day. For a very long time, there is no hope, no sign of renewal. In essence, day after day, people and places disappear.[10]

Those who remained in the South Bronx were forgotten by the city and stigmatized by their place of residence. In addition, they had to pay the social and economic costs of housing abandonment, depopulation, and commercial and industrial flight. They had to work harder to live less well. They had to walk farther for food and transportation; they had to travel farther for all their needs. (No one delivered in the South Bronx, including the *New York Times*; taxies generally would not go there.) Residents became members of a still large, but diminishing, community that received minimal services and minimal attention from the city. In terms of the basic, everyday accoutrements of modern living (plumbing, heat, basic repairs), life was simply more difficult in the South Bronx.

Community Efforts: The Strengths of the Community

The media and academic sources have generally depicted the communities in the South Bronx as passive, if not contributing, forces in

110

the devastation of the South Bronx.[11] This view ignores the long-term existence of stable Puerto Rican communities in the South Bronx. These communities had existed for decades in very old tenement housing before large-scale abandonment and decay began. These communities produced writers, artists, professionals, and leaders (as well as ordinary, productive citizens) who have since gone on to make positive contributions to society. These communities were poor, but they were intact. They provided the stability and strength to persevere. They allowed for the networks that enabled families and friends to help one another.

Also ignored in this conventional view are those common, every-day activities integral to the life and functioning of the community that were also destroyed. These activities often provided the spiritual and social sustenance that helped community members cope with larger societal injustices. These established communities have always had nurturing networks, in the form of social clubs, religious organizations and activities, street games, impromptu musical groups, domino-players' groups, athletic teams, bingo games, numbers runners, and other informal networks of information and support (Sánchez-Korrol, 1983; Padilla, 1958). In addition, there were the more formalized *bodegas* (grocery stores), *botánicas* (herbal/spiritualist stores), *cuchifrito* stands (eating places), dance clubs, churches, and spiritual healers. This combination of informal and formal activities and organizations that constituted the substance of community life often died or was disabled when the communities were destroyed.

These and other similar activities were carried on in those residentially unified communities, unnoticed by the world outside and taken for granted by those within. Many of these activities engaged entrepreneurial energies and organizational abilities. Residents took them so much for granted that they were missed only when they were gone. Sadly, it appears to some today that these entrepreneurial efforts never occurred; that, indeed, there is a lack of entrepreneurial interest or skill on the part of Puerto Ricans and that this distinguishes the Puerto Rican migration from other migrations. Extensive research documenting the historical existence of Puerto Rican-run businesses is not available—although a number of works allude, in passing, to the prevalence of *bodegueros* and small store owners in the early communities (Handlin, 1959: 72 ff.; Padilla, 1958; Mills et al., 1950; Gosnell, 1945). Moreover, even after all the devastation, there is still evidence of the entrepreneurial spirit in the U.S. Census Bureau figures. These show that Puerto Ricans owned 34% of all Latino-owned firms in New York City in 1982 (National Congress for Puerto Rican Rights, 1987; see also Institute for Puerto Rican Policy, August 1987).[12]

This is not to argue that all in the community were busily being aggressive entrepreneurs or social and political organizers; rather, it is an illustration that structures existed within the communities and encompassed a variety of people. The communities were not made up exclusively of noble urban fighters struggling against injustice and decay, but neither were they completely apathetic, passive, and dependent. They were heterogeneous communities with strengths as well as problems.

The South Bronx Survivors

Also generally absent from depictions of these communities are stories of the survivors of the South Bronx: how they coped with arson, no hot or (often) no running water, no heat, no garbage services, no lights, no housing maintenance, no interest from outside agencies, and no psychic or monetary support. These survivors are as much successes as those who fled the neighborhoods, for they never gave up, never stopped struggling against insuperable odds. The countless, now nameless, heros and heroines of the streets deserve their due. They may not have had a choice whether to stay or go, but they stayed and survived. (If, in the future, the area is gentrified, they will be the first to be asked to leave.) There are stories of great sadness and stories of joy, but the major story of these survivors is that the communities were torn apart yet the members of some communities persevered and carried out reconstruction against great odds.

Drugs and Housing

Last but not least are the struggles of the community to combat the forces of decay within it. These too are generally ignored in depictions of the South Bronx. Perhaps one of the earliest and most valiant struggles was the struggle against drugs. Drugs, especially heroin, arrived on the scene in the middle and late 1950s, after the Korean War. Drug use intensified in the early and late 1960s. Few immigrant communities in the United States had ever before experienced such a destructive plague. Drug traffic contributed to the destruction of buildings as well as of people. Puerto Rican churches and community leaders tried to deal with the destruction of Puerto Rican youth during this first period of neighborhood and housing devastation. These grass-roots efforts have generally gone unrecorded.[13]

These efforts were particularly striking because they were made at a time when drug use had not been acknowledged as a widespread social problem. Indeed, from the city's perspective, the problem was viewed mainly as a case of social containment within the *barrios*. The only facilities for dealing with drug abuse were correctional institutions, and even these were not held responsible and appeared to care little about whether these (essentially young) men improved. (One dramatic example of this interlocking grid of personal despair and institutional indifference is the account of the distraught mother whose addicted son escaped from Riker's Island Detention Center and returned home. After three days, realizing she could not trust him at home and that he had escaped a legally sanctioned institution, she decided, with guilt and fear, to turn in her own son. She called Riker's, only to discover that the institution was completely unaware that he had been gone. They simply informed the woman that she should tell her son to come back. This routine, ineffective handling was tragic, comic, and ironic, compounding the mother's tragedy with bureaucratic ineptitude.)

The Costs of Urban Change

Despite the efforts of Puerto Rican communities to cope with urban devastation, there were many costs that had to be borne. This type of (forced) geographic mobility undoubtedly had a great impact on individuals and families. Such extensive change placed a great strain on the ability of the community to progress. It affected earnings, as jobs disappeared and people had to travel further to find employment. It affected education, as it created an atmosphere in which study was difficult. It affected familial and friendship support networks,[14] and it affected the development and maintenance of community organizations.[15] In the past, Puerto Ricans have been displaced from their homes because of housing abandonment and decline, and urban renewal; the question today is whether current gentrification will also result in a disproportionate amount of Puerto Rican displacement relative to other groups.[16]

The City's Response:
Benign Neglect and Planned Shrinkage

The city's reaction to the daily destruction of housing in the South Bronx was far from adequate to the size of the problem. Community groups accused the city of following an intentional policy of "planned shrinkage." Although this was denied, in effect, this was what occurred. The South Bronx shrunk "naturally"; housing fell and people, stores, and firms left. The city was paying more to have buildings destroyed than it was to have them repaired. The city devoted approximately $7 million a year to demolishing buildings in the South Bronx (South Bronx Development Organization, 1982).[17] Until the late 1970s, city legislation allowed landlords to forgo payment of taxes for three years before the city attempted to collect.[18] In 1975, the city had its fiscal crisis; if there had been little done before, now there was even less that could be done. Whatever efforts the city pursued during this time to counter the slide toward deterioration, it is evident that the South Bronx never became a priority issue.

The efforts of the city during this time may not have been very different from those of other municipalities facing severe urban blight. The failure of municipalities to halt the deterioration of these blighted areas is a reflection of the lack of political clout and the class position of the people in the blighted areas. But in many ways the South Bronx was different. It was different because of the extent and speed of devastation, and because it had developed a national and even international reputation as the foremost symbol of urban blight. It had become a campaign stop, a backdrop for speeches on urban decline, and a tourist stop for concerned visitors from abroad. World-famous figures such as Presidents Carter and Reagan and Pope John Paul II came and visited the South Bronx.

In part because of its national and international notoriety, the federal government proposed an extensive redevelopment project in the Charlotte Street area of the South Bronx, but the city rejected this attempt at reconstruction.[19] Herman Badillo, who was at the time deputy mayor responsible for overseeing the potential Charlotte Street project, left the city administration in protest. He charged that the mayor was forming a coalition with the middle class and creating a "beautiful fantasy world" in Manhattan while allowing the rest of the boroughs to turn into slums. He argued that the rejection by the New York City Board of Estimate of the federally funded project represented an endorsement of "planned shrinkage" (Peirce and Hagstrom, 1979: 1647–48). Subsequent studies have indeed shown that Manhattan was favored over the other boroughs in terms of city development support.

There were, undoubtedly, many reasons for not approving the Charlotte Street project and for following the many procedures and practices that had a negative impact on the South Bronx. A lifetime could be spent discussing all the detailed pros and cons. However, after all was said and done, one would still be left wondering why more was not done to avert the overall destruction. Why didn't the city act aggressively to save the South Bronx, indeed to save the whole Bronx? One is left with the sad awareness that, from the city's point of view, the South Bronx was not worth saving.

In 1978, after the worst had occurred, something was done. With the incentive of federal and state monies, the city established the South Bronx Development Organization (SBDO) to "study" the problem. In 1980 the SBDO incorporated; by 1982 it was receiving $3 million per year; $1 million from the federal government, $1.5 million from the state, and $.5 million in in-kind services from the city (SBDO, 1983; Peirce and Hagstrom, 1979: 1647).[20] In 1983 the city finally came up with its own plan. True, it was still with federal monies, but it *was* Mayor Edward I. Koch's idea. The Reagan administration provided the city with $300,000 "to improve the image of various neighborhoods, including the Bronx—by pasting cheerful vinyl decals over the smashed, gaping windows of abandoned buildings."

These decals poignantly underscore the city's attitude. Koch told reporters, "A clean bandage is much, much better than a raw or festering wound." But apparently the bandage was less for the victims than it was for the observers. As one commentator put it, "Drivers on the Cross Bronx Expressway will no longer have their sensibilities ruffled, because windows facing the road—and only those windows, not the ones Bronx residents see —will be covered up by pictures of shutters, venetian blinds, and potted plants." Scenes of desolation were being vinyled over to give suburban commuters peace of mind. The South Bronx was being "covered up."[21]

These highlights do not do justice to the variety of activities that occurred in the South Bronx. What they do underscore, however, is (1) the distance between the policymakers and the people of the area and (2) the passivity and reactive posture of the administration during a time of aggressive destruction and progressive decline in South Bronx neighborhoods and commercial areas. It is important that these contextual factors be understood as part of the historical experience of Puerto Ricans. The revitalization policy instituted after the fiscal crisis favored Manhattan and big business. Decline in the Bronx continued, although the rate of decline has been arrested, and signs of revival have appeared. The South Bronx has bottomed out,[22] but the history lived there will remain a bitter chapter for all concerned.

Conclusion

The South Bronx was not the only place where Puerto Ricans lived, but it was where more Puerto Ricans lived. Indeed, it was the densest and largest Puerto Rican community in the United States. It was also an area that contained more Puerto Ricans than any other group. Both these facts make the destruction of this community not just a bitter chapter but a real obstacle to progress for the Puerto Rican community. More research is needed to determine the extent to which the South Bronx experience has been repeated in other Puerto Rican communities in New York City and in the country as a whole.

At present the perceptual evidence on housing is disturbing in its sharp contrasts. There are the well-kept homes in Puerto Rico (at all class levels) and the clear examples of successful, Puerto Rican-sponsored urban housing such as that of Villa Victoria in Boston (Uriarte-Gaston, 1987) and family-owned housing in the smaller towns throughout the Northeast, South, Midwest, and West Coast. And then there are other areas of Puerto Rican concentration, such as East Harlem, the Lower East Side, and Lincoln Center, where Puerto Ricans have experienced urban renewal, then urban devastation, and finally displacement as a result of gentrification.[23] These contrasts show that housing devastation does not always follow Puerto Ricans. But it plagued them in New York City and extracted a huge cost. More research is needed to understand the factors that have made for these contrasting housing pictures.

Notes

Author's Note: Some of the material in this chapter is excerpted from Rodríguez and Sclar (1983).

1 See, for example, New York Times (June 5, 1986: B1), Thurow (1986), and Wall Street Journal (January 23, 1986: 1).
2 That securing employment is a strong motivation for Puerto Rican migration is suggested by the results of a recent study of Puerto Rican migrants. The study reported that the majority (58%) left Puerto Rico for economic reasons, to work at a job or to find a job. Interestingly enough, the majority (60%) of those entering Puerto Rico came for the same reasons (Junta de Planificacion, 1986: 12).
3 In 1980, 37% of Puerto Ricans in New York City lived in the Bronx and 32% in Brooklyn. Of the total Bronx population, 35% was Hispanic; of these, 80% were Puerto Rican.
4 In 1970 there were 268,371 Hispanics, 258,767 Blacks, and 230,314 Whites living in the jurisdictions of the six community planning boards that make up the South Bronx. By 1980, 30,044 Whites were left, 191,019 Blacks, and 223,906 Hispanics. These figures are based on 1970 and 1980 census tract data developed by the South Bronx Development Organization, Health Services Unit (South Bronx Development Organization, 1983).

116

5   Figures on housing loss are based on the NYC Department of City Planning's Sanborn Housing Unit Change File, which used field surveys to make yearly counts of housing gains and losses. The survey defined a housing unit as "living quarters whether occupied or vacant, including abandoned or uninhabitable structures as long as a roof is present, as well as new construction once the foundations are in place." Thus, an abandoned building with a roof on it was included in the housing unit count. Data on housing were collected from this source by the Bronx Urban Resource Center, Fordham University (Correa Alejandro, 1982).

6   For specific numbers lost, see Rodríguez and Sclar (1983) and Correa Alejandro (1982).

7   The actual figures were 149,347 in 1970 and 96,530 in 1980. Census tract and district data on population were compiled from NYC Department of City Planning's Community District Portfolio (Correa Alejandro, 1982).

8   The districts referred to in this paragraph are, respectively, census tracts 375.01 and 375.02 in Community District 6, census tract 215.01 in Community District 5, and census tract 363 in Community District 6.

9   The following descriptions of the South Bronx are based on my 30 years of personal experience and direct observation; I grew up there, and later lived there for nine years, during the period of most extensive devastation, 1972–1981.

10 See Mohr's (1985) short story, "A Thanksgiving Celebration (Amy)," which describes the anxiety, confusion, and anger experienced by a Puerto Rican woman with three children in an area rapidly experiencing deterioration.

11 There are those who privately subscribe to what I call the "bongo" theory of destruction—that is, that it was the arrival of the bongo drums in the public parks and Puerto Ricans in general that destroyed the South Bronx. This view ignores the fact that bongos had been beating for generations in Latino communities that did not experience housing devastation.

12 According to Duany (1987), there has also been a decrease on the national level in the number of Puerto Rican *bodegas*: "From 1969 to 1972, a period in which Hispanic-owned firms grew in volume by 58 percent, Puerto Rican grocery stores in the U.S. decreased by 26 percent. However, these same firms grew in terms of average receipts per firm." He notes that some of the decline was due to ethnic transfer, that is, the sale of the *bodegas* by first-generation Puerto Ricans to newer immigrant groups.

13 Sánchez-Korrol (1985) provides an in-depth interview with one of the notable figures in these efforts, "Mama Leo." This woman minister of a Pentecostal church conducted an extensive campaign against drugs, which included picking up thousands of junkies at the church's doorstep, on nearby streetcorners, on release from prison, and on voluntary admission, and incorporating them into her church services. I personally witnessed the conversion to the faith and to the ministry of numerous hard-core addicts.

14 Jorge (1983: 219) points out that "the Puerto Rican community in New York was the victim of an unprecedented urban renewal program in the 1950s and 1960s. Urban renewal destroyed local Puerto Rican-owned businesses, primarily grocery stores, and forced people to live in twenty-story buildings. Furthermore, in order to acquire an apartment in public housing, the extended family concept had to be given up." Boarders could not live in public housing; if children worked, rents were increased. (Another example of the negative

impact of urban renewal on a flourishing Puerto Rican community in Lorain, Ohio, can be found in Rivera, 1987.)

15 The Housing Task Force of the Puerto Rican Center for Research and Information (1978) concludes that the past 30 years of urban renewal and planned shrinkage made the Puerto Rican community a highly transitory one, with Puerto Ricans in constant flight, continuously seeking out better low-cost housing. The task force notes the negative impact of this situation on the sustained development of community groups. Their analysis is based on NYC Board of Education records of student transfers.

16 There is some indication that Hispanics, in general, are more likely to be displaced as a result of gentrification because they often live in "buffer" zones (i.e., between Whites and Blacks) or in transitional areas. The Schill and Nathan (1983: 111) probit model shows that "Hispanic-headed households are most likely to be displaced." These authors looked at nine neighborhoods in five cities at two points in time. The gentrifying areas in New York City examined by Chall (1984) also had significant numbers of Latinos.

17 By 1984, over 70% of all housing units lost in the Bronx since 1970 had been demolished (*Newsletter of the Fordham University Bronx Urban Resource Center*, 1987).

18 Stevenson (1980), in a case study of the first building to be abandoned on the Grand Concourse in the South Bronx, details the roles the city and the landlords played in the process of housing abandonment. His analysis of fiscal records shows disinvestment and profiteering to have been key in the abandonment of the building. (See also these other works on housing abandonment in New York City during this time: Women's City Club of New York, 1977; Marcuse, 1979; SBDO, 1980; Sternlieb, 1973; Correa Alejandro, 1982.)

19 Upon reflection, it is ironic that the reasons given for not approving the Charlotte Street project included that the Board of Estimate wanted to concentrate on "areas of strength" (Peirce and Hagstrom, 1979). Indeed, this became the major philosophical orientation of the city, as the subsequent title of the South Bronx Development Organization's (1980) development plan showed: "Areas of Strength, Areas of Opportunity." The Charlotte Street area had been written off.

20 The distance of the SBDO from neighborhood and community people was legendary. Indeed, a major criticism of the plan was that it proceeded as if there were no people living in the South Bronx—the SBDO eventually built middle-income housing for low-income people. Then it found it difficult to lure the middle class into the 90 ranch-style, manufactured, single-family homes it built in the middle of the South Bronx.

21 Quotes on the South Bronx are taken from "Window Dressing" in the *New Republic* (December 5, 1983: 7). The *New York Times* (June 14, 1987: 42) indicates that only $70,000 was used for the vinyl decal program; this suggests that even this effort was not fully carried out.

22 On the return of the Bronx, see Cammarosano (1981), Jonnes (1986), Peirce and Hagstrom (1979), Wiseman (1981), Goldman (1981), and Malinconico (1983). Although there has been improvement in the Bronx, "some 36,863 units were restored and 12,780 more built with government funds . . . [These] efforts do not come close to replacing the 100,000 units lost." In addition, the city has only recently articulated a plan to build "affordable housing" and

proposed in its first phase to build 3,400 new units in the Bronx by the end of the decade. The cost of these units, however, does not appear to be within reach of the average renter's income in the Bronx (*New York Times*, June 14, 1987: 42).

23 For a case study of gentrification in a long-established Puerto Rican neighborhood, Atlantic Avenue, Brooklyn, see Kazinitz (1983).

6

EDUCATIONAL DYNAMICS

This chapter addresses the educational experience of Puerto Ricans in New York City. In so doing, it explores (1) the results of the educational experience, as reflected in student achievement; (2) a number of theories often advanced to explain student outcomes; (3) the historical context and its effect on education; (4) the response of the Hispanic community to the problems in education; and (5) some ideas on how to improve the current educational situation. An important theme in this chapter is that within the educational system an educational dynamic has been institutionalized that involves a number of components in an assimilation dialectic. These components are the system (teachers, schools, and the values they try to inculcate) and the new entrants (students, parents, and their values and aspirations). These interact to create the results (educational outcomes and changes in the system).

What the Records Show

Reading, Math, and English

The reading and math scores of students in predominantly Hispanic school districts have continued to lag behind those of students in New York City as a whole.[1] This is true at every grade[2] (Hayes and Grether, 1983; U.S. Commission on Civil Rights, 1972; Fitzpatrick, 1971; more recent figures derived from the NYC Board of Education, 1984a, 1984b). The number of school districts in NYC that are predominantly Hispanic (i.e., that have 50% or more Hispanic students) has increased from 3 in 1969 to 11 in 1983. Less than half of the children (45.51%) in the Hispanic districts are reading at or above grade level, while just over half (54.19%) are performing at or above grade level in math (NYC Board of Education, 1984a, 1984b).[3]

Limited English Proficiency

Students who are limited in their English proficiency (i.e., classified as limited English proficient or LEP students) numbered over 110,000 in 1985 (Educational Priorities Panel [EPP], 1985b). There have always been a large proportion of Hispanic students in all grades who were termed "English-poor," that is, who spoke little or no English or spoke it hesitantly, or with a heavy accent. In 1960, these students totaled 104,482, or 9.25% of the total student population (U.S. Commission on Civil Rights, 1972). By 1985, they constituted 12% of the total school population, or 113,831 (EPP, 1985b: 3).

Despite the now legally mandated requirement that these students receive bilingual instruction, 40% of those entitled still do not receive it. Of the 60% who do receive language instruction, only 30% are exposed to a fully bilingual instruction program (EPP, 1985b). What happens to LEP children—particularly those who are not served? According to some reports, they drop out and at higher rates than other students (EPP, 1985b; Calitri, 1983; Santiago-Santiago, 1984b). In addition, they are over-represented in zoned high schools and underrepresented in optional education programs (Advocates for Children, 1985). In sum, they end up in the educational tracks that often have the fewest rewards.

The LEP figures are expected to swell with increased numbers of language minority students entering the system (Smith, 1987: 9). However, this figure includes only students who score below the twentieth percentile on an English proficiency test. Only these students qualify for special English-language instruction. Hispanics constituted 72% of the LEP group in 1984 (EPP, 1985b: 9) and LEP students constituted approximately 26% of all Hispanics in the public school system (EPP, 1985b; New York City Board of Education, 1984a). The remaining 74% of Hispanics who scored above the twentieth percentile did not qualify for LEP instruction, even though they might have placed anywhere from the twenty-first to the sixtieth percentile. The needs of these children are not addressed.

Dropping Out

There are numerous and differing ways to measure school dropout rates (Valdivieso, 1986: 12; Santiago-Santiago, 1984a; Hernández, 1976;

Calitri, 1983; Reyes, 1984; Smith, 1987). Different studies produce slightly different figures, depending upon who is classified a "dropout." The Board of Education, for example, does not count as dropouts those who leave and enroll in a GED or equivalent program, although few of those enrolled in these programs ever attain high school diplomas. The U.S. Commission on Civil Rights (1972) estimated a Puerto Rican dropout rate of 67% in New York City in 1970–71, but argued that this was a conservative estimate because untabulated transfers and migrations underestimated the true dropout rates for Puerto Ricans while inflating those of Whites. Calitri (1983) found an 80% dropout rate for Hispanics and Puerto Ricans in New York City. A New York State study put the rate of Hispanic dropout at 62% (*New York Times*, March 15, 1987: 22). There is also no agreement on the dropout rate for all students in New York (*New York Times*, March 9, 1986: 40; February 26, 1987; March 1, 1987; Calitri, 1983: 4).

Under any definition, Hispanic and Puerto Rican youth have for some time been dropping out at higher rates than any other group in the city. High Hispanic dropout rates are not just a New York City problem—they are a national problem (Valdivieso, 1986; Hispanic Policy Development Project, 1984a, 1984b; National Center for Education Statistics, 1981; Carnegie Council on Policy Studies in Higher Education, 1979; Michigan State Board of Education, 1986). However, significant variations in Puerto Rican/Hispanic dropout rates by city have also been found (Hernández, 1976; Valdivieso, 1986). Thus, some school systems are better than others in retaining Hispanic students.

In New York City, we see the effect of the high Hispanic dropout rates when we look at ethnic composition by grade level. As Figure 6.1 illustrates, Hispanics and Blacks have the largest shares at each grade level up to the ninth grade, when Hispanics decline precipitously (and Blacks more evenly), while Whites increase. By the twelfth grade, Whites outnumber Hispanics and equal Blacks. Thus, at the formal exit point, so many Hispanics have left that the compositions of graduating classes do not reflect the schools from which they graduated.[4]

Segregation

Segregated schools and the accompanying correlates of reading retardation, low four-year college attendance, and low diploma completion continue to be a severe problem in NYC schools.[5] The majority of elementary and junior high school Hispanic students attend schools in districts that have high proportions of Hispanic students. In fact, 68% of Hispanic children in New York City attend schools in districts that are 30%

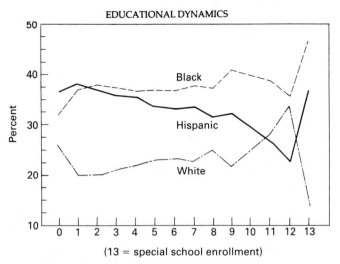

Figure 6.1 Groups by Grade, 1983–1984
Source: New York City Board of Education (1984a).

or more Hispanic, while only 10% attend schools in districts that have 10% or fewer Hispanic students.[6] Others attend schools that have high proportions of Black students. At the high school level, where residence is less of a factor, there is a similar segregation.[7] Many Hispanics attend high schools where there are large proportions of other Hispanics and Blacks. In these high schools, they face the correlates of segregated schooling—the odds are that most of their peers will be below grade level in reading, are less likely to receive diplomas, and are less likely to go on to four-year colleges (see Table 6.1).[8]

Colleges

The high dropout rates found at the junior high and high school levels continue on into college. As the National Congress for Puerto Rican Rights recently pointed out: "If we start with a hypothetical 100 Puerto Rican

Table 6.1
Correlation Coefficients, Random Sample of New York City High Schools

	Two years behind in school	Graduates going on to 4-year colleges	Diplomas granted
Whites	−.845	.4	.672
Hispanics	.41	−.014	−.142
Blacks	.628	−.467	−.642

Source: New York City Board of Education (1984b).
Note: Systematic random sample of high schools; N = 15.

123

students, the best case scenario has 55 graduating from high school, 25 entering college, and 7 graduating from college" (cited in Puerto Rican Council on Higher Education, 1986: 7). This depressing situation represents the "best case" scenario because it assumes a relatively optimistic dropout rate of 45% for Hispanics. If we use the 80% dropout rate found by Calitri (1983), then only 2.5 of the original 100 would graduate from college.

In New York State undergraduate colleges, Hispanics had the lowest retention rates between 1973 and 1981 when compared with Whites, Blacks, Asian/Pacific Islanders, American Indians, and Alaskan natives (Prieto, 1984). Indeed, between 1978 and 1980, the proportion of Hispanic students in New York State who stayed and completed their undergraduate degrees declined from 58% to 55%, while the retention rates for Whites increased (91% to 94%) and that of Blacks stayed the same (63%). On the positive side, total Hispanic enrollment during the 1976–82 period increased slightly (43,842 to 56,506). Also increasing during this period were the numbers of Hispanics in graduate and professional schools and the number of degrees conferred (Prieto, 1984). Thus, it appears that at the state level more Hispanics are getting through the undergraduate colleges than before, but the proportion dropping out has increased and remains higher than for any other group.

The picture at the city colleges, where most Hispanics attend, is similar.[9] Retention rates are low and, correspondingly, dropout rates are high. This generalization does not appear to be affected by method of entry, that is, whether students entered "under the rigorous admissions standards in force at the university during the 1960s" (Lavin et al., 1986: 3) or whether they came in under an open admissions plan in effect during the early 1970s.[10] Hispanic students lagged behind Whites and Blacks in the proportion completing their baccalaureate programs at the City University of New York (CUNY) regardless of their mode of entry.

Indeed, as the chancellor of the Board of Higher Education has pointed out, there appears to be a "bleaching phenomenon" that takes place within the CUNY system: the longer you're at CUNY, and the higher up you go, the more likely you are to be White (Murphy, 1986: 5–6). This is true for students and faculty alike.[11] Thus, in 1985, 65% to 75% of entering freshman students were members of minority groups (35% Black, 25% Hispanic, and 5% to 10% Asian). Yet, over the past few years, 64% of those awarded baccalaureates were White (Murphy, 1986: 6). Although there has been a slight increase in the proportion of Hispanic students in graduate schools—from 5.5% in 1978 to 7.2% in 1983—Hispanics are still vastly underrepresented at this level (City University of New York, 1983: 131).

Standardized Test Scores

Puerto Rican mean scores on exams taken when applying to most college and graduate schools—the SAT and the GRE—are also not encouraging. Table 6.2 shows the mean scores of Puerto Ricans relative to non-Hispanic Whites. All scores are at least one standard deviation below the mean. There has been significant improvement in the last few years— between 1980 and 1985, Puerto Ricans in the states experienced the greatest positive change in verbal SAT means and the second highest increase in SAT math means compared with all students, Whites, Asian-Americans, Mexican-Americans, American Indians, and Blacks (Ramist and Arbiter, 1986: xii). However, there is still a very large lag. In effect, even the group that graduates and is college or graduate school bound has not narrowed the educational achievement gap measured by these tests.

Table 6.2
Standardized Mean Test Scores

| | Scholastic Aptitude Test (SAT) | | Graduate Record Exam (GRE) | | |
	Verbal	Math	Verbal	Quantitative	Analytical
Puerto Ricans	356	387	389.42	417.71	384.7
	(6,849)	(6,848)			
Whites	442	482	511.5	525.08	528.73
	(720,010)	(719,891)			
Mexicans	372	413	418.82	422.14	412.26
	(14,169)	(14,167)			

Source: Duran (1983: 61, 66). SAT figures are based on 1979–80 scores; GRE figures are based on 1978–79 scores (College Entrance Examination Board data).

Note: Figures in parentheses are population figures; these were unavailable for the GRE columns.

It is important when reviewing SAT scores to bear in mind that there is a great deal of debate about whether these tests accurately measure Hispanic students' intelligence or potential to do well in college or graduate school. According to Verdugo (1986), what these scores measure more than anything else is students' "knowledge of middle class culture." These test results are seen to be a reflection of the class status, culturally bound experiences, and placement in educational tracks of most Hispanics in the United States. This positioning of Latinos in schools and in the economy may influence test-taking skills, such as familiarity with vocabulary, test anxiety, speed, and guessing skills (Ballesteros, 1986).

The influence of language on scores is also evident, for when the SAT scores are controlled for best language spoken by student, considerable differences can be seen (Ramist and Arbiter, 1986: xxiii). This holds true for non-Hispanic Whites as well as for Puerto Ricans and Mexican-Americans (Durán, 1983: 65–66). In addition, the predictive nature of these tests has been found to be considerably lower for Hispanics than for Anglos; there are lower correlations between standardized test scores and first-year grade point averages for Hispanos relative to Anglos (Durán, 1983: 102). The lack of a relationship between these tests and college outcomes has led Verdugo (1986) to argue that intelligence tests are a form of racism and that they should not be used until their predictive power is conclusively proven.

There is one very interesting exception to the general lack of predictive validity of these standardized tests for Hispanics. This is to be found in Puerto Rico. There, standardized Spanish-language tests are as useful in predicting college success for Puerto Ricans in Puerto Rico as their English-language equivalents are in predicting success for non-Hispanic Whites in the United States (Durán, 1983: 93). If high school grades are combined with test scores in Puerto Rico, these variables are *better* predictors of college success for Puerto Ricans in Puerto Rico than they are for non-Hispanic whites in the United States (Durán, 1983: 94). This exception to the rule for Hispanics in the United States raises interesting questions about the relationship between the validity of these tests and the geographic and social contexts within which they are taken. Why should equivalent tests and grades have great predictive validity in Puerto Rico but not in the United States?

Explanatory Theories

Numerous explanations are offered for Hispanics' low achievement in the school system. In this section, many of these are reviewed and critiqued; I then present an argument for a more historical approach to understanding the dynamics of Hispanic/Latino education. It is postulated that a dialectic has evolved and been institutionalized that has typified the struggle between entering students from another culture and a school system charged with molding them into the U.S. society and economy. (Thus, while macro theories may explain the goals and outcome of the educational system, the historical dialectic helps us to understand the process of immigrant education.) I argue that the educational experience of many, but especially that of immigrants, in New York City has been marked by a dialectical struggle that has historically occurred on several levels: between students and teachers, between parents and schools, and between communities and school systems.

A Lack of Money

Liberals often argue that poor educational outcomes are the result of insufficient funding. However, it is not a simple question of money. New York State is *second* in the nation in terms of per-pupil expenditures and *seventh* in terms of teacher salaries. Yet, the system cannot hold on to its students; New York is 46th (out of 50 states) in terms of retention (Hodgkinson, 1985: 11). It has the highest dropout rate of any northern state (*New York City Sun*, November 26–December 2, 1986: 5). Interestingly, other states that also rank low in retention are ethnically more diverse and more urban as well. In general, money spent on teachers' salaries and per-pupil expenditures does *not* greatly influence retention in any state (Hodgkinson, 1985). Money is not the problem—at least not as it is currently disbursed.

Blaming the Victims

Another explanation blames the students and their parents for the disappointing outcomes, while the system itself is absolved. The assumption is that Puerto Ricans and Hispanics have just not been able, or wanted, to "make the grade." This perspective does not explain how both academic successes and failures can occur within the same family, a common occurrence within Hispanic families, and denies the experiences of a great many Latinos. The experience of successful Latinos in the school system has often led them to conclude that they "made it" *despite* the system. Others have concluded they might have gone further but for the system. Finally, almost all Latinos have had experiences with or have known someone who could have made it, but did not because of the way the system functioned.

A more benign version of the blame-the-victim perspective argues that it is the student's fault, but only because the system has failed. Thus, because education is such a dismal failure, students are pushed or pressured to seek other alternatives that seem preferable to the lifeless and dulling monotony that school represents. The educational process has so eroded the self-esteem of students that they no longer care what happens

127

to them, so they turn to drugs or they become pregnant. This perspective may account for some outcomes but it does not explain why so many others who have not sought these alternatives still graduate with only minimal levels of literacy.

The Payoffs to Education

Another argument is that Hispanics do not excel in school, or drop out altogether, because they have little confidence that there will be any significant payoff for their investment of time. To the extent that young people correctly perceive their future income potential, there may be some truth to this. Most studies have shown that greater education may yield somewhat greater income for minority group members, but not at parity with native Whites (Mindiola and Gutierrez, 1982). Indeed, a recent census analysis of Puerto Ricans within the states says, "What is especially distressing about the earnings gap by educational levels is the evidence that the differentials between native White and Puerto Rican men *increase* rather than decrease at higher levels of schooling." Although the earnings gap is smaller for Puerto Rican females, their income levels are considerably lower (Tienda, 1985).

It is unclear from the research what effect education has on Puerto Rican employment. Earlier work had found that Puerto Rican dropouts had a greater chance of being employed than Puerto Rican high school graduates (Brown et al., 1981). Hernandez (1983) also found that education was not as significant a factor in Puerto Rican youth employment as might be expected. However, Vélez and Javalgi (1986), using a different sample of Puerto Rican youth, found education (as well as age) to be important in predicting employment. A number of other studies have utilized the Survey of Income and Education (SIE) to examine the relationship between education and income or employment for Hispanics (Reimers, 1984a, 1984b); Abowd and Killingsworth, 1985; Tienda, 1981, 1983a, 1983b; Tienda and Glass, 1985; Tienda and Guhleman, 1985; Tienda and Neidert, 1984; Bean et al., 1985; Borjas, 1983; DeFreitas, 1985).[12] Unfortunately, the results of these studies with regard to Puerto Ricans have been inconclusive. The best that can be said is that Puerto Ricans do not appear to fit the models developed.

Puerto Ricans do not fit some models because the distinction between foreign and native birth makes a big difference for most Hispanic groups, especially with regard to education and experience. However, this distinction makes practically no difference for Puerto Ricans—that is, it has little relationship to economic outcomes (Borjas, 1983). This may be due to the fact that the distinction between foreign and native is less clear for Puerto Ricans because of Puerto Rican migration patterns. It may be that, to a significant but as yet unmeasured degree, foreign-born Puerto Ricans (i.e., those born in Puerto Rico) cannot automatically be assumed to be foreign-raised. Similarly, those born in the states may not have been raised in the states. Thus, both (statistical) groupings may face a similar employment structure. (See Falcón-Rodríguez, 1987, for an analysis of the differences between the economic attainments in New York City of mainland- and island-born Puerto Ricans.)

Data Deductions

Another explanation has to do with what the data are measuring. Many of the available data report Hispanic, not Puerto Rican, performance. One perspective holds that Puerto Ricans have improved their performance over time, but that the data continue to show poor performance because of the influx of newer Hispanic immigrants into the school system. It is also speculated that successful Puerto Ricans either migrate to other states or become more successful when they migrate. This would leave not only fewer Puerto Ricans in the Hispanic pool, but it would leave those less successful in New York. Thus, the educational experience of Puerto Ricans would appear to be more consistently depressed than it actually has been.

However, we cannot test this hypothesis with available data because the only data collected by the NYC Board of Education with a Hispanic category is the Annual Ethnic Census of Schools, which is a simple head count of students disaggregated only to the district level. Thus, in addition to having no separate data on Puerto Ricans, we have had no data on Hispanic dropout rates, graduation rates, types of diplomas received, scores on regents' exams, students left back, special program or GED enrollments, applications or acceptances to specialized high schools, or passing rates on equivalency exams (Reyes, 1984). The Board of Education can tell us nothing about how Puerto Ricans are doing in any of these areas.

Self-Fulfilling Prophesies

It is also argued that there is an attitude problem within the schools, that the attitudes of teachers and staff lead to self-fulfilling prophecies of failure (for themselves and for students).[13] In turn, these attitudes feed student attitudes of resistance, alienation, and underachievement.[14]

129

That expectations are important in Hispanic student achievement is evident in a study conducted by Thomas and Gordon (1983),[15] which shows that educational expectation (i.e., the highest education level high school seniors thought they would achieve) was the variable that most determined Hispanic occupational attainment. This was especially true for Hispanic women. (Educational expectations were not important determinants for White or Black students.) Hispanic educational expectations were more important than standardized test scores, occupational expectations, attendance at two- or four-year colleges, college GPA, college major, and college and high school racial composition. It would seem, then, that what Hispanics (especially Hispanic women) *expect* to achieve, in terms of education, influences the jobs they eventually do attain. Latino student aspirations continue to be important, regardless of generation (Buriel, 1988).

Although educational expectations are important in the occupational achievement of Puerto Rican youth, the educational aspirations of Puerto Rican high school youth have been found to be lower than those of White or Black youth (Nielsen and Fernández, 1981: Table 2.2; Ramist and Arbiter, 1986: xiv). Teachers, parents, and peers all play a role in determining educational expectations;[16] in particular, parental career values have been found to be closely related to the career expectations of Puerto Rican youth[17] (Dillard and Campbell, 1981). If these aspirations are low, then it becomes all the more important for the schools to emphasize high educational aspirations.

But there appears to be a problem. On the one hand, there appears to be selective receptivity for Hispanic elementary students on the part of teachers. Gumbiner et al. (1981) found Mexican-American children ages 7 to 11 to be more attuned to praise from teachers, and to have higher self-esteem, when teachers asked a lot of questions and listened well. On the other hand, the U.S. Commission on Civil Rights (1983) found that teachers in the classroom did not positively reinforce Mexican-American students as often as they did Anglo students. Teachers directed praise or encouragement at Anglo students 36% more often than at Mexican-American students, built on the spoken contributions of Anglo students 40% more often, and asked Anglo students 20% more questions than they asked Mexican-American students.

That classroom interactions influence student expectations, motivation, and achievement is also suggested by Durán (1983), Torruellas (1986), and Cummins (1986). Durán (1983: 56) concludes: "The quality of classroom interactions for Hispanic children may be poorer than for Anglo children. Specifically, evidence was cited that teachers may have lower academic expectations and lower social esteem for Mexican American children than for Anglo children."[18] Torruellas (1986: 4) cites low teacher expectations and a lack of socially and culturally relevant curricula as factors that discourage the overwhelming majority of Black and Puerto Rican students in New York City:[19]

> Low teacher expectations with respect to educational achievement compound the problem [of differing linguistic styles], leading to loss of self-confidence and, ultimately, internalization by students of the belief that they cannot succeed in school. . . . It is essential that schools create an educational environment where success and self-esteem, not failure, is the expectation for our children.

The way to create this environment, Torruellas argues, is to acknowledge, respect, and draw upon the values, experiences, and resources that students bring to the school, so that their culture and natural language ability skills are reinforced.[20] Cummins (1986), speaking from a broader perspective, echoes these statements. He argues that educators, in teaching "dominated societal groups," subtract cultural/linguistic dimensions, exclude community participation, and follow a straight line toward transmission and legitimation of information. Furthermore, according to Cummins (1986: 33), schools continue to reproduce in their interactions with students the power relations that characterize the wider society and make minority students' academic failure inevitable.

Social Reproduction

The social reproduction theorists argue that schools are driven by the capitalist economy, and thus reproduce the dominant ideology and an inherently unequal structure. The role of public education is to sort students carefully so that the existing social order is reproduced (Bowles, 1976). Within the social reproduction model, the effects of class and race combine to pull Puerto Ricans and other Hispanics down into the lower educational tracks, which serve as preparation for entry into the secondary labor market (Barrera, 1979; Olivas, 1983). Once "finished" with school, Puerto Ricans and other tracked groups move on to take positions in society similar to those their parents had occupied. The sectors where they work and the jobs they perform might change, but the position of the jobs on the social and economic scale remain about the same.

Thus, public education results in a useful inequality for the capitalist system. The existence of competing racial-ethnic and gender groups with low educational attainment contributes to the persistence of a permanent industrial reserve force that serves to maintain low wages. The talented one-tenth (or less) of the group that "succeeds" (i.e., moves up the socioeconomic ladder) illustrates that the system does work for a few, and also serves a useful societal purpose; they are often mediators, middlemen, and service providers to the remaining 90%. Social reproduction theorists say that these are the exceptions that prove the rule.

Tracking

Social reproduction can occur even without formal tracking. As noted in the section on self-fulfilling prophesies, teachers may have different expectations of students depending on their class, race, or gender. With different expectations, the behavior of both students and teachers is bound to be influenced. The net effect may not be explicit tracking, but differential group outcomes. These outcomes are often indistinguishable from the systematic ordering of Hispanic students into nonacademic, nondemanding, or special education tracks. However, even those who do not subscribe to the social reproduction theory agree that tracking does exist. They see the placement of lower-achieving students in less demanding classes to be an "unfortunate" but "functional" aspect of the educational system. In the past, tracking provided alternative routes to—but not necessarily through—high schools for those judged less able.

Tracking appears to be a rather permanent feature of the New York City school system, which, since at least the turn of the century, has had separate tracks for different kinds of students. During the early period, some ethnic groups predominated in the lower tracks (Ravitch, 1972). As the system became increasingly minority, minority groups were found to be disproportionately represented in the lower tracks and in "special education." (See the Appendix for a discussion of the tracking of Hispanics in special education and in vocational schools.) Although there have been changes, in the 1980s it still appears that tracking exists, although the forms it takes have been altered.

According to one recent report, what has evolved within the NYC system in the 1980s is a "Tower of Babel"—a confusing matrix within which there are to be found various courses of study within high schools and various routes for getting into these programs (EPP, 1985a). The academic-zoned high school—where 70% of all students ended up going in the 1980s—became, in many cases, the dumping ground for those traditionally in the lower tracks, while those schools with more popular and effective educational option programs moved into the upper tracks (EPP, 1985a: i). The multiplicity of programs, combined with vague or undefined admissions criteria, enabled individual high schools to exercise a great deal of control over who entered which tracks (Advocates for Children [AFC], 1985). The high school admissions process became a labyrinth, and public schools developed private admissions practices.

It also appears that White- and middle-class students receive preference with regard to admissions, while minority students from low-income homes and areas tend to be excluded. Limited English proficiency students are the least successful at getting into selective programs. These students tend to reside in the "excluded" low-income areas and homes, and they require special English-language instruction. They tend not to apply to these new upper tracks (and they are rarely accepted when they do apply). As a result, LEP students are overrepresented in zoned schools and underrepresented in nonzoned programs (AFC, 1985: 33).[21]

In addition, Advocates for Children (1985: 1) contends that the New York City educational system had made an "enormous number of accommodations" to keep White students in the school system:[22]

> AFC finds that students from impoverished, segregated minority neighborhoods have a much poorer chance of obtaining acceptance to a selective school than those in more affluent, integrated, or predominantly white neighborhoods. Minority students' odds are particularly bad at schools that are seeking to maintain a white majority pursuant to the policies of the Office of Zoning and Integration.

Thus, it appears that the Board had developed a policy, indeed, an office, that required certain schools to maintain White majorities.[23] This is an educational system that had had minorities as its majority population for the last 19 years. Some argue that rather than doing away with tracking, the school system found a more sophisticated way of conducting it.

Tracking apparently also has taken on more informal forms in the 1980s. For example, even though race and ethnicity are not generally reported in applications to selective public schools, the student's name, address, school, and district on the application give "the savvy high school admissions officer a great deal of information about the student's likely ethnicity, race, and socioeconomic status" (AFC, 1985: 38). These ethnic and class clues cue many admissions personnel to accept or reject students. The net result of this process is continued ethnic and racial queueing and tracking. The bias against minorities from low-income areas is so strong that concern is expressed in the AFC (1985) study that even the best from these areas did not get into the more selective programs (p. 42).

A Complex Equation

Each of the theories and explanations presented above doubtless holds a grain of truth. Together, they contribute to an understanding of the educational situation of Puerto Ricans and Hispanics in New York City. However, the situation is complex and has been so for some time. As Durán (1983: ix) has pointed out:

> A simplistic and culturally chauvinistic interpretation of the situation would conclude that Hispanics' educational attainment is a function of their ability or inability to adopt the sociocultural values and language of mainstream America. An equally naive view, at another extreme, would be that failure of Hispanics to succeed is due exclusively to prejudicial bias against Hispanics in the educational system and to deliberate exclusion of Hispanics from educational institutions.

What is perhaps most important is an understanding of the historical context that Puerto Ricans and other Latinos entered when they came to the United States and within which they have evolved.

The Assimilation Dialectic

From the earliest history of the United States, a continuous flow of immigrants, especially to New York City, has made for a continuing encounter between immigrant students and more assimilated teachers. As a result of this ongoing encounter, an educational dialectic has evolved and has become a part of the public school system (Rodríguez, 1973). In New York City schools, this dialectic involves an ongoing struggle between two forces: the assimilated and assimilating teacher (thesis) and the newly arrived student (the antithesis). The student is almost always from an ethnic background different from the teacher's, and often resists assimilation. The synthesis, narrowly defined, is when the student leaves the system—through graduating, transferring, or dropping out—often as a "hyphenated" American.

The melting-pot ideology legitimized the early functioning of the dialectic. Jews were taught to be publicly non-Jews, yet to remember that they were Jews (Podhoretz, 1968). The same was true of Italians, Germans, and other immigrant groups. Having experienced this assimilating process, these same "now-assimilated" ethnics would come to defend the system that had broken them in. They would expect the newer immigrants

134

to undergo the same painful initiation. Perhaps, more correctly, they would never see or accept an alternative to this method of initiation. After the newer ethnics were fully educated, they were, as the ethnics before them had been, closed to public acknowledgment of (even) obvious ethnicity. At the same time, they were privately alert to ethnic cues. The message these "former" ethnics transferred to all newcomers was the fear of difference, as well as the shame or embarrassment of one's own difference. It was in this way that ethnicity became America's worst kept secret.

The details of this dialectic have changed with time. In the nineteenth century, teachers were Protestant and students Catholic, for example. Although each immigrant group's historical conditions varied, its involvement in the basic dialectic did not. The dialectic was institutionalized and served to make legitimate the cultural hegemony of the United States as well as to control immigrant populations. A central tenet of the assimilationist thrust in the dialectic was the emphasis on White, middle-class Anglocentric values, perspectives, and styles.[24] This suggested, in turn, a certain negativism—albeit unacknowledged—about those who did not conform to this value. This sometimes led to the rupture of family ties. This process was articulated by a prominent educator who had been an Italian immigrant child in the New York City public school system during the 1920s and 1930s:

> We soon got the idea that Italian meant something inferior and a barrier was erected between the child of Italian origin and their parents. This was the accepted process of Americanization, we were becoming Americans by learning to be ashamed of our parents. (Covello, 1969: 59)

With few exceptions, those most assimilated or assimilating were sifted out as the brightest, most successful, and so on. Those who did not conform dropped out, or didn't learn.[25]

The Dialectic and People of Color

It may be argued that all people of color experience the educational dialectic quite differently than European or White immigrants to the United States. Historically, conquered groups such as Blacks, Native Americans, and Chicanos have not fared as well in this country in terms of economic or educational attainments or in terms of political influence as have European groups who immigrated in the nineteenth and twentieth centuries. (Conquered groups are groups who did not come to the country

135

out of choice, but who had "the country come to them"; Daubon, 1987). European groups became "hyphenated" Americans—Italian-Americans, German-Americans, or Irish-Americans—or just plain "Americans." The more visible minorities did not, in the main, become hyphenated Americans, but remained clustered as Black, Hispanic (i.e., Chicano, Puerto Rican, New Yorican), Asian, or Indian.

Thus, the educational dialectic "Americanized" Puerto Ricans, and other people of color, but it did not de-ethnicize them. These groups were conquered, coerced into coming, or pushed to immigrate. With time, they became national minorities. The expectation for White immigrants was that with greater time in, or exposure to, the United States, these hyphenated Americans would lose their ethnicity and become "Americans." The end product of the assimilation process for the others was that they would become native minorities. These minorities might succeed economically to greater or lesser degrees. For example, the fabled Asian propensity for hard work would earn them eventual success. But even after eight generations of hard work, they would still be seen— as one Chinese-American youth in California said—to be "Chinese."

People of color would keep their "ethnicity," despite the fact that they might lose their immigrant origins, their language, and even their communities. This has clearly been the case with the "model minority"— Japanese-Americans, who can no longer point to geographically based Japanese-American communities. White immigrants, on the other hand, would succeed or not succeed, but their ethnic origins would become symbolic, highly blurred, or totally lost; that is, these origins would not be directly relevant to their definition as Americans.

Thus, the conflicts that surfaced between Puerto Ricans and teachers were part of an ongoing historical process and continuing conflict that was, in part, based on class and, in part, based on difference. In the history of the Puerto Rican community, there have been some bitter resolutions of the dialectic, and there have been some resolutions that have sweetened the lives of those involved. Most Puerto Rican experiences were somewhere between these two extremes. The experiences varied mainly with teachers, but were also affected by peers, schools, and personal or familial situations. But all were involved in this dialectic.

The dialectical process was not solely responsible for the achievement levels of Puerto Rican and other Latino students, but these dynamics were critical and pervasive in the educational process. Despite the fact that the dynamics of the dialectic received little attention, they informed the dialectics of resistance that were sometimes found in the educational arena and in other areas. However, most people, teachers included, were unaware that they were participants in this dialectic or that they had an assimilationist ideology. Simultaneously, they were unaware of any alternatives to it.

The Empirical Literature

The empirical literature provides some insight into the dynamics of educational dialectics as they occur in the classroom, between parents and schools, and between communities and school systems. A number of generalizations emerge from this review of the literature.[26] In general, the literature on Hispanic student and teacher interactions suggests that (1) a student's being Hispanic affects teacher perceptions and (2) the smaller the "difference" perceived by the teacher, the more favorable, or fair, is his or her treatment of the student (Rosenthal and Jacobsen, 1968; Fleming, 1971; M. Ramírez, 1981; Durán, 1983: 50; Torruellas, 1986; A. G. Ramírez, 1985; Roberts et al., 1985; Tobias et al., 1982; Moore, 1983; Soto, 1983).[27] These generalizations seem to coincide with the assimilationist thrust of the dialectic noted above.

Given that being "different" is a variable in the educational process, are there significant cultural differences between Hispanics and others, and do these differences affect the learning process? Unfortunately, there has been little serious research on the role of culture in education. It may be that it is not important to most researchers, who tend to be culturally consistent with the majority culture. Or it may be that monocultural researchers are not able to address the bicultural issues involved adequately. Perhaps the dialectic has functioned so well that culture, or cultural difference, is just not seen as a serious or significant variable worthy of study. It is curious that this area has not surfaced more often in research circles.[28]

Nonetheless, there is a generalization that emerges from the studies on cultural differences that have been carried out: Hispanics and Anglos differ significantly on cultural orientations (Triandis et al., 1985a, 1985b; Powers and Wagner, 1983; Wurzel, 1983). While this may hardly seem surprising, when seen in the context of the general denial of specific cultural differences, it is significant.[29] In the classroom, Hispanic and Anglo students respond differently to, and Hispanic and Anglo teachers use, different teaching styles and classroom structures (Ramírez and Castañeda, 1974; Marín et al., 1983; Gumbiner et al., 1981; Muñoz-Hernández and Santiago-Santiago, 1983).[30]

Another generalization that emerges is that explicit or positive acknowledgment of Hispanics' or other minorities' cultural base is important and valuable. For example, in the educational arena, Comas-Díaz et al. (1982) find a strong relationship between exposure to a Puerto Rican cultural awareness program and enhanced self-concepts of Puerto Rican children. The use of culturally relevant modalities has been particularly important in the mental health area (Comas-Díaz, 1985; Constantino and Malgade, 1984; Canino and Canino Stolberg, 1980; de la Cancela, 1986; Teichner and Berry, 1981). Thus, the more culturally relevant the components utilized, the better the self-concept, the better the response, and the more effective the treatment or process. The opposite has also been found—that is, the more the Anglo middle class dominates power within the school (which means the smaller the cultural component), the more negative the attitudes of Hispanics toward themselves and other Hispanics (Iadicola, 1981; Cummins, 1986).[31]

The last generalization is more specific to the Puerto Rican situation. It concerns the lower self-concept and educational achievement that some studies have found among Puerto Ricans raised in New York compared with those raised in Puerto Rico (Martínez, 1979; Prewitt-Díaz, 1983; Thiel, 1977; Greene and Zirkel, 1971).[32] This parallels findings of immigrant versus native or national minority educational achievements in other countries (Cummins, 1986: 21 ff.; Ogbu, 1978). In general, immigrants have tended to do better in U.S. schools than have "indigenous" minorities. The question is whether the difference between those born in the host country and those who immigrate is due to (1) their cognitive/academic skills on arrival possibly having a better foundation or (2) their lack of experience with the devaluation of their identity in the societal institutions of the host country, mainly the schools (Cummins, 1986). Data from Europe indicate that students who immigrate late—at about 10 years of age—do better than children of immigrants who were born in the host country (Cummins, 1986: 23).

To sum up, the literature reviewed here seems to say that there are unique cultural differences between Hispanics and Anglos. Acknowledging Hispanic culture in a positive and direct way appears to be important in the treatment of the mentally ill, in enhancing the self-concept of children, and in predicting academic success. Its absence leads to more negative self-concepts and negative attitudes toward one's group. Members of the Puerto Rican population who have been most exposed to corrosive cultural forces—those raised in New York City—appear to have lower self-concepts and to achieve less in school than their counterparts who were raised in Puerto Rico. Given these findings, it seems important to deal with the cultural dimensions that Hispanics present.

Hispanic Struggles

Hispanics have not been passive recipients in the educational process. Both Latinos and the educational system have been engaged in a dialectic similar to that found in the classrooms. As Olivas (1983: 127) notes:

> The history of Hispanic education has been one of struggle against insensitive government agencies and school boards, those organizations responsible for governing education systems.

Indeed, within the Puerto Rican community there is an emerging awareness of this history of struggle. Moreover, there is a growing sense of pride in that history(González and Ortiz, 1987: 17; Uriarte-Gaston, 1987; Rivera, 1987; Morales, 1986; Pérez, 1987; Padilla, 1987a). It is as if throughout this history there have been two goals. The Hispanic goal has been to change the system so that Hispanic students would do well, stay in school, graduate, and go on to college; the system's goal has been to get Hispanics to do better, but without changing the system.

The term *struggle* may convey a combative orientation, while the demands made and the alternatives sought by Puerto Ricans may be interpreted by some as a reflection of a disinclination to assimilate and hence as evidence of disinterest in "making it." For some, the struggles of Hispanics may be seen as part of the problem, when in fact they have been part of the search for a solution. Puerto Ricans have participated in these struggles not because they wanted to struggle, but because they felt there were no other alternatives. Furthermore, it was because Puerto Ricans wanted to succeed, and to have their children succeed, that these battles have been fought, that these demands have been made. Puerto Ricans have pressured for reforms because the system has been inadequate, as demonstrated by a history of failure. Puerto Ricans have sought alternatives because the programs in place have not worked for the majority of their children.

The History of Struggle

The pressure to change the educational system can be divided into three historic periods. In the first phase of struggle, Puerto Ricans pressured for studies to examine the "problems" (Santiago-Santiago, 1987). Then, during the 1960s, the community developed agencies and organizations that more directly addressed the difficulties Puerto Rican children were having in the schools.[33] Finally, in the 1970s, the community, having exhausted its patience, turned to the courts. What has become clear with time is that the changes that have taken place would not have come about but for the struggles of the community.

The studies. As early as 1954, the New York City Board of Education received Ford Foundation support to study the "Puerto Rican problem" (Jorge, 1984). The final report of this study recommended proper screening and placement of non-English-speaking children. These recommendations were ignored (Jorge, 1984; Santiago-Santiago, 1987; Vásquez, 1971). A subsequent study by Jenkins (1971) described the difficulties Puerto Rican children met in the schools and the embarrassingly inadequate measures taken by the Board of Education to meet their needs. The findings were again ignored, and the study was not released for more than a year after its completion. Since then, there have been numerous studies. The most recent, by the Educational Priorities Panel (1985b), documented the school system's failure to serve students with limited English proficiency, as is now required by law and court order.[34]

The legal suits. In the second phase, the Puerto Rican community moved into litigation strategies.[35] Puerto Ricans, seeking to obtain equal educational opportunity for their children, sued the NYC Board of Education in 1972. This suit resulted in the Aspira Consent Decree, which required that the NYC Board of Education implement a transitional bilingual program for all LEP students (Santiago-Santiago, 1987). Aspira of New York and the Puerto Rican Legal Defense Fund also filed an *amicus-curiae* brief with the Supreme Court in the *Lau v. Nichols* case. The decision in this case also resulted in significant regulatory changes at the federal level for linguistic minority children.

In this way, the community won some attention for its limited-English-proficiency students, but only after "bitter resistance" from the New York City Board of Education (Santiago-Santiago, 1987). Changes were "almost begrudgingly" implemented, despite their being mandated by the courts (Santiago-Santiago, 1987). The subsequent record of the NYC Board of Education in meeting its court-mandated commitments to LEP students has been "less than sterling" (EPP, 1985b).

The Struggles Over Programs

In education, there have been many struggles (Fuentes, 1984a, 1984b; Caballero, 1986). Only three will be highlighted here: bilingual education, access to postsecondary education, and ethnic/Puerto Rican studies programs. These struggles illustrate how difficult it has been to alter the NYC system so that it will do a better job with Hispanics. They also reflect the capacity of the system to resist change, so that in effect very little change takes place. Struggles within the established programs illustrate the continuing functioning of the dialectic and the resistance of the system to these changes. Hispanics have had to continue their struggles to protect the programs established and to ensure that they progress. These are "wars of maneuver" (Barón, 1985) that must constantly be fought to assure a "seat at the table" for these programs.

Bilingual education.   Originally conceived by Puerto Rican and other Latino advocates as a comprehensive approach to children whose first language and culture were Spanish, bilingual education quickly became translated as the more general "teaching of English as a second language." The cultural components were lopped off, nonnative speakers were employed, and funds (originally secured because of the difficulties of the large numbers of Spanish-language children) went into programs that serviced smaller minority groups that (as groups) had not demonstrated serious difficulties in the educational system. Thus, the system incorporated the change thrust upon it, as a result of Hispanic struggles, by altering the nature of the change. It created and proposed its own programs for groups it determined to be deserving.[36] It altered the symbolic meaning of the original concept of bilingual education: the strengths of bilingualism and biculturalism came to be viewed as disabilities.[37]

Access to postsecondary education.   A second major struggle of the Hispanic community was the expansion of educational opportunity in postsecondary education. Puerto Ricans fought alongside Blacks and other minorities to institute an open admissions system in the public city university system. This resulted in increased numbers of not just Puerto Ricans but other Latinos attending and graduating from two- and four-year colleges. As Georges (1988: 12) notes, "Access to the university system of New York City, especially during the open admissions period of the seventies, was critical to the formation of a Dominican leadership." It was, when measured in these terms, a "successful" experiment.

But that was only an experiment. In 1975, the year of New York City's fiscal crisis, the open admissions access route was closed off. In addition, the CUNY administration imposed tuition, for the first time in its history.[38] Thus, it was no longer sufficient to be bright and talented; immigrants now had to have some money if they were going to receive the benefits of a postsecondary education. Previous immigrants had been allowed to attend based only on merit.[39]

Ethnic studies/Puerto Rican studies. Puerto Ricans also struggled for and successfully established Puerto Rican studies programs at the college level. Although some college presidents were subsequently fond of expounding on their perspicacity for taking the initiative to establish them, these programs would not have been conceived or, in some cases, established without pressure from students, faculty, and the Puerto Rican community. The pressure was sometimes subtle, sometimes violent, but never distant.

The struggle for Puerto Rican studies was similar to that for bilingual education, in that the original purposes were, from the system's point of view, perceived as antithetical to the way in which things had always been done. When Puerto Rican studies programs were first established, their thrust was to debunk, clarify, or critique the theories and teachings that were commonplace in the university that tended to portray Puerto Ricans and other racial or ethnic groups in a distorted fashion. In this regard, Puerto Rican studies and other ethnic studies programs challenged the accepted thinking in academic circles.

These programs brought to the universities what they otherwise lacked. They enriched the curriculum, although they also challenged it. In addition, because of the factors of historical birth, thrust, and the newness of the field, Puerto Rican studies was seen by some in the early days as illegitimate or non-academic. It was distrusted by some; many were threatened by these new modes of thought. However, the field of Puerto Rican studies has overcome many of these problems. It has succeeded in educating others not simply about Puerto Ricans, but about the United States and about other groups as well, for the Puerto Rican experience contains important lessons.

The struggles of the Puerto Rican community appear to have had positive second-order effects for other groups as well. As Georges (1988: 8) points out in speaking of the cadre of new Dominican leadership: "While in school, many of these young Dominicans participated in student associations which brought them in contact with other Hispanic, particularly Puerto Rican activists. They established ties and became imbued with social activist ideologies which subsequently guided their career choices and forms of political participation." These programs have also served a number of other important but informal roles vis-à-vis universities and their students—in community and public relations, in committees of programs dealing with the "disadvantaged," and in minority student advising (Rodríguez, 1981).

Developing Alternatives

Puerto Ricans have consistently pursued alternatives that are intended to reinforce cultural price and linguistic heritage. These thrusts continue; for example, there are growing numbers of Hispanics and non-Hispanics who take the position that language minorities have the legal right to sustain and encourage their native language in the United States. They argue that these rights have been recognized by all the organic laws formalizing the relationship with Puerto Rico, all of which have acknowledged a Spanish-speaking citizenship; the treaties annexing former Mexican territories in the Southwest and those made with Native American nations; the U.S. Constitution, which does not recognize any official language; the Universal Declaration of Human Rights of the Charter of the United Nations, of which the United States is a signatory; and the amended Voting Rights Act of 1965, which protects language minority groups (Daubon, 1987; González and Ortiz, 1987).

This is not to say that Puerto Ricans and other Hispanics are reluctant to become as competent and proficient in English and the American culture as possible.[40] It is apparent that proficiency in English is necessary for success in a country that is English dominant and that promises to be so for quite some time. Some see a contradiction in arguing for cultural and linguistic retention as well as absorption of the English language and the American culture; this is discussed in the next section.

The English-Only Movement

The U.S. English organization is opposed to the establishment of bilingual education and the bilingual ballot. Originally headed by Senator S. I. Hayakawa (R-CA), this organization seeks to limit bilingual education to a transitional role, to restore the English-only ballot, and to pass legislation (including state and federal constitutional amendments) that would establish English as the official language of the United States. It has been quite successful in raising funds "to restore English to its rightful place as the language of *all* Americans."[41] As of August 1987, 13 states had adopted English-only bills, 33 states had considered such bills, and there were five separate English-only language bills in Congress (*San Juan Star*, August 2, 1987: 16).

U.S. English represents a defense of the old assimilation dialectic. The driving force of the organization is not, apparently, to help non-English speakers learn English, but rather to suppress their languages and cultures. If the former were the case, English as a second language (ESL) classes would be advocated (*San Juan Star*, August 2, 1987: 16). In its mailings, the organization raises the specter of language minorities becoming permanent power blocs in the context of the "largest wave of immigration" the United States has experienced "in its history." Thus, it appears the real issue is not language or assimilation, but power. Those seen as most resistant to assimilation are Hispanics, because they "reject the melting pot concept, resist assimilation as a betrayal of their ancestral culture and demand government funding to maintain their ethnic institutions."

The English-only movement seems to be rooted in fear—that others will be speaking in a language that one cannot understand. If this movement succeeds, then speaking Spanish in public settings will become a political act. It appears that U.S. English perceives bilingual education as equivalent to an antiassimilation movement. Their mailings state, "We have embarked upon a policy of so-called 'bilingualism,' putting foreign languages in competition with our own." However, advocates of bilingual education have seldom argued that students should not learn English; *bilingual* means capable of speaking *two* languages.

Bilingualism and the United States

In light of the real polyglot, multilingual history of the United States, U.S. English's harking back to a time when English reigned supreme is amusing. The group's goal of restoring English to its "rightful place as the language of all Americans" and the fears expressed in its literature that the nation will be turned into a polylingual "Tower of Babel" both deny and contradict the history of the United States. According to Keller and Van Hooft (1982), bilingual education was common during the 1700s. It was not until after the Revolutionary War that English came to assume a greater importance. During the eighteenth and nineteenth centuries, many immigrants received instruction in bilingual schools; in some cases, these schools received public monies.

It was with the advent of public education, in the latter part of the nineteenth century, that English assumed prominence as the language of instruction. However, German was also often used; six states permitted or mandated bilingual education in German. French was a second language in Louisiana, and Spanish in New Mexico. It was with the large migrations from southern and eastern Europe that rigidity set in with regard to English as the only language of instruction (Klass, 1971). After World War I, the United States abandoned interest in bilingual education and in the study of foreign languages. Between 1950 and 1965 there was renewed interest in bilingual education (especially stirred by the U.S.S.R.'s launch of *Sputnik* in 1957), and in 1967 the Bilingual Education Act was passed by Congress. Bilingual education is not a Hispanic invention, although Hispanics have struggled hard to reestablish it in the United States.

What Works

All One System

It is easy if you are not poor, if you are not a minority group member, and if you have the option to go (or send your children) to private schools, to ignore the difficult situation of Latinos in education. You may learn about the severity of the situation, perhaps even feel sympathy or pity, or blame those in the situation, but then move on to things that are of direct concern to your own life. Like many, you may believe that minorities and the urban public schools have very little to do with those outside that system.

But, as Hodgkinson (1985: 13) has so aptly pointed out, that world is inextricably linked to all other worlds. We are all part of a continuum wherein changes at one point will have direct and predictable consequences for others. Even if we discount the observed relationships between high school dropouts, crime, and public expenditures (Smith, 1987: 17 ff.), there are still the unchangeable demographic facts. As Hodgkinson (1985: 2) poignantly states, "Our aging white middle class will find its retirement income generated by an increasingly nonwhite work force." According to Hodgkinson, by the year 2000 one of every three persons in the United States will be non-White (p. 7).[42] With fertility rates higher and median ages lower among minorities, non-Whites will be in the work force when middle-class baby-boom Whites are in retirement. As he says, "If they do not succeed, all of us will have diminished futures" (p. 18). The economic loss to the society must also be considered, including lower productivity of future workers, lower earnings, lower levels of consumption, and consequently lower economic growth. (The current threat to our international competitiveness further underscores these concerns.)

Quality, Concern, and Effective Teaching

What is to be done? While it is not possible to present a solution here, the material reviewed suggests a number of possibilities. There is obviously a need for an alternative educational process that is more interactive, more culturally and linguistically inclusive, and that involves and integrates the community from which Hispanic students come in a more positive and reinforcing way.[43] Studies of effective schools have shown that they usually demonstrate high expectation levels, concern for

145

students, and an interest in a job well done (Edmonds, 1984).[44] These same features also translate into better achievement for Hispanics (García, 1988; Moll, 1988). Urban magnet schools, which were developed as a way of coping with segregated school districts, have also been quite successful at producing educational excellence. Studies of these schools corroborate the strong relationship found between expectations and academic achievement in other schools (Blank et al., 1983; ERIC/CUE, 1984: 24).[45]

In addition, an extensive study involving 15,000 hours of observation in ordinary secondary schools yielded the conclusion that student-student and student-teacher cohesion, a strong academic emphasis, high teacher expectations, positive attitudes of teachers toward their students, stress on positive rewards, and consistent and shared values and standards make for an ethos that contributes to the academic success of urban minority students (Rutter et al., 1979; ERIC/CUE, 1982: 14). The greater success (Coleman et al., 1982) and retention (Calitri, 1983) of Hispanic students in parochial and private schools also indicates that where these more qualitative dimensions are in place, Hispanic students fare better.

Hodgkinson's (1985) finding that teacher-student ratios were better predictors of retention than money spent is also of interest in this regard. Low teacher-student ratios allow more time for teachers, but they also allow teachers more time with students. High teacher-student ratios, on the other hand, put other considerations first, such as order and group control; individual attention is less possible. These findings suggest that an effective solution must include what the Hispanic Policy Development Project (1984b) referred to as a more qualitative, concerned approach to teaching.

Changing the Teachers Is Not Enough

Altering the color or ethnicity of the teaching staff will not by itself correct the attitudinal problems noted earlier, for a number of reasons. Although the role of teachers in the functioning of the educational system is obviously a critical one, it is not the only one. Discriminatory assessment of students is often carried out, at various levels, by "well-intentioned individuals who, rather than challenging a socioeducational system that tends to disable minority students, have accepted a role definition and an educational structure that makes discriminatory assessment virtually inevitable" (Cummins, 1986: 30). All those involved in the educational system play complementary roles. No one group can be blamed for the failings of the institution. Guidance counselors, clerical and administrative personnel, central board bureaucrats, testing experts, and paraprofessionals are all important.

146

It is also not just a question of race or ethnicity. Recently hired educators from minority groups also take and enforce their legacies as rigidly as (and sometimes more rigidly than) did their predecessors (Smith, 1987: 1–2). In the end, everyone's role is to a very great extent determined by the total workings of the institution. The system works to perpetuate relations of dominance that exist in the greater society. The ideology articulated and enforced by the system legitimates and advances that structure of dominance. It is important for all to recognize (a) how and why the system works the way that it does and (b) how to keep it from running counter to the survival and achievement of dominated groups.

Bilingualism and Educational Achievement

The struggles of Hispanics to establish bilingual education have been rooted in a perhaps unarticulated, but strong, awareness that solid knowledge of two languages is a superior base upon which to build additional knowledge. Research shows that bilingual education should be strongly considered as part of any solution to the problems of Hispanics in public schools. The most recent data on Hispanic high school students shows, interestingly enough, that those students who are most proficient in Spanish and in English are also those who have the best educational attainment. Nielsen and Fernández (1981) analyzed 6,698 Hispanic high school sophomores and seniors, and found that those who were highly proficient in Spanish performed better on reading, vocabulary, and math achievement tests and tended to be less delayed in school and to have higher educational aspirations. As expected, those highly proficient in English also had positive correlations with measures of educational achievement.[46]

Nielsen and Fernández hypothesize that high Spanish proficiency may be an indicator of general verbal ability. They also note positive correlations between Spanish and English fluency. Cummins's (1986:23) review of the literature on bilingual programs leads him to state, "The most successful bilingual programs appear to be those that emphasize and use the student's L1 [first language]." Nielsen and Fernández (1981: 54) suggest that "proficiency in two languages does not require a trade-off in which proficiency in one language can be increased only at the expense of the other." Indeed, Cummins (1984: 112) hypothesizes that speaking only English at home may lower the quality of parent-child interaction and may expose children to poor models of English.

High school students in bilingual programs also have significantly higher attendance rates (90%) and lower dropout rates (16%).[47] School

147

administrators report that participation in bilingual programs enhances self-esteem and contributes to a more positive self-concept (Cardenas, 1986; Brice-Heath, 1986). Bilingual programs have been doing a good job of keeping students in school—something the regular school system has not been able to accomplish. However, scores on standardized tests have not been consistent across programs, and some programs have had superior scores. This may be due to the diversity of structures, personnel, and support these programs have received.

Full bilingual-bicultural programs have, in the main, not been fully supported; they have been tolerated. When they have gone beyond the "soft money" stage, they have suffered the same fate as the Puerto Rican or ethnic studies programs in the colleges—that is, they have often been marginalized from the mainstream of activities and their status has not been seen as equivalent to that of other programs. Furthermore, they have often been unsupported and overworked. As new programs, they had to start from scratch in developing appropriate curricula, tests, and content materials—tasks that might have been easier in a system that had no institutionalized assimilationist dialectic.

Bilingualism and Our Multicultural World

Santiago-Santiago (1987) presents another very important argument for bilingual education. She argues that bilingual programs, if supported, can provide a more successful, alternative program model for students to learn. If successful, they can also produce superior educational products.[48] In addition, she argues that the public's interest is best served by schools that implement comprehensive and effective models of bilingual/ multiethnic education (see also Banks, 1981):

> The multi-ethnic education model . . . enables schools to incorporate ethnic minorities more successfully, improve cross-cultural and inter-racial understanding, and prepare all children to function in a pluralistic society. (p. 178)

In addition to the advantages Santiago-Santiago notes, it seems to me that such a model is the best way of meeting the concerns raised in the literature. It also seems the best way to educate children who will live in a world that has an international economy. Moreover, bilingual education capitalizes on the strengths of Hispanic children and develops a natural national resource, the Spanish language, along with other languages. It enables children who speak a language other than English to develop fully the superior cognitive abilities that come from complete mastery of more than one language.

Bilingual education has the potential to provide society with better educated, cognitively superior graduates. It could also be implemented with relative ease, because of the concentration of Hispanic children in certain areas, schools, and districts. A bilingual, multicultural education can be a superior education, as many other countries and upper-income families have known for some time. Today's Latino youth see no contradiction in being bilingual, bicultural, and American (Ramos and Morales, 1985).[49]

Notes

1   In this chapter the term *Hispanic* will often be used when discussing Puerto Ricans because the educational data combine all Spanish-origin groups into one category. (The NYC Board of Education eliminated the "Puerto Rican" category in 1978.) Most of the studies and other data cited also use this term.

2   On the national level, the educational attainments of Hispanics, as a group, are generally below those of non-Hispanic Whites and, in some cases, non-Hispanic Blacks (Hispanic Policy Development Project, 1984b; Durán, 1983; Fligstein and Fernández, 1985; Valdivieso, 1986; Brown et al., 1981; Nielsen and Fernández, 1981).

3   When we compare districts with 40% or more Hispanic students with districts that have 40% or more White students, we find significant differences. Thus, districts with significant numbers of Hispanics are below the city averages in reading and math; they are significantly behind those districts with predominantly White school student populations.

4   The dropout situation in NYC high schools is so bad that Fine (1985: 44) acknowledges that, although she set out to study why students dropped out, in the midst of her research, she was confronted with a new question: "Why do they stay?"

5   Berne (1988) finds high negative correlations in NYC schools between the percentage of Black and Hispanic students and the percentage reading at or above grade level. He notes that the correlations have become slightly weaker since 1976–77, but they were still very high in 1982–83. The correlations become stronger in the higher grades. Similar associations were found between poverty and reading scores. See also Buriel (1987), who finds that greater racial segregation in schools reduced the achievement of both first- and second-generation Mexican-American students in junior high schools in California.

6   Some districts in New York City were overwhelmingly Hispanic in 1984; for example, District 6 had 79.4% Hispanic students; District 1, 73.6%; District 32, 70.0%; District 14, 69.3%; District 12, 68.4%; District 7, 67.7%; District 4, 59.7%; District 10, 58.4%; District 8, 55.6%; and District 9, 50.7%. In fifteen high schools more than 50% of the students were Hispanic (New York City Board of Education, 1984a). In contrast, the majority (77%) of schools in New York State did not have any Hispanics (Prieto, 1984).

On the national level, there has been little change in the segregated schooling of Hispanics. Noboa (1980: 24–28) found that in half of the school districts Hispanic segregation had increased between 1968 and 1978. Orfield (1987: 6) found that Hispanic students were more likely than Blacks to attend a class where less than half the students were White; he also found Hispanic segregation to have increased since 1968.

7   As of 1984, there were 33 high schools with student bodies 40% or more Hispanic, and 3 with student bodies over 70% Hispanic. Of the 78 academic high schools in New York City, 14% have student bodies over 50% Hispanic (NYC Board of Education, 1984a).

8   A systematic random sample by the author (N = 15) of the 78 academic high schools in New York City revealed the following relationships. The proportion of Black students in a high school was positively correlated with the number of students being two or more years behind (r = .63) (see Table 6.1). The proportion of Hispanic students in a high school had a more modest positive relationship (r = .41). However, the proportion of White students in a school was negatively correlated with the proportion of students in a school that were reading two or more years behind grade level (r = −.85).

The percentage of diplomas granted in high school graduating classes showed a similar relationship. The correlation coefficients were White, .67; Black, −.64; and Hispanic, −.14. The same pattern existed for college attendance at four-year colleges, although all the coefficients were smaller. The correlation between percentage White and percentage of graduates attending four-year colleges was .40; it was −.47 for Blacks and a negligible −.01 for Hispanics.

These correlations do not imply causation, but association. The association calculated is the one most people mentally calculate: the greater the proportion of Whites in a high school, the lower the proportion of students who are below grade level and the higher the proportion of graduates who go on to four-year colleges. On the other hand, the greater the proportion of Black students in a high school, the greater the proportion who are below grade level and the lower the proportion who receive diplomas and go on to four-year colleges. Hispanics follow the Black pattern, but in a less accentuated fashion.

9   The proportion of Hispanics within the City University system has also increased—from 7.8% in 1970 to 23.6% in 1983. However, Hispanics are still concentrated in community colleges. Indeed, it is in community colleges (two-year or junior colleges) that Hispanics have shown the greatest increase between 1970 and 1983. (Whites, on the other hand, have shown sharp declines within CUNY at both the four-year and community college levels.)

10   Lavin (1973), in a comparison study of open admissions and regular admissions students in the City University system, found lagging graduation and completion rates for Hispanic students at both the community college and four-year college levels. Moreover, transfer rates from community colleges to four-year colleges were also lowest for Hispanic students. Lavin et al.'s (1986) more recent analysis of three freshman cohorts entering the City University system between 1970 and 1972 shows that Hispanics had the lowest graduation rate and the lowest completion rate even when a longer time frame for completion of college was used (i.e., 12–14 years after entering). This was true for Hispanic students who entered as open admissions students and for those who were regular entrants. In essence, open admissions Hispanic

students trailed White and Black open admissions students, and regular Hispanic students trailed White and Black regular students.

11 With regard to faculty, 18% are minority group members; of these, 26% are Hispanic. However, only 10% of full professors are non-White (Murphy, 1986: 6). Thus, whether we look at undergrads in two-year or four-year colleges, at graduate students, or at faculty, it appears that the higher one's level of education within CUNY, the greater the likelihood that one is not Hispanic.

12 These studies used a common data base and similar methodological approaches—in the main, probit, multiple regression, and multiple classification analysis techniques. They also focused on differences between Hispanic origin groups and attempted to ascertain the extent to which human capital variables accounted for the variance of their chosen dependent variable. Education was one of the human capital variables examined. In some cases, regional or market variables were included in the equations.

13 An example of the subtle fatalism that sometimes afflicts those in charge and in supportive service positions can be seen in the following remark of a South Bronx junior high school principal. After discussing the high dropout, absenteeism, truancy, and left-back rates and low reading and math scores of his students, he went on to focus on the success of one student, saying, "If only one succeeds . . . it's all worthwhile." The expectations inherent in the comment become quite clear if we reflect on whether we, or any responsible administrator, would be satisfied if "only one makes it." To accept such a perspective is to pretend that the system is functioning effectively, even though 99 out of 100 students are not successful. The comment of this principal passed unnoticed, as do others like it every day. Indeed, at the time this comment was made, this particular principal was regarded by other educators as "one of the best" in the South Bronx.

An interesting counterpoint to the "if only one succeeds" philosophy is millionaire industrialist Eugene Lang's program of guaranteeing kids a paid college education if they stick to their schoolwork. His position is that they can all succeed if they try. The success of his idea is evident in the fact that it has been replicated in 15 cities beyond New York (New York Times, June 21, 1987: 1).

14 Fine (1983) found in her study of 170 teachers and counselors that their own disempowerment was highly correlated with disparaging attitudes toward students. She concludes that the disempowered teacher may help to produce the disempowered student, who often drops out.

15 The Thomas and Gordon (1983) study was a two-stage probability sample. Subsamples ranging from 50 to 136 Hispanics, 116 to 750 Whites, and 69 to 54 Blacks were drawn. They were interviewed in 1972 and again in 1979. Results were analyzed using multiple regression techniques, with educational and occupational attainment as independent variables.

16 Fligstein and Fernández (1985) found that mother's education was significantly related to Hispanic school attendance and school delay. This held even if the mother was foreign-born and educated elsewhere.

17 Dillard and Campbell (1981) found, in their sample of 608 parents and adolescents, that the relationship between Puerto Rican adolescents' career expectations and their parents' career values was significant. This was contrary to the results for White and Black teens.

18 Although not ignoring the sociocultural and socialization roles of parents in

affecting Hispanics' school achievement, Durán (1983) suggests that teachers' stereotypical beliefs about cultural attributes of Hispanics could lead to teachers' lowered educational expectations of Hispanic children relative to their expectations of Anglo children.

19   Torruellas (1986) also cites other, more commonly mentioned, factors: understaffed, ill-equipped, and overcrowded schools and traditional, repetitive teaching methods.

20   Bruno's (1983) study of the sources of stress for 400 teachers is intriguing in this regard. A majority of the teachers working in predominantly Black or Hispanic high schools experienced high to unbearable stress (65% of those in predominantly Black schools, 52% of those in predominantly Hispanic schools), while only a minority (20%) of those in White high schools experienced this level of stress. Bruno found that the most significant sources of stress for teachers in predominantly Hispanic high schools in the inner city were administrators and "unmotivated" students.

Does the perception of students as "unmotivated" imply low teacher expectations? Why are the students unmotivated? If educational expectations influence occupational attainments, and if Hispanic students are not motivated, is that not a clear signal of alienation and distress? What is it about the school system that makes for low motivation?

21   The Board of Education recently altered admissions practices for the "educational option" programs (New York Times, September 18, 1986: 1; September 21, 1986: IV, 9). It is worth noting that this change was instituted despite the opposition of the principals of the schools, who were concerned that random selection would lead to a slipping of academic quality. One principal spoke quite honestly when he said, "This school can be a dominant minority school and continue to be a strong school. . . . Unfortunately, the public may not see it that way" (New York Times, September 18, 1986: B31).

22   This policy (to keep certain schools at least 50% White) was first adopted in 1976 as a way of preventing "White flight" from the schools. Its defenders argued that the policy enabled the city to avoid forced busing and redistricting. However, the policy also tended to benefit White students. Since the entering pool of students consisted of less than 50% White students, White students were at an advantage in applying to unzoned schools. The Board of Education is considering ending this policy in view of a now 83% minority population (New York Times, August 17, 1988: 1).

23   The concern with racial balance is not new. As early as 1967—when the school system first became majority-minority—Dr. Nathan Brown, executive deputy superintendent of schools, said, "The Board of Education has attempted through a number of procedures to promote ethnic balance in the schools . . . but the 'continuing increase' in the number of Negro and Puerto Rican pupils . . . makes it more difficult for us to provide the kind of integrated education that we would like to provide for every section in the city" (New York Times, March 15, 1967: 1). At the same time, an editorial in the New York Times underlined the "futility of demands to legislate racial 'balance' in the schools."

24   Most Hispanics in the nation underwent similar Americanization experiences, particularly in the prebilingual program period. Brez Stein (1985) refers to this period as the "sink or swim era" for Hispanics. He describes assimilationist policies that aimed to force acculturation, ban the use of Spanish, and channel Hispanic children into programs that virtually guaranteed that they would

pursue low-status occupations: "Americanization seemed to fit into a kind of 'stay where you are' policy. The young people would be trained for low-level jobs and at the same time they were given a strong dose of acculturation" (p. 190). Girls, for example, were trained to become domestics and garment workers in the "Anglocentric" school system.

For a detailed analysis of the early establishment of bilingual education programs in the early 1970s, see Santiago-Santiago (1978: 20 ff.).

25 The modern-day equivalents of this process are well described by Richard Rodríguez, a Mexican-American, in his book, *Hunger of Memory* (1982); see also Rodríguez (1974c).

26 The studies reviewed in this section were selected because they focus on Puerto Ricans and Hispanics in educational settings, and on issues relevant to educational, usually classroom, settings. The studies are, in the main, empirically based and contemporary. However, some of these studies deal with Hispanics as a generic category or with Mexican-Americans who live outside of New York City. Although there are a great many differences among Latino groups, there are also a great many similarities. Thus, three common areas were emphasized: student-teacher interactions, the role of "culture" or "Hispanicity" (Padilla, 1985), and the role of expectations and motivation in achievement. Differences between Puerto Ricans in New York and those in Puerto Rico were examined separately.

27 Consistent with these generalizations is the finding that Hispanics were viewed by teachers as interacting less frequently with teachers and peers (Roberts et al., 1985). This perception of Hispanics as more distant may reflect actual Hispanic student behavior, or it may reflect the perceptions of the teachers. It may also be an interactive variable—that is, the more they are perceived as distant, the more distant they are and vice versa. (However, Fairchild and Cozens, 1981, find that Hispanics do not view themselves this way.) In all of these studies, difference and distance appear to go together.

28 "Culture" has often served, however, as a good catchall to explain the problems of Hispanics. (See, for example, Lewis, 1966; Glazer and Moynihan, 1970; Galli, 1975; Sowell, 1981. For critiques of these studies, see Valentine, 1968; Rodríguez, 1974b, 1984b; Rodríguez and Rodríguez, 1975.) This use of "culture" has been so extensive it has led to articles critiquing works that use cultural deficit models and to articles that discuss common methodological problems in the research or treatment of Hispanics. (See Andrade, 1982; Baca Zinn, 1979; Becerra and Zambrana, 1985; Marín and Marín, 1983; Santiago-Santiago, 1986a. Within the medical arena, see Brazil, 1972; de la Cancela and Zavala-Martínez, 1983; de la Cancela et al., 1986; Rendon, 1984; Rivera, 1986; Rogler et al., 1983; Zavala-Martínez, 1981.) Indeed, the term *revisionist school* has been applied to those who take issue with works that have based much of their analyses on this broad use (or misuse) of culture. For a critical perspective that examines cultural behavior as the result of class status, see de la Cancela (1986).

29 See, for example, Triandis et al. (1985a), who find that, in their sample of U.S. Navy recruits, Hispanics tended to use *simpatía* as a cultural script, while for Anglos neither the script nor an English-language equivalent to the concept exist. Powers and Wagner (1983) found that in their sample Hispanics had greater internal locus of control compared to Anglos, who manifested greater external locus of control. Triandis et al. (1985b) found Hispanics to have more

153

cooperative as opposed to competitive orientations. They also found that Hispanics and Anglos differed on orientations to work and family. Wurzel (1983) found that in his sample of 59 (12–13-year-olds in Boston, Puerto Ricans were more hierarchical and fatalistic than their Anglo classmates.

30 Gumbiner et al. (1981) found that Mexican children's responses to teaching styles were different from those of Anglo children. For example, Mexican students were more comfortable with a structure that called for greater interdependence with peers, while Anglo students preferred a more individualized structure. The social orientation of Mexican students was less affected by teacher behavior than was Anglos' orientation. Muñoz-Hernández and Santiago-Santiago (1983) found qualitative differences in the ways in which Hispanic and White teachers expressed praise and disapproval. Although the reported findings were preliminary, they found that Hispanic teachers tended to use more indirect forms, conditional tenses, personal appeals, and polite forms, while White teachers used more direct forms. Marin et al. (1983) found that undergraduates in Los Angeles differed in their responses to the same questionnaire item depending on whether the question was asked in English or in Spanish.

31 This was found in Iadicola's (1981) California study of 220 sixth graders in desegregated schools. Cummins (1986), in his review of the literature on bilingual programs, also concluded that to the extent that the patterns of interaction in the school reverse those that prevail in the society at large, minority students will succeed educationally.

32 Martínez (1979) found that island-born Puerto Ricans achieved significantly higher grade point averages than their mainland-born counterparts. Dropout rates were also higher for the New York-born group. Prewitt-Díaz (1983) found that his sample of new arrivals from Puerto Rico, with one year in bilingual education, had higher self-esteem scores than their counterparts who were not in bilingual education programs and were not new arrivals. An earlier study by Thiel (1977) also found that inner-city schoolchildren had more negative self-concepts than their counterparts on the island, and Greene and Zirkel (1971) found self-concept among Puerto Ricans to be significantly related to academic achievement. However, Wurzel (1983) found no significant differences between Puerto Ricans raised in Puerto Rico and those raised in Boston with regard to perceptual or relational modalities and fatalistic and hierarchical orientations.

33 Many of these organizations still exist; see APRED (1987) and Office of Puerto Rico (1987) for listings and descriptions of Puerto Rican community agencies.

34 Although some progress has been made, a contradiction persists between the severity of the Puerto Rican situation and the lack of attention and significance attached to it. For example, when a report was issued by Mayor Koch's Commission on Hispanic Concerns, the mayor himself publicly stated his opposition to its recommendations (New York Times, July 24, 1986:B1; August 3, 1986: B1), including a recommendation that the mayor appoint a Hispanic member to the Board of Education. Despite the fact that one out of three students in the school system is Hispanic, the Hispanic community did not have a seat on the seven-member Board of Education. The major declared, after removing the one Hispanic member, that he saw no need to name a Hispanic person to the Board because the chancellor (whose office is subject to the Board) was, he said, Puerto Rican. Mayor Koch said, "I believe that the

Board of Education should reflect the most able people in the field of education, who can enhance the education of the children without regard to race, ethnicity, religion or sex" (*New York Times*, August 3, 1986: B1). As Fuentes (1984b) points out, typically, this "color-blind" approach leads to all-White results.

35 For an analysis of legal struggles between the educational system and Puerto Ricans, see Santiago-Santiago (1978, 1987).

36 The positive side to this was that many other groups who had not participated in these struggles benefited from the existence of these programs. Their transition to English was eased because of these struggles. The negative side was that there never seemed to be enough for everybody.

37 Dr. Maria J. Canino, a Puerto Rican member of the CUNY Board of Higher Education, takes note of the need to change this deficit conception of bilingualism. She also refers to bilingual education as "a basic democratic right of our community, a pedagogically sound approach, which provides equal opportunity to a large segment of the university's future population" (Puerto Rican Council on Higher Education, 1986: 8).

38 Resistance to the recision of open admissions and free tuition, as well as to faculty retrenchment, was made manifest in the many student protest activities of the time. Strongly in the lead, and in the ranks, of these opposition movements and actions were Puerto Rican students and faculty.

39 Open admissions benefited students of Italian and Irish descent more than it did Hispanics or Blacks—proportionally more were admitted and more graduated (Lavin, 1973). White working-class students were less often the recipients of low faculty expectations, however, because open admissions policies were perceived as being for Blacks and Hispanics. García et al. (1981) confirm the tendency to associate "special admissions" programs with lower evaluations of minorities. In their study, minority applicants to schools with affirmative action programs were perceived (by nonminorities) as less qualified than comparable White student applicants. (Minority applicants to schools without affirmative action programs were perceived as more quali-fied.)

40 The educational concerns of Hispanic parents and educators have a long history. For a sampling of these concerns, see U.S. Congress (1970).

41 The phrases in quotes are taken from materials distributed by U.S. English. The fund-raising letter says: "We have enough problems as a nation, without having to talk through an interpreter. We can still reverse our misguided course, and secure for ourselves and our children the blessings of a common language." The organization is described—in an accompanying article it sends out with its literature—as an organization that will "try to speak for those who don't want to see this English-speaking nation turned into a poly-lingual babel."

42 For slightly different estimates, see Bouvier and Davis (1982) and Valdivieso (1986).

43 The Hispanic Policy Development Project (1984b: 13) found that "the effectiveness of schools is improved when schools, parents and students work together to define needs and develop programs." They also recommend that schools take the initiative in building links to the communities they serve.

44 These studies have found that effective schools differ from ineffective schools in the following ways: (1) teachers in effective schools expect students to learn

and (2) the leadership in effective schools expects instruction to take place. These qualitative dimensions of schools are often lost or not actualized when there are large numbers of children in classes, or when there is little interest or hope that children can succeed.

An interesting by-product of these characteristics of effective schools is that they also have greater discipline (Edmonds, 1984). Valdivieso (1986: 23) notes two additional characteristics of effective schools: (1) student acquisition of basic and higher-order skills takes precedence over all other school activities, and (2) frequent and consistent evaluation of student progress is performed. Although the effective schools movement had a number of adherents, models of effective schools cannot easily be transplanted to new sites. Nonetheless, the principles of operation of effective schools are still well worth implementing.

Some of these principles apparently have worked for Middle College, an alternative high school that sends 85% of its "at-risk" students to college and that has a dropout rate of only 15%. The student body is made up of students with previous records of academic failure; the school has a limited enrollment of 450 and a student:teacher ratio of 18:1. According to the students, the school works because "it provides a supportive, nurturing environment where the teachers and staff know them and care about them" (*New York Post*, April 17, 1986).

45 The magnet schools were originally instituted to attract students from a variety of districts through their more unified curriculas. They sought to enhance academic performance by drawing together students and staff with the same aptitudes and interests. The first national study of magnet schools concluded that they share a number of characteristics with effective schools: they tend to have strong leadership, a cohesive curriculum, high expectations, and a consensus among faculty, students, and parents about the goals of the school (Blank et al., 1983; ERIC/CUE, 1984: 24). Although class and selection variables are not controlled in magnet schools, Blank et al. (1983) find only moderate association between the degree of selectivity of a magnet school and reading and math achievement scores.

46 Spanish usage was, however, negatively related to educational achievement. Nielsen and Fernández present two possible explanations. One is that those who are more active users of Spanish may be involved with more code-switching, which may have deleterious effects on achievement. The other is that the institutional context within which Spanish is used may influence alienation and therefore achievement. For example, students in bilingual/ bicultural programs may be less alienated from school and therefore may achieve better. Since few students are to be found in these settings, greater Spanish use appears to be negatively related to achievement.

47 The attendance results are based on Title VII evaluations that compared students in bilingual programs with other students in the same schools. Attendance for bilingual program students averaged 90% in 1983–84 and 91% in 1984–85. Dropout results are based on Title VII data for 1984–85. Dropout rates of students in bilingual programs is 16% versus the citywide average of 42% (in González, 1986).

48 For evidence that those who successfully master two languages develop superior cognitive abilities, see Hakuta and Díaz (1984) and Hakuta (1984a, 1986); for a specific study of Puerto Rican children in Connecticut, see Hakuta

(1984b). Veltman (1981), using the 1976 SIE, found that native-born Hispanic-bilingual children had higher educational attainments than native-born English-monolingual Hispanic children. See Ramírez (1985: 193–201) for a review of research showing the cognitive superiority of bilinguals in different countries. One concept clarified in this review is the need for a threshold level of knowledge in both languages in order for the cognitive superiority of bilinguals to be evidenced. Also clarified in this study are the specific advantages of competent bilinguals over monolinguals, for example, "cognitive flexibility," "divergent thinking," and higher levels of reasoning and verbal abilities.

49   It should perhaps be clarified that what is intended in this model is not a "sterile cultural pluralism in which peoples dwell together but remain locked in worlds apart, in which as time passes, people know less rather than more about each other" (Bonilla, 1988: 14).

7

THE MENUDO PHENOMENON: AN UNWRITTEN HISTORY

The Visible and the Invisible

There is a large distance between what is depicted or known about the Puerto Rican community among outsiders and what is lived or experienced within it. This gap between what is and what is seen is best illustrated in the cultural realm. Here, in the literary, visual, and performing arts, we can clearly see the contradiction of "unperceived realities." We see, in essence, that there are realities (i.e., cultural productions) that go unnoticed or unrecognized.

The Puerto Rican community in New York, almost from the moment of its inception, has developed its own rich traditions in literature and the arts. Jesús Colón, Bernardo Vega, Piri Thomas, Nicolasa Mohr, Edward Rivera, Ed Vega, Miguel Algarin, and others, residents of the early barrios, began to depict the unique and rich experiences of Puerto Ricans from a literary vantage point. Puerto Rican poets provided more distilled versions of the experience. All affirmed in their writings their intent to persevere and to cultivate their existence, and to defend their cultural birthright (Esteves, 1987). The writings of these authors are extensive, but they are not well known outside of the Puerto Rican community. They are not included in most American anthologies, nor are they required reading in the school systems.

The cultural presence and impact of Puerto Ricans has long been felt, although it has seldom been accurately or adequately acknowledged. Bernardo Vega notes that Puerto Ricans, in the first significant migration of Spanish-speaking people to New York, took Hispanic/Spanish culture out of the universities and put it on the streets of New York (Iglesias, 1980: 28). Puerto Ricans have made New York a bilingual city in the same way that Cubans made Miami a bilingual city (Mohr, 1987: 160). Moreover, as Mohr notes, Puerto Ricans have created a "benchmark in New York City culture" that is echoed throughout the nation, as Puerto Ricans have recreated communities in new cities. The Puerto Rican diaspora—from Puerto Rico and then from New York—has meant that "Puerto Ricans are no longer an island people" (Mohr, 1987: 160). The addition of new Latino immigrants has added to the ever-widening bands of Spanish threads in the fabric of many cities. However, acknowledgment of this fact has been nominal.

In the visual arts, the Puerto Rican community boasts another long tradition and a number of prominent institutional accomplishments. A full-service museum called El Museo del Barrio (The Community's Museum), on Fifth Avenue's "museum row," represents the community that gave birth to it. For over a decade it has exhibited the art of Puerto Rican and other Latin American artists. But for its presence, these artists would have received far fewer showings. Furthermore, as a result of the efforts of concerned Puerto Rican and Hispanic leadership, and aided by sympathetic supporters, the Bronx Museum of the Arts has also become a leader and an important outlet for the exhibition of Puerto Rican and other Latino art.[1] Satellite galleries have accompanied both museums, so that art has become more accessible to all community residents.

In addition, a unique form of art evolved in the 1960s and 1970s as a result of the fusion of artists from Puerto Rico and New York. This "cubical" art was reproduced via silk-screen methods for community consumption. A number of "tallers" (workshops-studios) taught design methods to community youth and thus encouraged their creative expression. At least one taller is still producing excellent work. Such institutions and activities owe their existence to the efforts of Puerto Ricans who sought to create channels for their creative energies and to assist others to develop themselves. Yet, they've received little attention from the larger artistic community, which is, like them, centered in New York.

The development of music in the community is another example of the breach that exists between New York Puerto Rican cultural production and the world outside. As early as 1928, Rafael Hernández, the most famous of contemporary Puerto Rican composers, was creating music on the sidewalks of East Harlem. Here was written "Lamento Borincano," the most popular of his folk-rhythm and lyrical compositions (Salazar, 1984), which was embraced by many in Puerto Rico with an affection befitting a national anthem. The evolution of other musical forms, such as Latin jazz or salsa, followed a clear, but similarly uncredited, course.[2] Clearly a musical development of sustained substance, Latin jazz (today referred to by some as salsa) remained largely unknown beyond the community and a ring of sophisticated jazz musicians (Paredes, 1984). The more commercial dimension of Latin music has consistently filled dance halls, home parties, and festive occasions with throbbing energy. Yet, the intense involvement of Puerto Ricans in Latin music was surpassed only by its relative obscurity in the mass media.[3]

There have been myriad artistic activities in the Puerto Rican community. It is impossible to do justice in one chapter to the many long-established Puerto Rican agencies and theater companies, the established Puerto Rican colleges in New York (Hostos and Boricua), and the multitude of social clubs and village associations that have all been involved in extensive cultural programs or that utilized the visual arts. (These few examples were chosen because of their institutionalized nature and because of my own familiarity with them.) This very short review of cultural accomplishments has been offered only to point up the breach that exists between what is or has been in the Puerto Rican community and what has been seen by outsiders.

The Menudo Phenomenon

To provide a better basis for understanding the distance that exists between what occurs within the Puerto Rican community and what is visible to those outside it, I move now to an in-depth focus on a major social phenomenon that took place within the Puerto Rican community that was also nearly invisible to those outside of the community: the Menudo phenomenon, that is, the reaction within the community to the folk-rock group Menudo.[4] My intent is not to argue the aesthetic or cultural attributes of the phenomenon. Rather, by focusing on Menudo, I will demonstrate how events and activities that were commonly known within the Latino/Puerto Rican communities were largely unknown outside of these communities. In so doing, I will highlight the strengths, resources, and untapped talents that are also common in these communities.

The Focus on Menudo[5]

It might be argued that this focus on a popular cultural phenomenon trivializes more serious cultural productions and accomplishments of Puerto Ricans—that, indeed, by focusing on the reactions to this one pop group, I neglect the cultural expressions of Puerto Ricans in literature, theater, music (both popular and classical), oral folklore, and so on that more truly reflect the community's spirit of survival and its sense of pride and positive accomplishments. These concerns are legitimate, but my choice of Menudo as a focus for this chapter is based on the group's position as a popular phenomenon, not on its "importance" as a contribution to art.

Clearly, coming from Puerto Rico, Menudo did not reflect the community's experience, nor was it a by-product of the U.S. community. Moreover, the response to Menudo by Puerto Ricans and others represented a response to advertising, commodity capitalism, and popular culture. In spite of these facts, it is important to focus on the Menudo phenomenon in the United States because Menudo was one of the most significant popular culture influences in Latino communities in the early 1980s. At that time it would have been difficult to find a member of the Latino community who did *not* know about Menudo.

Menudo also penetrated the mainstream media network—as a totally Spanish-language production. Although other Latinos have managed this crossover (and at present there appears to be a trend toward "Hispanicizing" American music), Menudo followed a different trajectory. In contrast to earlier groups, Menudo first took off in a significant way in Latino communities and not in the mainstream media. Menudo also differed in that, early on, it had international influence—that is, Menudo was creating a stir in the United States, Mexico, and Central and South American countries as well.

But the more important reason to study Menudo is the grass-roots reactions the group elicited within Latino communities. These reactions are detailed in the following pages; they included the mass production of instantaneous identity symbols, the development of an invisible but lightning-quick communication system without formal networks, increased use of Spanish, and the spontaneous creation of mini-Menudo groups. (These reactions, in turn, further contributed to the group's success.) It is in these reactions that one can glimpse a sense of Latino consciousness and identification. There may be debate over whether this consciousness or identification is consistent with more acknowledged Latino cultural traditions, but it is clear that the response occurred, that it occurred strongly, and that it hasn't occurred in the same way with other pop groups or idols.

Method of Study

Before proceeding with a discussion of the reactions to Menudo, I should point out that this analysis uses a number of methodological approaches. In addition to a review of the relevant literature, three sources were used as a basis for the observations made here. The first was a case study of a mini-Menudo group, which involved over a year and a half of participant observation with the group members and their families. This included open-ended interviews, participation at various functions, and visits to Menudo contest sites and outlet stores. The second was a computerized search of the major press outlets, including United Press International and the Associated Press, for the years 1981–1984. The third was a monitoring of the Spanish-language press and other English-language media covering Menudo.

Menuditis

Menudo was a group of five Puerto Rican rock singers who were, and to some extent still are, very popular in Latino communities in the United States and in Central and South America. The following (somewhat dramatized) account conveys more of the essence of Menudo, particularly for young Latina women in the early 1980s:

"Bigger than the Beatles," said—of all people—Mayor Koch of NYC. . . . Broke all records at the Felt Forum. . . . Three killed in stampede at concert in Mexico. . . . Mobs tying up traffic at the airport. . . . A key to the city is presented to Menudo. . . . 5,000 girls mob City Hall for a glimpse of Menudo. . . . ABC is interested . . . Hollywood calls. . . . Menudo buttons . . . Menudo mania!!!!![6]

In 1983, a new term entered the Spanish-English vocabulary: *Menuditis*. It referred to a newly discovered illness that afflicted young Latina girls whenever they were in the electronic or actual presence of Menudo. Symptoms included fainting, yelling, screaming, and moaning in long, loud wails whenever the group was mentioned or near.

There was no known remedy. Treatment consisted of acquiring Menudo paraphernalia and specialty Menudo items at one of the newly established Menuditis stores or in newly developed sections of novelty or music shops. It was also advisable to attend Menudo concerts and to watch Menudo on television when possible. Although there was no known cure for Menuditis, it was expected to diminish with age if contracted early. There was no hope for older victims.

Mass-Produced Identity Symbols

Menudo buttons appeared on the street. "I love Menudo," "I love Miguel," or Charlie, or Ricky, or Johnny, or Xavier—pronounced *Savier*, not *H*avier, because that was how it was "supposed" to be pronounced, that was the way his mother intended it. Girls wore many at once; 99 buttons were counted on one young woman.[7] A row of 6 to 8 buttons running down the side of one's pants was "cool" and common. Menudo buttons were precious possessions, guarded, stolen, given only as gifts of love—mainly between women. These prominently and proudly displayed emblems silently communicated the Latina woman's love for, and pride in, *their* group. Every Menudo button seen on the street multiplied the declaration of Latino pride and identity.

Buttons proliferated. Age was irrelevant to the wearing of Menudo buttons; they were seen on 6-month-olds in baby carriages to 76-year-olds at concerts. Surprising was the adoption (in some working-class and Black areas) of Menudo buttons by non-Latinos. Also surprising was the introduction of "I hate Menudo" buttons, often worn, interestingly enough, by Latino boys. The buttons were but the leaders in the now typical marketing blitz that follows "hot" commodities.[8] Everything was Menudo—you could wear Menudo boots, pants, T-shirts, hats, belts, jackets, neck chains, and sunglasses while you carried Menudo bags, key chains, and pocketbooks. The more you had, the better you felt.

Communication without Formal Networks

The Menudo phenomenon hit the press and the Latino community quickly and strongly. Without formalized information networks, the Menudo fans (thousands of them) knew when Menudo was coming, where they would be, and what they would be producing next. Madison Square Garden spent weeks telling thousands of callers they had no information on when Menudo was to appear, and therefore could not sell tickets. But the Menudo fans knew they were coming and kept calling. When the appearance was announced, the concerts were sold out in three days. Fans began lining up at 3:00 in the morning; the line stretched for blocks. Tickets for the Menudo concert were selling on the street for $90 apiece, and they were being purchased by people who didn't have a lot of money.

Such teenage phenomena are not uncommon. What is surprising is the speed with which information about Menudo moved in what had always been perceived, when it came to rock music, as a quiescent and privatized community. Information about available Menudo goods, whether material products or performances, permeated all circuits, all ages, generations, boroughs, and neighboring states. Women learned that Menudo belts were available, or that Menudo would be coming back into

New York in June, often before public confirmation or actual availability of the goods. Fan clubs developed overnight and grew quickly beyond their own abilities to handle requests for membership. It was a display of lightning communication without formal networks.[9]

The Spanish Language

Among the more dramatic developments that directly resulted from the Menudo phenomenon was the development of Spanish-language readership. *Las Noticias del Mundo*, a little-known paper (owned by Rev. Moon, but published without reference to the Unification Church), increased its circulation dramatically. Young girls who had never read or studied Spanish were buying *Las Noticias del Mundo* so that they could read the Menudo articles that appeared every day.[10] Working their way through those articles, they learned more Spanish than they could acquire in a year's schoolwork. They were interested.

The articles often included the words to recently released Menudo songs, and the fans learned the songs in this fashion. Intense debates took place regarding the correct pronunciation of certain Spanish words. Second- and third-generation Latina girls who had previously spoken little Spanish became fluent and educated in the cultural images of the island, for instance, "El Coqui." "Cielito Lindo," a song of Mexican origin, became identified as Puerto Rican because it was sung by Menudo. How did these women know that *Las Noticias del Mundo* or specific English- and Spanish-language magazines had articles on Menudo? Word of mouth was the explanation.

It is important to bear in mind that the Menudo phenomenon was distinct from "Beatlemania" or other teenage crazes because it was initially a totally Spanish-language production. The original members of Menudo spoke English hesitatingly, while many of their fans spoke Spanish hesitatingly. Yet they were idols. The original members had minimal experience in the United States, although a number had been born here. Yet, they appealed with great strength and intensity to the Latinas in New York, Chicago, New Jersey, Connecticut, Miami, and Los Angeles.

Mini-Menudo Groups: Las Fórmulas

Perhaps the most important, and also the least well-known and least anticipated, reaction to Menudo was the spontaneous creation of hundreds of mini-Menudo groups. These groups sang and danced the

Menudo songs in local talent shows and in the barrios of New York. The following is a case study of one such group: Las Fórmulas. This group illustrates the spontaneous generation of talent and energy that was part of the Menudo phenomenon.

I first saw Las Fórmulas in professional action at the Teatro Puerto Rico, a long-established movie house in the South Bronx that generally showed Spanish movies and some variety acts. On this occasion, an amazing 122 mini-Menudo groups were to perform, and the place was buzzing with excitement.

I marveled, Where did these 122 groups come from? There was no advertising for this performance, but everyone knew that groups selected at this tryout would perform in a subsequent show (for which flyers would be distributed). From whence did so much talent spring? How did they get here? How did they find out about it? How did they organize themselves for this endeavor? How did they come to think of themselves as capable of standing in front of a large audience and performing?

The groups generally consisted of five girls, although a few were larger and some were smaller. Thus, there had arisen, without any significant encouragement, publicity, or formal leadership that I could detect, about 610 working-class girls who were saying, by virtue of their presence at the theater that day, that they wanted to, and felt they could, perform on stage in honor of their idols. How had this come to be?

I reflected on the group I was observing. Five girls (11–12 years of age) who knew each other as friends because they all attended a parochial school in the most devastated (in terms of housing and population loss) area of the South Bronx. *They* had decided they wanted to have a group. *They* came up with their name, Las Fórmulas, from a Menudo song. *They* came up with the ideas for their costumes. *They* rehearsed their dance steps, improvising the choreography from their viewing of Menudo on TV and in concerts. Like most of the other groups there, they had never performed before an audience.

They dragooned a still single (and therefore with some free time) aunt of one of the girls to be their "manager." She did very little in terms of teaching the girls, but she was an adult who could represent them to the talent scout, when necessary. Despite the presence of the "manager," it was the members of Las Fórmulas who found out about the next talent show, came up with costume ideas, worked out their routines, and perfected their singing.

Most of the other groups were from public schools and had what appeared to be greater family ties. Ages within the groups ranged from 6 to 17. Most groups, including Las Fórmulas, sang to the accompaniment of Menudo records that they brought with them, but the girls' voices could generally be heard above the recorded voices of Menudo. Menudo's own democratic style of switching leads was incorporated into the mini-Menudo groups' style. Similar, but sometimes very different, dance steps were developed. In this regard, the performances of the mini-Menudo groups were not an imitation of Menudo, but distinct performances, taking off on Menudo's performance. As a matter of fact, each group was evaluated by the others on the extent to which they performed not just well, but uniquely.

Las Fórmulas' name was well chosen; they had the formula, for they went on to win first prize at a subsequent show. In the process of rehearsing and performing, they refined their acuity with regard to musical notes, their awareness of the quality of electronic recordings, their self-discipline, their dance and voice synchronization, their stage presence, and their general awareness of the workings of "show biz"—all without any teachers or trainers.

Most of the other groups were good, too. There was a handful of all-male groups, all older than the average age of the girl groups. (They were pursued as Menudo "stand-ins" by the girls during intermission.) Although the overwhelming majority of the groups in the show were mini-Menudo groups, it was here that I also first saw the electric boogey and some break dancing—later to move to Hollywood. There were also, in other shows I attended at clubs or social halls, guest spots for non-Menudo-type soloists. The multifaceted, generally unknown, talents of the community were displayed in these shows.[11]

International Appeal

That Menudo was an international phenomenon was also missed in most mainstream media. The internationalization was due mainly to the creative use of the means of cultural production. It was possible for the New York fans to see that women in Central and South American countries were interested in their favorite group. It was reported (and subsequently seen on televised broadcasts) that Menudo had played to packed stadiums (of sometimes more than 100,000 people) in many Latin American countries. Coverage of thousands of swarming Menuditis-afflicted girls in these various countries was broadcast to the fans in New York. The enthusiastic reception given to the (Puerto Rican) "ambassadors" of goodwill and good entertainment was highlighted on Spanish-language TV stations. (This, by the way, was the first and perhaps only time that many of these predominantly second-generation young girls tuned in to Spanish-language stations.) The international acclaim of Menudo was not lost on the U.S. Latino audience, and further affirmed the cultural pride the group had developed among Latinos in the United States. Thus, Spanish-language television conveyed international recognition, which validated Puerto Rican/Latino identity in the United States.

Menudo and Other Teen Idols

Although the excitment over Menudo was in many ways like other teenage crazes, in some ways it was not. Menudo was much like Elvis Presley, the Beatles, and Michael Jackson in that it was very marketable and profitable and underwent a similar process of commercialization. In its use of the advanced means of cultural production available today—television via satellite, videos, films, and electronic recording gimmicks—Menudo, like other groups, created a commodity that was very successfully sold.

Yet, most significant about Menudo are the ways it differed from previous individual or group idols:

(1) it was originally (and successfully) a totally foreign-language (i.e., Spanish) production;
(2) its popularity spread (originally) without formal networks, that is, without the aid of "mainstream" media channels;
(3) it had an appeal to Latino identity;
(4) it appealed to Latinos in the United States and in Latin America at the same time, validating Noriega's (1983) conception of Hispanics as the majority population in the hemisphere;
(5) it produced an active response among its fans (e.g., in mini-Menudo groups); and
(6) it produced a unique gender response (i.e., Latina women used Latino men as role models—women loved Elvis and the Beatles, but they didn't try to be like them).[12]

A Recognized Commodity

The Menudo phenomenon was unprecedented in the Latino communities of the United States. These communities have had many successes within the cultural sphere, but these have been, in large part, "contained" within the barrios. For example, other Latin music developments or fads enjoyed tremendous popularity among young Latinos—salsoul, salsa, the boogaloo, Latin jazz, the pachanga, and charanga—yet they received minimal mainstream media attention. The Puerto Rican Day parade has been a huge success, in terms of numbers attending, for over 25 years,[13] but it too has consistently received minimal mainstream media attention. Similarly, the electric boogey, rapping, and break dancing received minimal media attention until they became commodities.

New Markets and Global Capitalism

The unanticipated and unique reactions that Menudo ignited within Latino communities (and that, in turn, contributed to the group's success) would not have been enough by themselves to warrant mainstream media attention. Menudo received attention because it was perceived as capable of making *more* money than previous Latino groups.[14] It was perceived as capable of generating greater revenues through the exploitation of new markets within the United States and Latin America.[15] The English-dominant media marveled at the fact that the group could gross $21 million in such a short period of time.[16] Indeed, the attention given to the marketing apparatus that created Menudo received almost as much attention as the group itself.[17]

In essence, there was a larger context within which the Menudo phenomenon occurred, that of global capitalism. Menudo illustrates the search for new markets (in other countries) and the recognition of racial-ethnic markets in the United States. Menudo was transported from Puerto Rico (the periphery) to New York (the center) and to Central and South American countries (other peripheral areas) via the modern instruments of cultural production (satellite TV and other forms of the electronic and print media).[18] The media network of the English-dominant world moved quickly to incorporate and further exploit this new commodity in large part because it was profitable. The corporate backers of Menudo also seized upon the opportunity to further expand the market for their commodity and moved to change the group so that it would have greater appeal to non-Latino households.[19] In turn, the strong appeal Menudo originally had for Latinas began to wane. With the changes, Menudo may have become bigger, but it had become less a part of them.

Summary of the Impact

Nonetheless, the Menudo phenomenon can legitimately be said to have generated among large numbers of Latinas

(1) increased use of spoken or sung Spanish;
(2) increased literacy in Spanish;
(3) increased circulation of Spanish-language papers and magazines;
(4) increased identification with Latino cultural traditions and increased cultural pride;
(5) cross-national identification with Latina women in Latin America;
(6) development of highly efficient informal and formal (in the case of talent shows and fan clubs) communication links among Latinos, especially Latinas;
(7) increased knowledge about and proficient use of electronic media, such as tapes, records, videos, films, and photography; and
(8) the spontaneous creation of a multitude of independent, highly energized, and very organized musical groups, with all the attendant skills training in the areas of choreography, costume design, discipline, voice training, and organization and management.

The reactions elicited by Menudo in Latino communities showed that, despite economic oppression, there is strength, and there are resources. These resources were displayed by the quickly mobilized, highly energized mini-Menudo groups.

In addition, Menudo triggered in the larger Latino community a sense of pride and positive accomplishment. In many minds, the group's success was identified with the possibility of success for all Latinos, as Latinos. Very simply, Menudo's success indicated that Latinos were not all failures—that a Latino could succeed in a context where most Latinos do not succeed. Most Latinos liked Menudo; subsequent attention by the mainstream media press further reinforced their liking for Menudo and their pride in Menudo's accomplishment.

Menudo went on to cross over (successfully at first) into the English-language or bilingual music world. Their popularity within the Puerto Rican community was initially sustained, but then the strong appeal that Menudo had for Puerto Rican women began to wane. As Menudo became bigger, more "Hollywood," they became less a part of the community. The Menudo phenomenon exemplifies the gap that exists between occurrences within the community and those outside of it and an attempt to bridge that gap through alterations in the commodity produced. The story of Menudo provides insight into the strengths, vigor, and wealth of undeveloped talents that are common in the community.

Unknown, Unwritten

This chapter is subtitled "An Unwritten History" because its underlying message is about a history that has been lived, a culture that has been produced and reproduced, but that remains largely unwritten and unknown. We need to begin to acknowledge many different dimensions of that history. An article by José Lumen Roman, published December 14, 1986, in the Spanish-language daily *El Diario-La Prensa*, discusses this need. A long-time community activist and lawyer, Roman describes "the true history of the Puerto Rican community" (p. 17). He proposes "to retrace the history carved out by Puerto Ricans—without pretense of using a historian's guise—so that the road hewn by our Latin American brothers may be smoother." He begins:

Among the Hispanic communities, we were not the first to establish ourselves in the northeast United States. However, it was we, the Puerto Ricans, who came in major numbers. . . . We were poor in material riches. But we were rich in faith, hopes, and spirit. . . . They were difficult times. . . . Our constitutional rights, to which we as American citizens were entitled, had to be fought for.

Roman names dozens of people and describes their accomplishments, but goes on to say:

We can continue to name dozens of people. But the real heroes, those who truly wrote with pain, blood and tears the pages of our history are those who with warmth or bitterness had to superimpose themselves against the discrimination, the abuse, the exploitation, the lack of English and the insults to forge a better life. . . . It was they who suffered. It was they, the unknown today, those who are barely remembered. They are the true heroes. . . . Those "boricuas" [Puerto Ricans] who came here to work day and night . . . so that we could today enjoy what their efforts and work facilitated [author's translation].

There is growing awareness of the struggles that have been fought and of the many unsung heroes of these struggles; there is also a growing sense of the unfairness of these oversights.[20] There is a great need to begin to recognize what has and is being done, as well as a need to disseminate this information outside the Puerto Rican community. It is incumbent upon all of us (Puerto Rican and non-Puerto Rican alike) to begin to write of the history and the reality, so that the next generation can go beyond the struggle to survive.

The first generation of Puerto Ricans in the United States were the pioneers. Those in the second generation have been the "survivors," and they have grown strong and confident because of their struggles against great adversity. But they have earned many scars along the way; for many, the wounds are deep. If the members of the next generation are to be (as one student said) the "achievers," their work must begin in earnest. A large part of that work should be to write a cultural history; an even larger part will be to bring the Puerto Rican community to center stage. The work must begin immediately and with great intensity, devotion, and commitment.

Notes

1 See, for example, these works of the Bronx Museum of the Arts: *The South Bronx: Devastation/Resurrection* (1980), *Building a Borough* (1986), and *The Work of Our Hands* (1984).

2 For further analyses and descriptions of Latin music, see *Latin New York* magazine, Padilla (1987a), Salazar (1984), Duany (1984), Paredes (1984), and Ramírez (1974).

3 Indeed, a recent film, *Crossover Dreams*, depicts the sad trajectory of an attempt by a Latin musician to bring his Latin music sound to a mainstream audience. Coming from the exploited world of Latin musicians, he attempts to sell his brand of music. In the process, he is "transformed" into an American commodity with more "appeal." After crossing over, he eventually fails and returns to his "home" ground. The film is illustrative of the phenomenon of segregated communities. It focuses on the gap between the two communities, on the differences between the Latino and English-language communities.

Lately, salsa is found with greater frequency in popular music; however, it tends to cross over in disguised fashion. Many Hispanic groups rise to popularity as non-Hispanics, or with their Hispanic/Latino origins blurred, for example, Sheila E. or the Miami Sound Machine.

4 *Menudo* means small change, as in nickels and dimes, in Spanish. It is unclear why this name was chosen for the group; it may have referred to the fact that the members were all young boys under the age of 15. All Menudo members had to leave the group when their voices changed (usually by their fifteenth birthday) and were replaced by new boys. Thus, the group never aged; Menudo was patented as a commodity with perpetual life.

5 I am indebted to an anonymous reviewer for raising issues concerning the focus on Menudo. I would like to thank him or her for several valuable points that have been incorporated into the text.

6 Documentation of these dimensions of "Menudo mania" can be found in the following news accounts:

Menudo was hailed as "bigger than the Beatles" by Mayor Koch (*New York Times*, November 19, 1983: I, 29).

Menudo set a record in ticket sales at Radio City Music Hall in February 1984 (Associated Press [AP] August 21, 1984). Stadiums were also sold out in Mexico, Peru, Argentina, and Venezuela (United Press International [UPI], July 26, 1983). During their 1983 tour, they played to sellout crowds across the country. Their tour in 1984 included New York, Boston, Chicago, Los Angeles, Houston, Dallas, and Miami (UPI, August 30, 1984).

Three people were trampled to death as 40,000 fans were leaving a Menudo concert in Puebla, Mexico (AP, November 3, 1983).

Newspaper accounts of the popularity of Menudo and of the crowds that gathered whenever Menudo appeared were many. See, for example, articles in the *Christian Science Monitor* (December 20, 1984), the *Washington Post* (September 17, 1984), the *New York Times* (February 3, 1983: II, 3; February 23, 1983; June 12, 1983: I, 42; June 15, 1983: II, 4; November 15, 1983: II, 3; November 19, 1983: I, 29; December 15, 1983: II, 3; February 19, 1984: I, 2, 68; July 2, 1984: II, 1), UPI (February 20, 1984; September 4, 1984; September 17, 1984), and AP (September 4, 1984).

AP (November 2, 1983) estimated that 5,000 fans were at the airport to meet Menudo when the group arrived in New York.

Menudo signed a contract with Norman Lear and Embassy Productions for up to five pictures and several television productions (*New York Times*, July 27, 1983: III, 18). RCA signed a long-term recording contract with Menudo comparable to the company's multimillion-dollar agreements with Kenny Rogers and Diana Ross (*New York Times*, November 23, 1983: II, 18).

7 A personal observation made September 28, 1984, Radio City Music Hall, New York City. It should be noted that the impact of Menudo in Puerto Rico was less intense than in Latino communities in large cities in the United States.

8 Modern-day capitalism now has the ability to mass produce "symbolic" commodities quickly through mere imprinting. These mass-produced identity goods facilitated the spread of the Menudo phenomenon. That Menudo and Michael Jackson dolls were headliners at the 1984 Toy Fair (UPI, February 21, 1984) illustrates the commodification as well as the success of the group.

9 The Associated Press (November 3, 1983) reported that 5,000 "screaming adolescent girls" flooded Kennedy airport as Menudo arrived. How did 5,000 girls come to know the exact time, place, and date of Menudo's arrival?

10 Citing the "craze among young Hispanics for Menudo," Manny Rosa, a special assistant to Bronx State Assemblyman Joe Serrano, credited the Moon organization for using this knowledge of the Menudo mania to perfection. He said, "Kids were always picking up the paper" (Rothmyer, 1984: 29).

11 Although the spirit and strength of these young women was impressive, there were more economically based activities that fueled and exploited Menudo mania. The organizers of the talent shows charged the groups who participated. The audiences (who consisted in large part of friends and family of the participants) paid admission. Concession stands sold food, and Menudo regalia, "autographed" pictures, and other commodities associated with Menudo were also sold. Unfortunately, the organizers appeared to be more interested in making money than in discovering or creating talent—there were

no hookups to Broadway outlets, to schools of acting or dancing, or to agents (there was not even a hookup to the corporate Menudo organization). The main prizes tended to be symbolic, or tickets to the next Menudo concert. But these were apparently enough.

12 Interestingly enough, the girls in the groups often referred to one another by the names of their special Menudo idols. When they sang songs for which a particular Menudo sang lead, they were that Menudo; that song was to be performed by the girl-Miguel or the girl-Charlie, and so on. Did this reflect a new gender openness, or perhaps an androgynous approach? Why were the groups usually formed by young women? Obviously, more research is needed on these questions.

There was also an interesting dialectic at work between Latinas and Menudo—as one young girl said when interviewed on television as she waited to catch a glimpse of her idols, "They make me feel proud." Another said, "I feel that when they move, they're telling me that they love me." Someday, someone may psychoanalyze the reaction of working-class Latinas to Menudo. They may find that this clean-cut, well-mannered but fun-loving and princely group of teenagers spoke to the sexual fantasies of young and/or prepubescent girls. They may also find that Menudo's soft fusion of American rock and traditional Latin words and feelings appealed to unresolved identity issues in Latinas. Whatever the underlying psychological causes of the Menudo phenomenon, the fact remains that tens of thousands of Latinas are "more Latina" today because of the Menudo phenomenon.

13 See Estades (1984) for a description of the origins of the Puerto Rican Day parade.

14 A number of factors added to this perception. The Latino population in the United States had grown by more than 60% between 1970 and 1980. Numerous projections on continued growth were made; there was general agreement the Latinos would soon become the largest minority group in the United States. The Latino market in the United States was virgin territory—young, unexplored, and fertile. Developing it was also seen as a step toward opening up Central and South American markets. Menudo, as the first hemispheric group, exemplified the possibilities for expansion. Some would argue that Menudo went beyond its hemispheric image and became international role models when they were anointed UNICEF's first youth ambassadors (see *Washington Post,* September 17, 1984: 4). They subsequently toured Japan, as have many other popular groups.

15 The press chronicled (albeit more circumspectly) the search for bigger or new markets in depicting Menudo's rise to mainstream media stardom. See *U.S. News & World Report* (August 8, 1983: 42), *New York Times* (November 23, 1983: II, 18), and UPI (August 30, 1984).

16 According to the *Washington Post* (September 24, 1984: 3), by September 1984, 8 million records had been sold since the group began in 1977.

17 This was particularly true in the Spanish-language media, where Menudo's director, Edgardo Díaz, was interviewed almost as often as the members of the group. Paquito Cordero, head of Padosa (Menudo's production company), also received eminent billing. The English-language media interviewed these behind-the-scenes personnel less than the Spanish media did, but were in many ways more intrigued with the financial success of the business enterprise.

173

18 Prior to the discovery of Menudo by the English-language world, the Menudo operation itself had used, very effectively, the more advanced means of cultural production to catapult Menudo to stardom and to generate a profitable operation. The main instruments of commercialization included television via satellite: Menudo had a weekly half hour show that aired both in Puerto Rico and in New York on the Spanish-language network. Also, a soap opera starring Menudo, ran in Puerto Rico, the United States, and some Latin American cities. Films were made and released in the United States and in Latin American markets. The group's record albums and videos were broadcast using all these outlets. Concerts in the United States and Latin America were taped and often came to constitute the content of the weekly shows. Menudo guest appearances on English-language shows furthered the success of these means. Finally, Padosa moved to control all profits from the sale of symbolic identity goods—T-shirts, buttons, and so on. Shops selling Menudo goods not licensed by Padosa were ordered to cease such sales (*National Law Journal*, August 1983: 2).

19 The introduction of Robbie, the first New York Puerto Rican Menudo, was just such an adjustment. Robbie was raised in New York and could thus ease the projected transition to a more "bilingual" production, meaning more songs in English, and more performances and sales to more English-dominant audiences and markets. Soon after Robbie joined the group, Menudo's first English-language releases were in the top ten—meaning "mucho dinero" again. Menudo's production company shared with other firms in the new service-based economy the characteristic of "flexible specialization." However, it is possible that this very changeability had an adverse effect on some fans, contributing to the decline of Menudo's popularity.

20 On political inequities, see, for example, the following authors, who argue that Puerto Ricans have been ignored by the political parties in New York during the past few decades despite their right as citizens to vote: Baver (1984), Fuentes (1984b: 131 ff.), and Jennings (1984b). Jennings (1984b: 85 ff.) makes note of this in Boston as well as in New York. This is in contrast to the treatment generally afforded immigrants, who in the past have been courted by the political parties. In essence, Puerto Ricans have been kept out (Sánchez, 1988). (See Baver, 1984, for an analysis of why the political parties were not particularly interested in recruiting Puerto Ricans.)

APPENDIX:
TRACKING IN THE SCHOOL SYSTEM

For many years, tracking has been a fairly persistent part of school systems in general and the New York City school system in particular. In the past, lower tracks were represented by the vocational schools. However, all high schools—academic, commercial, and vocational—also had internal tracking systems. For example, within the High School of Fashion and Design, the upper track had a predominance of White students; it fed students into the designer, marketing, and buyer fields. The lower track, where Hispanics and Blacks were concentrated, fed into the garment industry, where girls could get jobs as sewing machine operators (Hillsman, 1970). These were jobs their mothers had acquired without high school diplomas.

There were also tracks in academic high schools. The upper track, the academic track, was considered preparatory for college. There were few Puerto Ricans in the college prep track, as a 1963 study showed; of those Puerto Ricans in academic high schools, only 20% received academic diplomas (PRCDP, 1965). The remainder received commercial and general diplomas. The course of study leading to a commercial diploma prepared students for office jobs, while a general diploma was the result of a nonspecialized course of study. Students who graduated with a general diploma had to take additional noncredit courses at night if they wanted to go on to college. The commercial track often led to the same racial-ethnic differentiation noted above at the High School of Fashion and Design— that is, there was a greater predominance of working-class Black and Hispanic women at the lower-level file clerk positions, while White middle-class men and women predominated at the higher paying, more prestigious secretarial, receptionist, and bookkeeping positions.

Changes in the Tracking System

Recently, the form of the tracking system has changed, although its essence remains the same. In the 1970s, in response to considerable pressures for reform, the Board of Education began granting only one diploma. However, although there is technically only one diploma, there are regents-backed diplomas and New York City diplomas, and some students receive only a "certificate of attendance." Moreover, there appear to be the same racial-ethnic differences in who tends to get which diploma (Calitri, 1983). The form of tracking has also changed because the academic-comprehensive high schools no longer represent the clear upper tracks; the proliferation of competitive, attractive educational option programs throughout all schools has altered this status. Finally, in the new technological service economy, the nature of the formerly "good" jobs has changed. Creeping credentialism and technological change have diminished the prestige formerly associated with these jobs (e.g., receptionist and executive secretary positions) and new "good" jobs have arisen in their place (e.g., technical analyst and administrative assistant). At the same time, the race and ethnicity of those moving into the formerly prestigious, now declining, jobs have also changed.

Hispanics in Vocational Schools

The concentration of Hispanics in the vocational tracks has altered only slightly over time. This has been true at the national level as well as at the local level. In 1980, 40% of all Hispanic high school students in the nation were in a general track, 35% were in vocational programs, and only 25% were in academic tracks (Hispanic Policy Development Project, 1984b; ERIC/CUE, 1985: 26). The negative correlations of such tracking are detailed by Valdivieso (1986: 9), who finds that the higher the participation rate in vocational programs, the lower the scores of students on the cognitive tests administered in the "High School and Beyond" national survey. Moreover, for many of those in these tracks and training received has little relation to the jobs they actually get. As Valdivieso (1986) notes, less than one-third of vocational high school graduates ever work in the occupations for which they were trained.

At the local level, Hispanics have constituted an increasing proportion of the students in vocational schools over the last two decades. Not only have the vocational schools become increasingly Hispanic, but significant proportions of Hispanics are in vocational schools. The scissorlike shape of the graph in Figure A.1 is striking; it shows the precipitous decline of Whites from a majority of 54.2% of students in these schools in 1961 to 14.6% in 1984. It also indicates the increase of Hispanics during the same period, from 21.6% to 35%, in the vocational-technical schools. To a significant degree, this reflects the general decline in the numbers of

176

White students in the system. However, when we look at the proportion of each population that is in vocational-technical schools, we see that the proportion of both groups in these schools has declined; but, in 1984, the proportion of Hispanics in vocational schools was still double the proportion of Whites in vocational schools (see Figure A.2). Thus, Hispanics are still overrepresented in these schools.

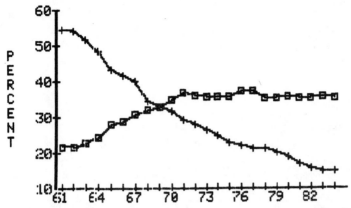

Figure A.1 Vocational High School Enrollment by Percentage, Hispanic and White, 1961–1984

Source: New York City Board of Education (1984a).

Note: Line with boxes represents vocational high schools by the proportion of Hispanic students over time; line with crosses represents vocational high schools by the proportion of White students over time.

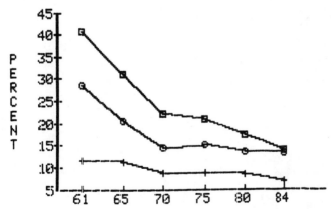

Figure A.2 Percentage of Each Ethnic Group in Vocational/Technical High Schools, NYC, 1961–1984

Source: New York City Board of Education (1984a).

Note: Line with boxes represents Hispanics, line with crosses represents Whites, and line with circles represents Blacks.

177

Vocational schools have in the past been criticized for training students for jobs that did not exist. In the last decade, some schools have made concerted attempts to train students for the changing job market. However, some of the same criticisms are still leveled at these vocational schools. "Critics charge that they teach outdated professional skills, while neglecting the basic language, math, and human relations skills that are increasingly important in the marketplace" (*New York Times*, December 4, 1986: B16). Hence, despite the changes instituted, these schools are still not looked upon with great confidence in some industries (*New York Times*, December 4, 1986: B16).

Academic High Schools

In the past, academic high schools were seen as the upper tracks. A look at the distribution of students in these schools over time shows the other side of the picture presented above. Although Hispanics increased their representation in these academic-comprehensive high schools, they were still underrepresented relative to Whites (see Figure A.3). Even in 1984 the proportion of Hispanics in academic high schools (80%) was smaller than the proportion of Whites (87%) was 23 years ago. Thus, even after a generational span, a much larger proportion of Hispanic than White students continue to be in the vocational schools, and a lower proportion attend academic high schools.

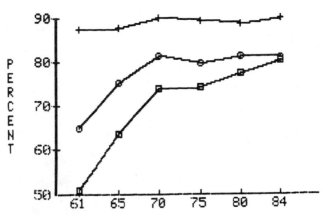

Figure A.3 Percentage of Each Ethnic Group in Academic High Schools, NYC, 1961–1984
Source: New York City Board of Education (1984a).
Note: Line with crosses represents Whites, line with circles represents Blacks, and line with boxes represents Hispanics.

Special Education

Some critics of the school system maintain that "special ed" is another tracking mechanism for Hispanics. Special education is technically for students who have "some handicapping condition" that limits their learning. Although there are a number of legal categories for those who are eligible for special education, in New York City the categories that are most generally referred to as "special ed" are the "emotionally disturbed," the "learning disabled," the "speech and language impaired," and "the mentally retarded." New York State leads the nation in the percentage of children assessed as emotionally disturbed or handicapped; 16.3% of New York's special education population is so classified (New York City Commission on Special Education [NYCCSE], 1985:11).

Overrepresentation

The question of whether Hispanics are overrepresented in special education because of misdiagnosis or tracking has long been an issue. In 1975, a federal court did find that Black and Hispanic youngsters were "discriminatorily and disproportionately placed" in day programs for emotionally handicapped students (*Lora v. the Board of Education of the City of New York* 1975; see NYCCSE, 1985: 52). A more recent review of special education programs in New York City found some improvement with regard to Hispanics. Hispanics were disproportionately represented in only one program, the Schools for Language and Hearing Impaired Children; they constituted 66% of the students in this program (NYCCSE, 1985: 53 ff.). However, the NYC Board of Education's Annual Census of 1983 still showed the proportion of Hispanics in special schools to be greater than the proportion of Whites. Hispanics also had more than their share of students (39%) in the largest program, the learning disabled program (NYCCSE, 1985: Appendix B, Table 7). The learning disabled constituted 54% of the special education population in the city.

Increased Numbers and Expenditures

Despite general declines in the school population over the years, and despite the high cost of educating students in special education, the total number of students in special education has been increasing. The special education population has more than doubled in five years; it now

179

constitutes 12.5% of total public school student enrollment, or 116,301 students in 1985. The growth has been mainly in the learning disability category (NYCCSE, 1985: 10–11). Special education is expensive—each evaluation or reassessment costs approximately $824, and the total NYC bill for the 1984–85 school year amounted to approximately $80 million. Thus, although special education students made up only 12.5% of the total school enrollment, these programs accounted for 23% of the entire school budget (NYCCSE, 1985: 15).

The question is why the numbers in special education have increased. To a degree, legal requirements, lack of alternatives, and the practice of placing students who are not up to grade level in special education classes so as to improve a school's academic image have all contributed to the increase (NYCCSE, 1985: 21). However, there is still the gnawing question of whether the children who are in special education really belong there. The New York City Commission on Special Education (1985: 30) says there are no data available to answer this critical question, yet the numbers continue to increase.

Some educators argue that there is a dual problem with special education placement—that is, that many of those who need special education don't get it, while many of those who are there shouldn't be (Carmen Fernández, personal communication, 1987). The referral process leads one to wonder. There is, on the one hand, the irony that the term *special ed*—devised perhaps as a way of ameliorating the possible stigma of the basically remedial nature of these programs—has sometimes been interpreted by newly arrived Hispanic parents as applying to programs for gifted children or programs designed to enrich regular students. They thus often quickly consent to having their children placed in "special ed" because they mistakenly think it is an award for their children's superior performance. Then there is the high rate of placement after referral. Although most of the referrals are made by teachers, the actual determination and placement of the children in special education is done by a special Committee on the Handicapped (COH). In 1983, the COH found 95% of the children referred to be eligible for special education (NYCCSE, 1985: 21). Because of a concerted attempt to reduce the growing numbers of special education students, in 1984, the eligibility rate was reduced to 85% (NYCCSE, 1985: 21).

If special education were effectively serving those in need, the money would be well spent. However, a recent review of special education programs in NYC questioned the "quality of education" in these programs. It also found "an overwhelming consensus" among special education advocates, school administrators, and educators in New York City that there may be "a significant number" of children in special education programs for the mildly or moderately handicapped who are not truly handicapped (NYCCSE, 1985: 31). Moreover, research elsewhere has found little or no difference between "slow learners" in regular classes and those in learning disabled classes (NYCCSE, 1985: 30).

Misclassification and Misplacement

With regard to Hispanics, the issue is even sharper. For some time, there has been concern over the misclassification and misplacement of linguistic minority students as learning disabled. This concern has been manifest at the national as well as at the local level. Argulwicz and Sánchez (1983) and Rodríguez et al. (1984) found that Hispanics were overrepresented in special education programs at the national level. However, in recent years there has been a shift in special education classification: Ortiz and Yates (1983) found that Hispanics were overrepresented in programs for the learning disabled and underrepresented in programs for the behaviorally disordered.

Wright and Santa Cruz (1983) also found Hispanics to be overrepresented in "specific learning disability" (SLD) programs in California. They suggest that SLD programs have come to substitute for the former mental retardation referral. Brosnan (1983) concurs with this finding of greater learning disability classifications and fewer mental retardation classifications among minorities, but she also found students from low socioeconomic districts to be overrepresented in mentally retarded and disability programs. Argulwicz (1983), however, argues that cultural/linguistic variables are more important than socioeconomic indicators in predicting the probability of special education placement. One small study found no significant relationships among race, socioeconomic status, and special education placement (Low and Clement, 1982).

Despite legislative mandates, court actions, and other safeguards, questionable special education placement practices continue (Vásquez Nuttal et al., 1984; NYCCSE, 1985). A recent study by Gottlieb of 752 special education referrals in NYC suggests one reason: Gottlieb found "substantial discrepancy between the verbal and performance I.Q. of Hispanic children," regardless of the language in which they were administered the intelligence tests. This suggests that Hispanic children may be referred for deficits that result from language delay rather than suspected learning disability (NYCCSE, 1985: 34). Further, it appears that it is the student who has reached the level of English necessary to perform cognitive tasks who is often misclassified as learning disabled, not the newly arrived monolingual speaker (Vásquez Nuttal et al., 1984: 45–48). Thus, special education referrals do not necessarily diminish with greater acquisition of English. Once placed, the student often stagnates at the level at which he or she first entered.

Tracked for Life

Once a student is referred for special education, it is almost certain that he or she will remain in that track throughout his or her school career (Fleischman Commission, 1970; ERIC/CUE, 1982a). The vast majority of students are referred while in grades 1–6. Black and Hispanic children are referred even sooner in their academic careers than are White children (NYCCSE, 1985: 27). The fact that referral to special education is an early and determinant decision makes the referral process a critical one. Concern over the impact of this placement and labeling on future employment and educational opportunities has been raised (NYCCSE, 1985), but it has yet to be assessed.

BIBLIOGRAPHY

Abowd, John and Mark R. Killingsworth (1985) "Employment, Wages and Earnings of Hispanics in the Federal and Nonfederal Sectors: Methodological Issues and their Empirical Consequences," in G. Borjas and M. Tienda (eds.) *Hispanics in the U.S. Economy*. New York: Academic Press.

Achebe, Chinua (1959) *Things Fall Apart*. New York: Fawcett.

Advocates for Children [AFC] (1985) *Public Schools: Private Admissions*. New York: Author.

Amastae, Jon and Lucía E. Olivares (eds.) (1982) *Spanish in the United States: Sociolinguistic Aspects*. New York: Cambridge University Press.

Anderson, Charles H. (1970) *White Protestant Americans*. Englewood Cliffs, NJ: Prentice-Hall.

Anderson, Elin (1938) *We, Americans*. Cambridge, MA: Harvard University Press.

Anderson, Robert W. (1965) *Party Politics in Puerto Rico*. Stanford CA: Stanford University Press.

Andic, Fuat M. (1964) *Distribution of Family Incomes in Puerto Rico*. San Juan: University of Puerto Rico.

Andrade, Sally (1982) "Family Roles of Hispanic Women: Stereotypes, Empirical Findings, and Implications for Research," in Ruth Zambrana (ed.) *Latina Women in Transition*. New York: Fordham University, Hispanic Research Center.

Andrews, Charles M. (1919) *Colonial Folkways*. New Haven, CT: Yale University Press.

Argulwicz, Ed N. (1983) "Effects of Ethnic Membership, Socioeconomic Status, and Home Language on LD, EMR, and EH Placements." *Learning Disability Quarterly* 6 (Spring): 195–200.

――― and D. Sánchez (1983) "The Special Education Evaluation Process as a Moderator of False Positives." *Exceptional Children* 49:422–428.

Aronowitz, Stanley and Henry Giroux (1985) *Education Under Siege*. South Hadley, MA: Bergin & Garvey.

Attinasi, John (1985) "Language Attitudes and Working Class Ideology in a Puerto Rican Barrio of New York." *Ethnic Groups* 5:55–78.

Baca Zinn, Maxine (1979) "Chicano Family Research: Conceptual Distortions and Alternative Directions." *Journal of Ethnic Studies* 7 (3):59–72.

――― (1986) "The Costs of Exclusionary Practices in Women's Studies." *Journal of Women in Culture and Society* 11 (21):290–303.

Baez, Joan (1987) *And a Voice to Sing With: A Memoir*. New York: Summit.

Baggs, William C. (1962) *Puerto Rico: Showcase of Development*. 1962 Britannica Book of the Year. Chicago: Britannica.

Ballesteros, Ernesto (1986) "Do Hispanics Receive an Equal Educational Opportunity? The Relationship of School Outcomes, Family Background, and High School Curriculum," in Michael Olivas (ed.) *Latino College Students*. New York: Teachers College Press.

Baltzell, Digby (1964) *The Protestant Establishment*. New York: Random House.

Banks, J. (1981) *Multiethnic Education: Theory and Practice*. Boston: Allyn & Bacon.

Baron, Harold M. (1985) "Racism Transformed: The Implications of the 1960s." *Review of Radical Political Economics* 17 (3) [special issue]:10–33.

Barrera, M. (1979) *Race and Class in the Southwest*. Notre Dame, IN: University of Notre Dame Press.

Barry, Daniel J. (1986) "The South Bronx: Revitalization through Economic Development." Princeton School of Architecture and Urban Planning. (unpublished)

Barry-Figueroa, Janis (1988) "An Investigation of the Labor Supply Determinants Among Puerto Rican Females by Headship Status." Paper presented at the Massachusetts Institute of Technology Seminar Series, "Puerto Ricans and the Changing Northeast Economy."

Baver, Sherrie (1984) "Puerto Rican Politics in New York City: The Post-World War II Period," in James Jennings and Monte Rivera (eds.) *Puerto Rican Politics in Urban America*. Westport, CT: Greenwood.

Bean, Frank D., C. Gray Swicegood, and Allan G. King (1985) "Role Incompatibility and the Relationship Between Fertility and Labor Supply Among Hispanic Women," in G. Borjas and M. Tienda (eds.) *Hispanics in the U.S. Economy*. New York: Academic Press.

Bean, Frank and Marta Tienda (1988) *Hispanic Population in the U.S.* New York: Russell Sage Foundation.

Beard, Charles A. (1968) *New Basic History of the U.S.* Garden City, NY: Doubleday.

Becerra, Rosina M. and Ruth E. Zambrana (1985) "Methodological Approaches to Research on Hispanics." *Social Work Research and Abstracts* 21 (2):42–49.

Bennet, Marion T. (1963) *American Immigration Policy*. Washington, DC: Public Affairs.

Berbusse, Edward J., S. J. (1966) *The United States in Puerto Rico, 1898–1900*. Chapel Hill: University of North Carolina Press.

Berne, Robert (1988) "Urban Education: A National Priority," in *An Urban Agenda for the 1990s*. New York: New York University, Urban Research Center.

Berthoff, Rowland (1968) *British Immigrants in Industrial America*. New York: Russell & Russell.

Betances, Samuel (1972) "The Prejudice of Having No Prejudice." *The Rican* 1:41–54.

Blanco, Tomas (1942) *El Prejuicio Racial en Puerto Rico*. San Juan: Biblioteca de Autores Puertorriqueños.

Blank, Rolf K. et al. (1983) *Survey of Magnet Schools: Analyzing a Model for Quality Integrated Education*. Cambridge, MA, and Washington, DC: Abt Associates and James H. Lowry and Associates.

Blau, Peter M. and Otis Dudley Duncan (1964) *The American Occupational Structure*. New York: John Wiley.

Blauner, Robert (1972) *Racial Oppression in America*. New York: Harper & Row.

Bluestone, Barry and Bennet Harrison (1982) *The Deindustrialization of America*. New York: Basic Books.

Bonacich, Edna (1986) The Sociology of Race Relations in the U.S.: Past and Future (Transforming Sociology Series of the Red Feather Institute, No. 123). Riverside: University of California.

Bonilla, Frank (1974) "Beyond Survival: Porque Seguiremos Siendo Puertorriqueños," in Adalberto López and James Petras (eds.) *Puerto Rico and Puerto Ricans*. New York: Schenkman.

————— (1985) "Ethnic Orbits: The Circulation of Peoples and Capital." *Contemporary Marxism* 10:148–167.

————— (1988) "From Racial Justice to Economic Rights: The New American Dilemma." Paper presented at the Dr. Martin Luther King, Jr., Birthday Celebration, Smithsonian Institution, Washington, DC, January 18.

————— and Ricardo Campos (1981) "A Wealth of Poor: Puerto Ricans in the New Economic Order." *Daedalus* 110 (Spring):133–176.

Borjas, George (1983) "The Labor Supply of Male Hispanic Immigrants in the United States." *International Migration Review* 17 (4).

————— (1987) "The Earnings of Male Hispanic Immigrants in the United States." *Industrial Labor Relations Review* 35 (3).

————— and Marta Tienda (eds.) (1985) *Hispanics in the U.S. Economy*. New York: Academic Press.

Borrero, Michael (1983) *Assessing the Impact of Federal Cutbacks on Employment and Training Opportunities for Puerto Ricans: Summary of a Seven-City Study*. Alexandria, VA: National Puerto Rican Coalition.

Bouvier, Leon F. and Cary B. Davis (1982) *The Future Racial Composition of the United States*. Washington, DC: Population Reference Bureau.

Bowles, Sam (1976) *Schooling in Capitalist America*. New York: Basic Books.

————— and Herbert Gintis (1986) "When Investment Capital Goes on Strike." *New York Times* (June 29): Forum.

Brau, Salvador (1894) *Puerto Rico y Su Historia*. Valencia, Spain: Francisco Viver Mora.

Brazil, Miriam (1972) "The Effects of Bilingualism and Culture Conflict on Diagnosis, Treatment and Care of Children in an Institution." Master's thesis, Smith College.

Brez Stein, Colman, Jr. (1985) "Hispanic Students in the Sink or Swim Era, 1900–1960." *Urban Education* 20 (July):189–198.

Brice-Heath, Shirley (1986) "Sociocultural Context of Language Development," pp. 143–186 in Sacramento Bilingual Education Office, *Beyond Language: Social and Cultural Factors in Schooling Language Minority Children*. Sacramento: California State Department of Education.

Bronx Museum of the Arts (1980) *The South Bronx: Devastation/Resurrection*. New York: Author.

———— (1984) *The Work of Our Hands: Photographs of a Resurgent Bronx* (Sandra Baker, curator). New York: Author.

———— (1986) *Building a Borough*. New York: Author.

Brosnan, Faye (1983) "Overrepresentation of Low Socioeconomic Minority Students in Special Education Programs, California." *Language Disability Quarterly* 6 (Fall):517–525.

Brown et al. (1981) *The Condition of Education for Hispanic Americans*. Washington, DC: National Council on Education Statistics.

Bruno, James F. (1983) "Equal Educational Opportunity and Declining Teacher Morale at Black, White, and Hispanic High Schools in a Large Urban School District." *Urban Review* 15 (1):19–36.

Buriel, Raymond (1987) "Academic Performance of Foreign- and Native-Born Mexican Americans: A Comparison of First-, Second-, Third-Generation Students and Parents." Report submitted to the Inter-University Program for Contemporary Latino Research/Social Science Research Council, University of Texas, Austin.

———— and D. Cardoza (1988) "Sociocultural Correlates of Achievement Among Three Generations of High School Seniors." *American Educational Research Journal* 25 (2):177–192.

Caballero, Diana (1986) "New York School Board Elections: A Fight for the Future of Our Children." Testimony presented by the Puerto Rican-Latino Education Roundtable at the New York State Assembly Public Hearing on School Board Election Reforms, June 5. (Newsletter available from Evelina Antonetty, Library, Centro de Estudios Puertorriqueños, Hunter College, New York.

Cabranes, Jose A. (1979) "Citizenship and the American Empire: Notes on the Legislative History of the United States Citizenship of Puerto Ricans." *University of Pennsylvania Law Review* 127: 391–492.

Calitri, Ronald (1983) *Racial and Ethnic High School Dropout Rates in New York City: A Summary Report/1983*. New York: Aspira of New York.

Cammarosano, Joseph (1981) *Industrial Activity in the Inner City: A Case Study of the South Bronx*. New York: Fordham University, Institute for Urban Studies.

Canino, Ian A. and Glorisa Canino Stolberg (1980) "Impact of Stress on the Puerto Rican Family: Treatment Considerations." *American Journal of Orthopsychiatry* 50 (3):535–541.

Capello, Doris (1986) "Puerto Rican Single Mothers: Stress and Coping Strategies." Doctoral dissertation, Fordham University.

Carby, Hazel V. (1982) "Schooling in Babylon," in Centre for Contemporary Cultural Studies, University of Birmingham, *The Empire Strikes Back*. London: Hutchinson.

Cárdenas, José (1986) "The Role of Native Language Instruction in Bilingual Education." *Phi Delta Kappan* (January):359–363.

Carnegie Council on Policy Studies in Higher Education (1979) *Giving Youth a Better Chance: Options for Education, Work and Service*. San Francisco: Jossey-Bass.

Caro, Robert (1974) *The Power Broker*. New York: Knopf.

Carpenter, Niles (1969) *Immigrants and Their Children*. Washington, DC: Census Monographs.

Carr, Raymond (1984) *Puerto Rico: A Colonial Experiment*. New York: New York University Press.

Carrillo, Emilio, Richard Levins, Joseph Regna, Ellen Rak, Maria Gordian, and Ruberto Diaz (n.d.) "Eco-Social Analysis: Evaluating the Health Relevant Social Environment of Migrant Latinos." (unpublished)

Carroll, Henry K. (1899) *Report on the Island of Porto Rico*. Submitted by the special commissioner for the United States to Puerto Rico to President William McKinley, Washington, DC.

Celso Barbosa, J. (1937) *Problema de Razas*. San Juan: Imprenta Venezuela.

Census of Population and Housing (1980). Tape file 1A. Puerto Rico.

Center for Popular Economics (1986) *Economic Report of the People: An Alternative to the Economic Report of the President*. Boston: South End.

Chall, Daniel E. (1984) "Neighborhood Changes in New York City During the 1970s: Are the Gentry Returning?" *Federal Reserve Bank Quarterly Review* (Winter).

Chang, Harry (1985) "Toward a Marxist Theory of Racism: Two Essays by Harry Chang" (Paul Liem and Eric Montague, eds.). *Review of Radical Political Economics* 17 (Fall):34–45.

Channing, Edward (1966) *A History of the U.S.* (Vol. 2). New York: Macmillan. (Original work published 1927)

Chenault, Lawrence (1938) *The Puerto Rican Migrant in New York City*. New York: Columbia University Press.

Chiswick, Barry (1977) "Sons of Immigrants: Are They at an Earning Disadvantage?" *American Economic Review* 67 (1).

Cifre de Loubriel, Estela (1960) *Catalago de Extrangeros en El Siglo XIX*. Rio Piedras: Ediciones de la Universidad de Puerto Rico.

Cinel, Dean (1969) "Ethnicity: A Neglected Dimension of American History." *International Migration Review* 3:58–63.

City University of New York (1983) "Trends in Ethnic Composition of Matriculated First Time Freshmen Fall 1970 . . . 1983," in *CUNY Data Book* (Fall). New York: Author.

Claus, Jeff (1987) "An Instance of Accommodation and Resistance Combined: Moving Resistance Theory Forward." Paper presented at the annual meeting of the American Educational Research Association, Washington, DC.

Coleman, James, Thomas Hoffer, and Sally Kilgore (1982) *High School Achievement: Public, Catholic, and Private Schools Compared*. New York: Basic Books.

Colleran, Kevin J. (1984) "Acculturation in Puerto Rican Families in New York City. *Hispanic Research Center Research Bulletin* 7 (July-October):3–4.

Colón, Jesús (1982) *A Puerto Rican in New York and Other Sketches*. New York: International. (Original work published 1961)

Colón-Warren, Alice E. (1984) "Competition, Segregation and Succession of Minorities and White Women in the Middle Atlantic Region's Central Cities Labor Market, 1960–70." Doctoral dissertation, Fordham University.

—— (1985) "Puerto Rican Women in the Middle Atlantic Region: Employment, Loss of Jobs, and Growing Poverty." Paper presented at the Yale Conference on Puerto Rican Migration, New Haven, CT, November 5.

Comas-Díaz, Lillian (1982) "Enriching Self-Concept Through a Puerto Rican Cultural Awareness Program." *Personnel and Guidance Journal* 60 (5):506–508.

—— (1985) "Cognitive and Behavioral Group Therapy with Puerto Rican Women: A Comparison of Content Themes." *Hispanic Journal of Behavioral Sciences* 7 (3):273–283.

—— Antonio L. Arroyo, and Juan Carlos Lovelace (1982) "Enriching Self-Concept and Bilingual Education Through a Puerto Rican Cultural Awareness Program." *Personnel and Guidance Journal* 60 (January).

Commonwealth of Puerto Rico Office (1964) *Documents on the Constitutional History of Puerto Rico*. Washington, DC: Author.

Constantino, Giuseppe and Robert G. Malgade (1984) "Verbal Fluency of Hispanic, Black and White Children on TAT and TEMAS, a New Thematic Aperception Test." *Hispanic Journal of Behavioral Sciences* 5 (June):199–206.

Corcoran, Mary, Greg Duncan, Gerald Gurin, and Patricia Gurin (1985) "Myth and Reality: The Causes and Persistence of Poverty." *Journal of Policy Analysis and Management* 4 (4):516–536.

Correa Alejandro, Nayda (1982) *Change in Number of Housing Units*. New York: Fordham University, Bronx Urban Resource Center.

Covello, L. (1969) "Interview with Leonard Covello." *Urban Review* 3 (January):53–61.

Cox, Oliver C. (1948) *Caste, Class and Race*. Garden City, NY: Doubleday.

Cruz-Monclova, Lidio (1958) *Historia de Puerto Rico* (3 vols.). San Juan: Editorial Universidad de Puerto Rico.

Cummins, Jim (1984) *Bilingual and Special Education: Issues in Assessment and Pedagogy*. San Diego, CA: College Hill.

—— (1986) "Empowering Minority Students: A Framework for Intervention." *Harvard Educational Review* 56 (February).

Darity, William and Samuel Myers (1987) *Transfer Programs and the Economic Well-Being of Minorities*. Madison: University of Wisconsin, Institute for Research on Poverty.

Daubon, Ramón (1987) "Statement by the National Puerto Rican Coalition Before the Educational Forum of the Pennsylvania English Plus Coalition." *National Puerto Rican Coalition Bulletin* (May 2).

de Anda, Diane (1984) "Bicultural Socialization: Factors Affecting the Minority Experience." *Social Work* (March-April):101–107.

de la Cancela, Victor (1986) "A Critical Analysis of Puerto Rican Machismo: Implications for Clinical Practice." *Psychotherapy* 23 (Summer):291–296.

—— Peter J. Guarnaccia, and Emilio Carrillo (1986) "Psychosocial Stress Among Latinos: A Critical Analysis of Ataques de Nervios." *Humanity and Society* 10 (November):431–447.

—— and Iris Zavala-Martinez (1983) "An Analysis of Culturalism in Latino Mental

188

Health: Folk Medicine as a Case in Point." *Hispanic Journal of Behavioral Sciences* 5 (3):251–274.

DeFreitas, Gregory (1985) "Ethnic Differentials in Unemployment Among Hispanic Americans," in G. Borjas and M. Tienda (eds.) *Hispanics in the U.S. Economy*. New York: Academic Press.

Degler, Carl N. (1959) *Out of Our Past*. New York: Harper & Row.

—— (1971) *Neither White nor Black: Slavery and Race Relations in Brazil and the United States*. New York: Macmillan.

del Valle, Manuel (1984) "Puerto Rico Before the United States Supreme Court." *Revista Juridica de la Universidad Interamericana de Puerto Rico* 19 (September-December):13–81.

Descartes, H. (1943) *Statistics of Puerto Rico*. San Juan: Bureau of Social and Economic Statistics.

Díaz, Manuel, Jr., chair (1986) *New York State Hispanics: A Challenging Minority* (Report of the Governor's Advisory Committee for Hispanic Affairs). New York: Progress.

Díaz, William (1984) *Hispanics: Challenges and Opportunities*. New York: Ford Foundation.

Díaz Soler, Luis M. (1953) *Historia de la Esclavitud en Puerto Rico*. Madrid: Ediciones de la Universidad de Puerto Rico.

Dietz, James L. (1986) *Economic History of Puerto Rico: Institutional Change and Capitalist Development*. Princeton, NJ: Princeton University Press.

Dillard, John M. and N. Jo Campbell (1981) "Influences of Puerto Rican, Black and Anglo Parents' Career Behavior on Their Adolescent Child's Career Development." *Vocational Guidance Quarterly* 30 (2):139–148.

Domhoff, William G. (1967) *Who Rules America?* Englewood Cliffs, NJ: Prentice-Hall.

Duany, Jorge (1984) "Popular Music in Puerto Rico: Toward an Anthology of Salsa." *Latin American Music Review* 5 (2):186–216.

—— (1985) "Ethnicity in the Spanish Caribbean: Notes on the Consolidation of Creole Identity in Cuba and Puerto Rico, 1762–1868." *Ethnic Groups* 6:99–123.

Duany, Luis A. (1987) "Fostering Puerto Rican Small Businesses as a Device for Economic Development." (unpublished)

Duncan, Beverly and Otis Dudley Duncan (1968) "Minorities and the Process of Stratification." *American Sociological Review* 33 (3):356–364.

Duncan, Otis Dudley and Stanley Lieberson (1959) "Ethnic Segregation and Assimilation." *American Journal of Sociology* 63:364–374.

Durán, Richard P. (1983) *Hispanics' Education and Background: Predictors of College Achievement*. New York: College Entrance Examination Board.

Economic Equal Opportunities Commission (1966) *Job Patterns for Minorities and Women in Private Industry*. Washington, DC: Author.

Edmonds, Ron (1984) "School Effects and Teacher Effects." *Social Policy* (Fall): 37–39.

Educational Priorities Panel [EPP] (1985a) *Lost in the Labyrinth: New York City High School Admissions*. New York: Author.

—— (1985b) *Ten Years of Neglect: The Failure to Serve Language-Minority Students in the New York City Public Schools*. New York: Author.

Ehrenreich, Barbara (1986) "Is the Middle Class Doomed?" *New York Times Magazine* (September 7): 44, 50, 62.

ERIC/CUE (1982a) "Developing Non-Biased Criteria for Mainstreaming Minority Students." Digest 13 (July).

—— (1982b) "Secondary School Ethos and the Academic Success of Urban Minority Students." Fact Sheet 14 (December).

—— (1984) "Urban Magnet Schools and Educational Excellence." Digest 24 (October).

—— (1985) "Raising Hispanic Achievement." Digest 26 (April).

Estades, Rosa (1984) "Symbolic Unity: The Puerto Rican Day Parade," in C. Rodríguez, Virginia Sánchez-Korrol, and J. Oscar Alers (eds.) *The Puerto Rican Struggle: Essays on Survival in the U.S.* Maplewood, NJ: Waterfront.

Esteves, Sandra Maria (1987) "Ambivalence or Activisim from the Nuyorican Perspective in Poetry," in Asela Rodríguez de Laguna (ed.) *Images and Identities: The Puerto Rican in Two World Contexts*. New Brunswick, NJ: Transaction.

Fairchild, Halford H. and Joy Asamen Cozens (1981) "Chicano, Hispanic or Mexican American: What's in a Name?" *Hispanic Journal of Behavioral Sciences* 3 (January):191–198.

Falcón, Angelo (1984a) "A History of Puerto Rican Politics in New York City," in James Jennings and Monte Rivera (eds.) *Puerto Rican Politics in Urban America*. Westport, CT: Greenwood.

—— (1984b) "An Introduction to the Literature of Puerto Rican Politics in Urban America," in James Jennings and Monte Rivera (eds.) *Puerto Rican Politics in Urban America*. Westport, CT: Greenwood.

Falcón-Rodríguez, Luis Miguel (1987) "Puerto Ricans on the Mainland: An Analysis of Labor Market Standing, 1970–1980." Doctoral dissertation, Cornell University.

Fanon, Frantz (1968) *The Wrteched of the Earth*. New York: Grove.

Faulkner, Harold U. (1957) *American Political and Social History*. New York: Appleton-Century-Crofts.

Featherman, David L. (1971) "The Socio-Economic Achievement of White Religio-Ethnic Subgroups: Social and Psychological Explanations." *American Sociological Review* 36 (2):207–222.

Federal Writers Project Guide to 1930s New York (1982) *The W.P.A. Guide to New York City*. New York: Pantheon.

Figueroa, Loida (1974) *History of Puerto Rico*. New York: Anaya.

Finder, Alan (1987) "In New York, 'Workfare' Gets Mixed Results." *New York Times* (March 23).

Fine, Michelle (1983) "Perspectives on Inequity: Voices from Urban Schools," in L. Bickman (ed.) *Applied Social Psychology Annual* (Vol. 4). Beverly Hills, CA: Sage.

—— (1985) "Dropping Out of High School: An Inside Look." *Social Policy* (Fall).

Fishman, Joshua A., Robert L. Cooper, and Roxana Ma (1971) *Bilingualism in the Barrio*. Bloomington: Indiana University Press.

―――― and Gary Keller (eds.) (1982) *Bilingual Education for Hispanic Students in the U.S.* New York: Teachers College Press.

Fitzpatrick, Joseph, S. J. (1971) *Puerto Rican Americans*. Englewood Cliffs, NJ: Prentice-Hall.

Fleischman Commission (1970) *New York State Commission on the Quality, Cost and Financing of Elementary and Secondary Education*. Albany: Author. (Officially published 1972)

Fleisher, Belton H. (1961) "Some Economic Aspects of Puerto Rican Migration to the United States." Doctoral dissertation, Stanford University.

―――― (1963) "Some Economic Aspects of Puerto Rican Migration to the United States." *Review of Economics and Statistics* 45 (3):245–253.

Fleming, James T. (1971) "Teachers' Ratings of Urban Children's Reading Performance." *Child Study Journal* 1 (2):80–99.

Fligstein, Neil and Roberto M. Fernandez (1985) "Educational Transitions of Whites and Mexican Americans," in G. Borjas and M. Tienda (eds.) *Hispanics in the U.S. Economy*. New York: Academic Press.

Flores, Juan (1984) "The Puerto Rico That Jose Luis Gonzalez Built." *Latin American Perspectives* 11 (3):173–184.

―――― John Attinasi, and Pedro Pedraza (1981) "La Carreta Made a U-Turn: Puerto Rican Language and Culture in the U.S." *Daedalus* 110 (Spring):193–217.

Fortney, Judith (1972) "Immigration Professionals: A Brief Historical Survey." *International Migration Review* 6 (17):50–61.

Friedlander, Stanley L. (1965) *Labor Migration and Economic Growth: A Case Study of Puerto Rico*. Cambridge: MIT Press.

Fuentes, Luis (1984a) "The Struggle for Local Political Control," in C. Rodríguez, Virginia Sánchez-Korrol, and J. Oscar Alers (eds.) *The Puerto Rican Struggle: Essays on Survival in the U.S.* Maplewood, NJ: Waterfront.

―――― (1984b) "Puerto Ricans and New York City School Board Elections: Apathy or Obstructionism," in James Jennings and Monte Rivera (eds.) *Puerto Rican Politics in Urban America*. Westport, CT: Greenwood.

Galbraith, John K. and Carolyn Shaw Soto (1953) "Puerto Rican Lessons in Economic Development." *Annals of the American Academy of Political and Social Science* 285 (January).

Galíndez, Jesús de (1969) *Puerto Rico en Nueva York: Sociología de una Immigración*. Buenos Aires: Editorial Tiempo Contemporaneo.

Galli, Nicholas (1975) "The Influence of Cultural Heritage on the Health Status of Puerto Ricans." *Journal of School Health* 45 (January):10–16.

García, Eugene E. (1988) "Attributes of Effective Schools for Hispanics." *Education and Urban Society* 20 (4):387–398.

García, Luis T., Nancy Erskine, Kathy Hawn, and Susanne R. Casmay (1981) "The Effect of Affirmative Action on Attributions About Minority Group Members." *Journal of Personality* 49 (December).

García, Philip (1984) "Dual Language Characteristics and Earnings: Male Mexican Workers in the U.S." *Social Science Research* 13 (3):221–235.

Georges, Eugenia (1988) *Dominican Self-Help Associations in Washington Heights: Integration of a New Immigrant Population in a Multiethnic Neighborhood* (New Directions for Latino Public Policy Research, Working Paper No. 1). Austin, TX: IUP/SSRC.

Giles, H., N. Llado, D. J. McKirnan, and D. M. Taylor (1979) "Social Identity in Puerto Rico." *International Journal of Psychology* 14 (3):185–201.

Gilkes, C. (1980) "The Sources of Conceptual Revolutions in the Field of Race Relations," pp. 7–31 in David Claubaut (ed.) *New Directions in Ethnic Studies: Minorities in America.* San Francisco: Century 21 Publishing.

Ginorio, Angela (1979) "A Comparison of Puerto Ricans in New York with Native Puerto Ricans and Native Americans on Two Measures of Acculturation: Gender Role and Racial Identification." Doctoral dissertation, Fordham University.

—— (1986) "Puerto Ricans and Interethnic Conflict," in M. Jerry O. Boucher, Dan Landis, and Karen Arnold (eds.) *International Perspectives on Ethnic Conflict: Antecedents and Dynamics.* Newbury Park, CA: Sage.

—— and Paul C. Berry (1972) "Measuring Puerto Ricans' Perceptions of Racial Characteristics" (Summary). *Proceedings of the 80th Annual Convention of the American Psychological Association* 7:287–288.

Giroux, Henry (1983a) "Theories of Reproduction and Resistance in the New Sociology of Education: A Critical Analysis." *Harvard Educational Review* 53 (3):257–293.

—— (1983b) *Theory and Resistance in Education.* South Hadley, MA: Bergin & Garvey.

Glazer, Nathan and Daniel P. Moynihan (1970) *Beyond the Melting Pot.* Cambridge: MIT Press.

Gockel, Galen (1969) "Income and Religious Affiliation: A Regression Analysis." *American Journal of Sociology* 74:632–649.

Goldman, John J. (1981) "South Bronx: Strength from Unity." *Los Angeles Times* (July 26):1.

Goldsen, Rose K. (1966) "Preliminary Report of a Housing Study in San Juan, Puerto Rico." Paper submitted to the Agency for International Development.

González, Angelo (1986) "Testimony Before the Board of Education of the City of New York," Hearing on the Chancellor's Budget Request, January 30, Aspira of New York.

González, Antonio J. (1966) "La Economía y el Status Político." *Revista de Ciencias Sociales* 10 (March):5–50.

González, Eddie and Lois Gray (1984) "Puerto Ricans, Politics and Labor Activism," in James Jennings and Monte Rivera (eds.) *Puerto Rican Politics in Urban America.* Westport, CT: Greenwood.

González, José Luis (1980) *El Pais de Cuatro Pisos y Otros Ensayos.* Río Piedras, Puerto Rico: Ediciones Huracan.

González, Juan D. and Hildamar Ortiz (1987) *The Status of Puerto Ricans in the U.S.: 1987.* New York: National Congress for Puerto Rican Rights.

Goodsell, Charles (1965) *Administration of a Revolution.* Cambridge, MA: Harvard University Press.

Gordon, David M., Richard Edwards, and Michael Reich (1982) *Segmented Work, Divided Workers: The Historical Transformation of Labor in the United States.* Cambridge: Cambridge University Press.

Gordon, Milton (1949) *Assimilation in American Life.* New York: Oxford University Press.

Gosnell, Patricia Aran (1945) "The Puerto Ricans in New York City." Doctoral dissertation, New York University.

Greeley, Andrew M. (1971) *Why Can't They Be Like Us.* New York: Institute of Human Relations Press of the American Jewish Committee.

Greene, J. F. and P. A. Zirkel (1971) "Academic Factors Relating to the Self-Concept of Puerto Rican Pupils." Paper presented at the annual meeting of the American Psychological Association, Washington, DC.

Grenier, Giles (1984) "Shifts to English as Usual by Americans of Spanish Mother Tongue." *Social Science Quarterly* 65:537–550.

Griffen, Clyde (1972) "Occupational Mobility in Nineteenth-Century America: Problems and Possibilities." *Journal of Social History* 5 (3): 318–327.

Gumbiner, Jann, George P. Knight, and Spencer Kagan (1981) "Relations of Classroom Structures and Teacher Behaviors to Social Orientation, Self-Esteem, and Classroom Climate Among Anglo and Mexican Children." *Hispanic Journal of Behavioral Sciences* 3 (1):19–40.

Guzman, Pablo "Yoruba" (1984) "Puerto Rican Barrio Politics in the United States" in C. Rodríguez, Virginia Sánchez-Korrol, and J. Oscar Alers (eds.) *The Puerto Rican Struggle: Essays on Survival in the U.S.* Maplewood, NJ: Waterfront.

Hakuta, K. (1984a) "The Causal Relationship Between the Development of Bilingualism, Cognitive Flexibility, and Social-Cognitive Skills in Hispanic Elementary School Children." Final Report, National Institute of Education.

——— (1984b) "Bilingual Education in the Public Eye: A Case Study of New Haven, Ct." *NABE (National Association of Bilingual Education* 9:53–76.

——— (1986) *Mirrors of Language: The Debate on Bilingualism.* New York: Basic Books.

——— and R. Diaz (1984) "The Relationship Between Bilingualism and Cognitive Ability," in K. E. Nelson (ed.) *Children's Language* (Vol. 5). Hillsdale, NJ: Lawrence Erlbaum.

Handlin, Oscar (1959) *The Newcomers: Negroes and Puerto Ricans in a Changing Metropolis.* Cambridge, MA: Harvard University Press.

Hanson, Earl Parker (1960) *Puerto Rico: Land of Wonders.* New York: Knopf.

Harris, Marvin (1970) "Referential Ambiguity in the Calculus of Brazilian Racial Identity," in Norman Whitten, Jr., and John F. Szwed (eds.) *Afro-American Anthropology.* New York: Free Press.

Hayes, Donald and Judith Grether (1983) "The School Year and Vacations: When Do Students Learn?" *Cornell Journal of Social Relations* 17 (1):56–71. (Original work published 1965)

Hayes-Bautista, David E. and Jorge Chapa (1987) "Latino Terminology: Conceptual Bases for Standardized Terminology." *American Journal of Public Health* 77 (January):61–68.

Herberg, Will (1955) *Protestant, Catholic, Jew*. Garden City, NY: Doubleday.

Herbstein, Judith (1983) "The Politicization of Puerto Rican Ethnicity in New York: 1955–75." *Ethnic Groups* 5:31–54.

Hernández, Jose (1976) *Social Factors in Educational Attainment Among Puerto Ricans in U.S. Metropolitan Areas*. New York: Aspira of America.

——— (1983) *Puerto Rican Youth Employment*. Maplewood, NJ: Waterfront.

——— (1985) "Puerto Rican Youth Empowerment," in *Puerto Ricans in the Mid '80s: An American Challenge*. Alexandria, VA: National Puerto Rican Coalition.

Higgenbotham, Elizabeth (1985) "Race and Class Barriers to Black Women's College Attendance." *Journal of Ethnic Studies* 13 (1):89–108.

——— (1987) "We Have Not Yet Arrived: Racial Discrimination Limits Options for Professional Black Women." Paper presented at the annual meetings of the Southern Sociological Society, Atlanta, GA, April.

Higham, John (1956) *Strangers in the Land*. New York: Atheneum.

Hillsman, Sally T. (1970) "Entry into the Labor Market: The Preparation and Job Placement of Negro and White Vocational High School Graduates." Doctoral dissertation, Columbia University.

Hiro, Dilip (1973) *White British, Black British*. Harmondsworth: Penguin.

Hirschman, Charles (1986) "The Making of Race in Colonial Malaya." *Sociological Forum* 1 (2):330–361.

Hispanic Policy Development Project (1984a) *Moving Up to Better Education and Better Jobs: A National Survey of Elected and Appointed Hispanic Officials Conducted by the Public Agenda Foundation* (Vol. 2). Washington, DC: Author.

——— (1984b) *Make Something Happen: Hispanics and Urban High School Reform* (Vol. 1). Washington, DC: National Commission on Secondary Education for Hispanics.

History Task Force, Centro de Estudios Puertorriqueños (1979) *Labor Migration Under Capitalism: The Puerto Rican Experience*. New York: Monthly Review Press.

Hodgkinson, Harold (1985) *All One System: Demographics of Education, K through Graduate School*. Washington, DC: Institute for Educational Leadership.

Hollister, Frederick J. (1969) "Skin Color and Life Chances of Puerto Ricans." *Caribbean Studies* 9 (3):87–94.

Hooks, Bel (1981) *Ain't I a Woman: Black Women and Feminism*. Boston: South End.

——— (1984) *Feminist Theory from Margin to Center*. Boston: South End.

Housing Task Force of the Puerto Rican Center for Research and Information (1978) *Housing and the Puerto Rican Community in New York City* (report funded by North Star Fund). New York: Author.

Hudson, Winthrop (1965) *Religion in America*. New York: Charles Scribner.

Hutchinson, E. P. (1956) *Immigrants and Their Children*. New York: John Wiley.

Iadicola, P. (1981) "Schooling and Social Control: Symbolic and Hispanic Students' Attitudes Toward Their Own Ethnic Group." *Hispanic Journal of Behavioral Sciences* 3 (4):361–383.

Iglesias, César Andreu (1980) *Memorias de Bernardo Vega: Una Contribucion a la Historia de la Comunidad Puertorriqueña en Nueva York.* Rio Piedras, Puerto Rico: Ediciones Huracan. (Also available in English, published by Monthly Review Press, 1984)

Institute for Puerto Rican Policy (1982) *Puerto Ricans in State Government: The Failure of Affirmative Action.* New York: Author.

—— (1985) *Selected Data on New York City and State Government Employment of Puerto Ricans and Other Latinos.* New York: Author.

—— (1987) *Puerto Rican- and Other Latino-Owned Businesses in the United States, 1982* (Datanote on the Puerto Rican Community 6). New York: Author.

Izcoa, Ada Elsa (1985) "A Comparative Study of the Self-Images of Puerto Rican Adolescents: Immigrants and Non-Migrants," in Hilda Hidalgo and Joan L. McEniry (eds.) *Hispanic Temas.* Newark, NJ: Rutgers University, Puerto Rican Studies Program.

Jaffe, A. J., Ruth M. Cullen, and Thomas D. Boswell (1980) *The Changing Demography of Spanish Americans.* New York: Academic Press.

Jasso, Guillermina and Mark R. Rosenzweig (1982) "Estimating the Emigration Rates of Legal Immigrants Using Administrative and Survey Data: the 1971 Cohort of Immigrants to the United States." *Demography* 19 (3).

Jenkins, Mary (1971) *Bilingual Education in New York City.* New York: New York City Board of Education, Office of Recruitment and Training of Spanish-Speaking Teachers.

Jennings, James (1984a) "The Emergence of Puerto Rican Electoral Activism in Urban America," in James Jennings and Monte Rivera (eds.) *Puerto Rican Politics in Urban America.* Westport, CT: Greenwood.

—— (1984b) "Puerto Rican Politics in Two Cities: New York and Boston," in James Jennings and Monte Rivera (eds.) *Puerto Rican Politics in Urban America.* Westport, CT: Greenwood.

Jennings, James and Monte Rivera (eds.) (1984) *Puerto Rican Politics in Urban America.* Westport, CT: Greenwood.

Jones, Maldwyn Allen (1960) *American Immigration.* Chicago: University of Chicago Press.

Jonnes, Jill (1986) *We're Still Here: The Rise, Fall, and Resurrection of the South Bronx.* Boston: Atlantic Monthly Press.

Jorge, Angela (1983) "Issues of Race and Class in Women's Studies: A Puerto Rican Woman's Thoughts, 1981," in Amy Swerdlow and Hanna Lessinger (eds.) *Class, Race and Sex: The Dynamics of Control.* Boston: G. K. Hall.

—— (1984) "The Puerto Rican Study 1953–57: Its Character and Impact on Puerto Ricans in New York City." Doctoral dissertation, New York University.

Joseph, Gloria (1981) "The Incompatible Ménage à Trois: Marxism, Feminism, and Racism," in Lydia Sargent (ed.) *Women and Revolution.* Boston: South End.

195

Junta Planificacíon de Puerto Rico (1986) *caracteristicas de la Población Migrante de Puerto Rico* (00942–9985, June). Santurce: Author.

Katzman, Martin (1978) "Discrimination, Subculture and the Economic Performance of Negroes, Puerto Ricans and Mexican-Americans." *American Journal of Economics and Society* 27 (4):371–375.

Katzman, Martin T. (1971) "Urban Racial Minorities and Immigrant Groups: Some Economic Comparisons." *American Journal of Economics and Society* 30 (1):15–26.

Kazinitz, Philip (1983) "Neighborhood Change and Conflicts Over Definitions: The Gentrification of Boerum Hill." Paper presented at the annual meeting of the Eastern Sociological Association, March 19, Boston.

Keller, Allan (1971) *Colonial America*. New York: Hawthorne.

Keller, Gary D. and Karen S. Van Hooft (1982) "A Chronology of Bilingualism and Bilingual Education in the U.S." in J. Fishman and G. Keller (eds.) *Bilingual Education for Hispanic Students in the United States*. New York: Teachers College Press.

Kirshenblatt-Gimblett, Barbara (1986) "Erasing the Subject: Boas and the Anthropological Study of Jews in the U.S., 1903–42." Paper presented at the Constructing America Seminar, New York University, Tisch School of the Arts, January 24.

Klass, H. (1971) *The American Bilingual Tradition*. Rowley, MA: Newbury House.

Kolby, Jerry (1987) "The Growing Divide: Class Polarization in the 1980s." *Monthly Review* (September).

La Ruffa, Anthony (1971) *San Cipriano: Life in a Puerto Rican Community*. New York: Gordon & Breach.

Lapp, Michael (in press) "The Migration Division of Puerto Rico and Puerto Ricans in New York City, 1948–1969." *New York Historical Society*.

Lavin, David (1973) "Open Admissions at City College of New York." Paper presented at a meeting of the CCNY Alumni Association, January.

—— Richard D. Alba, and Richard A. Silberstein (1981) *Right Versus Privilege: The Open Admissions Experiment at the City University of New York*. New York: Free Press.

—— James Murtha, Barry Kaufman, and David Hyllegard (1986) "Long Term Educational Attainment in an Open-Access University System: Effects of Ethnicity, Economic Status, and College Type." Paper presented at the annual meeting of the American Educational Research Association, San Francisco, April.

Lenski, Gerhard (1963) *The Religious Factor*. Garden City, NY: Doubleday.

Lewis, Gordon K. (1963) *Puerto Rico: Freedom and Power in the Caribbean*. New York: Monthly Review Press.

Lewis, Oscar (1966) *La Vida: A Puerto Rican Family in the Culture of Poverty—San Juan and New York*. New York: Random House.

Liden, Harold (1981) *History of the Puerto Rican Independence Movement, 19th Century* (Vol. 1). Maplewood, NJ: Waterfront.

Lieberson, Stanley (1963) *Ethnic Patterns in American Cities*. New York: Free Press.

———— (1980) *A Piece of the Pie: Blacks and White Immigrants Since 1880*. Berkeley: University of California Press.

Long, James E. (1977) "Productivity, Employment Discrimination, and the Relative Economic Status of Spanish Origin Men." *Social Science Quarterly* 58 (December): 357–373.

Longres, John F. (1974) "Racism and Its Effects on Puerto Rican Continentals." *Social Casework* (February):67–99.

López, Adalberto and James Petras (eds.) (1974) *Puerto Rico and Puerto Ricans*. Cambridge, MA: Schenkman.

López, Alfredo (1973) *The Puerto Rican Papers*. Indianapolis: Bobbs-Merrill.

Low, Benson P. and Paul W. Clement (1982) "Relationships of Race and Socioeconomic Status to Classroom Behavior, Academic Achievement, and Referral for Special Education." *Journal of School Psychology* 20 (Summer):105–112.

Lowry, Ira S. (1982) "The Science and Politics of Ethnic Enumeration," in Winston A. VanHorne (ed.) *Ethnicity and Public Policy* (Vol. 1). Madison: University of Wisconsin Press.

Maldonado, Edwin (1979) "Contract Labor and the Origins of Puerto Rican Communities in the United States." *International Migration Review* 13:103–121.

Maldonado, Rita (1976) "Why Puerto Ricans Migrated to the United States in 1947–73." *Monthly Labor Review* (September).

Maldonado-Denis, Manuel (1972) *Puerto Rico: A Socio-Historic Interpretation*. New York: Random House.

Malinconico, Joseph (1983) "Finally, Fordham Plaza Is at the Starting Gate." *New York Times* (October 2): section 8, p. 1.

Mann, Evelyn S. and Joseph J. Salvo (1984) "Characteristics of New Hispanic Immigrants to New York City: A Comparison of Puerto Rican and Non-Puerto Rican Hispanics." Paper presented at the annual meeting of the Population Association of America, Minneapolis, May 3.

Marcuse, Peter (1979) *Rental Housing in the City of New York: Supply and Condition, 1975–78*. New York: Office of Rent Control.

Marín, Gerardo and Bárbara Vanoss Marín (1983) "Methodological Fallacies When Studying Hispanics." *Applied Social Psychology* 3:99–173.

———— Hector Betancourt, and Yoshihisa Kashima (1983) "Ethnic Affirmation vs. Social Desirability: Explaining Discrepancies in Bilinguals' Responses to a Questionnaire." *Journal of Cross-Cultural Psychology* 14 (June):172–186.

Martínez, Angel R. (1988) "The Effects of Acculturation and Racial Identity on Self-Esteem and Psychological Well-Being Among Young Puerto Ricans." Doctoral dissertation, City University of New York.

Martínez, Robert A. (1979) "Dual Ethnicity: Puerto Rican College Students in New York." *Urban Education* 14 (2) 254–259.

Mathews, Thomas (1968) "The Question of Color in Puerto Rico." San Juan: University of Puerto Rico, Institute of Caribbean Studies.

McDill, Edward L., Gary Natriello, and Aaron M. Pallas (1985) "Raising Standards and Retaining Students: The Impact of the Reform Recommendations on Potential Dropouts." *Review of Educational Research* 55 (Winter):415–433.

McGahey, Richard (1982) "Poverty's Voguish Stigma." *New York Times* (March 12): A29.

Meléndez, Edwin (1986) "Divided America," in Center for Popular Economics, *Economic Report of the People: An Alternative to the Economic Report of the President*. Boston: South End.

———— (1987) "Vanishing Labor: The Effects of Industrial Restructuring on the Labor Force Participation Rate of Puerto Rican Women in New York City." Paper presented at the Conference on American Wages, Incomes and Public Policy, sponsored by the McCormack Institute of Public Affairs, University of Massachusetts, Boston, April 24.

Memmi, Albert (1965) *The Colonizer and the Colonized*. Boston: Beacon.

Meyerson, Ann (1986) "Deregulation and the Re-Structuring of the Housing Finance System" in Rachel Bratt et al. (eds.) *Critical Perspectives on Housing*. Philadelphia: Temple University Press.

Michigan State Board of Education (1986) *Hispanic School Dropouts and Hispanic Student Performance on the MEAP Tests: Closing the Gap*. Lansing: Author.

Miller Solomon, Barbara (1956) *Ancestors and Immigrants*. Cambridge, MA: Harvard University Press.

Mills, C. Wright, Clarence Senior, and Rose Goldsen (1950) *The Puerto Rican Journey: New York's Newest Migrants*. New York: Harper & Bros.

Mindiola, Tatcho, Jr., and Armando Gutierrez (1982) "Education and Discrimination Against Mexican Americans in the Southwest." *California Sociologist* (Summer).

Mintz, Sidney W. (1972) "Puerto Rican Emigration: A Three Fold Comparison," in E. Fernandez Mendez (ed.) *Portrait of a Society*. San Juan: University of Puerto Rico Press.

Mohr, Nicolasa (1985) *Rituals of Survival: A Woman's Portfolio*. Houston: Arte Publico.

———— (1987) "Puerto Ricans in New York: Cultural Evolution and Identity," in Asela Rodríguez de Laguna (ed.) *Images and Identities: The Puerto Rican in Two World Contexts*. New Brunswick, NJ: Transaction.

Moll, L. C. (1988) "Some Key Issues in Teaching Latino Students." *Language Arts* 63 (2):466–473.

Moore, Helen A. (1983) "Hispanic Women: Schooling for Conformity in Public Education." *Hispanic Journal of Behavioral Sciences* 5 (1):45–63.

Morales, Julio (1986) *Puerto Rican Poverty and Migration: We Just Had to Try Elsewhere*. New York: Praeger.

Morales-Carrion, Arturo (1952) *Puerto Rico and the Non-Hispanic Caribbean: A Study in the Decline of Spanish Exclusivism*. San Juan: University of Puerto Rico Press.

Morris, Michael (in press) "From the Culture of Poverty to the Underclass: An Analysis of a Shift in Public Language." *American Sociologist*.

Moviemiento Pro Independencia (1963) *Tesis Política: La Hora de La Independencia*. San Juan: Author.

Muñoz, Braulio (1982) *Sons of the Wind: The Search for Identity in Spanish American Indian Literature*. New Brunswick, NJ: Rutgers University Press.

Muñoz-Hernández, Shirley and Isaura Santiago-Santiago (1983) "Toward a Qualitative Analysis of Teacher Disapproval Behavior," in Raymond V. Padilla (ed.)

Theory, Techniques, and Public Policy on Bilingual Education. Rosslyn, VA: National Clearinghouse of Bilingual Education.

Murphy, Joseph S. (1986) "Statement on Affirmative Action." Delivered by the chancellor at the 148th Plenary Session of the University Faculty Senate, May 20, New York City Board of Higher Education.

Murray, Charles (1984) *Losing Ground: American Social Policy, 1950–1980.* New York: Basic Books.

Myrdal, Gunnar (1944) *The American Dilemma.* New York: Harper & Bros.

Nam, Charles (1954) "Nationality Group and Social Stratification in America." *Social Forces* (May):328–333.

Nash, June and María Patricia Fernández-Kelly, eds. (1983) *Women, Men, and the International Division of Labor.* New York: SUNY-Albany.

National Center for Education Statistics (1981) *Selected Statistics on the Education of Hispanics.* Washington, DC: Author.

National Committee on Pay Equity (1987) *Pay Equity: An Issue of Race, Ethnicity and Sex.* Washington, DC: Author.

National Council of Churches of Christ (1984) *Fact Sheets on Institutional Racism.* New York: Author, Division of Church and Society.

National Drug Abuse Center for Training and Resource Development (1979) "Racial Terminology Used in Puerto Rico," in *Puerto Rican History and Culture* (Participant Manual) (DHEW Publication No. [ADM] 80-00108P). Washington, DC: Government Printing Office.

Nelson, Candace and Marta Tienda (1985) "The Structuring of Hispanic Ethnicity: Historical and Contemporary Perspectives." *Ethnic and Racial Studies* 8 (January):49–74.

Nelson, Dale (1984) "The Political Behavior of New York Puerto Ricans: Assimilation or Survival," in C. Rodríguez, Virginia Sánchez-Korrol, and J. Oscar Alers (eds.) *The Puerto Rican Struggle: Essays on Survival in the U.S.* Maplewood, NJ: Waterfront.

New York City Board of Education (1984a) *Annual Pupil Ethnic Census.* New York: Author.

———— (1984b) *School Profiles, 1982–83.* New York: Author.

New York City Commission on Hispanic Concerns (1986) *Report of the Mayor's Commission on Hispanic Concerns* (Edgardo N. Vásquez, chair). New York: Author.

New York City Commission on Human Rights (1973) *The Employment of Minorities, Women and the Handicapped in City Government.* New York: Author.

New York City Commission on Special Education [NYCCSE] (1985) *Special Education: A Call for Quality* (Report to Mayor Koch; Richard I. Beattie, chair). New York: Author.

New York City Department of City Planning (1982) *The Puerto Rican New Yorkers: A Recent History of Their Distribution and Population and Household Characteristics.* New York: Association of Puerto Rican Executive Directors.

New York State (1986) *Report of the Task Force on Poverty and Social Welfare.* Albany: Author.

Newsletter of the Fordham University Bronx Urban Resource Center (1987) Vol. 5 (Summer).

Nielson, Francois and Roberto M. Fernández (1981) *Hispanic Students in American High Schools: Background Characteristics and Achievement*. Washington, DC: National Opinion Research Center, National Center for Education Statistics.

Nieto, Sonia (1987) "Self-Affirmation or Self-Destruction: The Image of Puerto Ricans in Children's Literature Written in English," in Asela Rodríguez de Laguna (ed.) *Images and Identities: The Puerto Rican In Two World Contexts*. New Brunswick, NJ: Transaction.

Noboa, Abdin (1980) "Hispanics and Desegregation: Summary of Aspira's Study on Hispanic Segregation Trends in U.S. School Districts." *Metas* 1 (Fall):1–24.

Noriega, Nino (1983) "Hispanic Americans Occupy a Pivotal Role in the Americas," in *1983 Hispanic Conventioneer*. Los Angeles: Caminos Corp.

Ogbu, John V. (1978) *Minority Education and Caste: The American System in Cross-Cultural Perspective*. New York: Academic Press.

Olivas, Michael A. (1983) "Research and Theory on Hispanic Education: Students, Finance and Governance." *Aztlan* 14 (Spring):111–146.

Omi, Michael and Howard Winant (1983a) "By the Rivers of Babylon: Race in the United States (Part One: Resurgent Racial Conflict in the 1980s)." *Socialist Review* 71 (September-October):31–66.

——— (1983b) "By the Rivers of Babylon: Race in the United States (Part Two: The Great Transformation)." *Socialist Review* 72 (November-December):35–68.

Orfield, Gary (1987) "School Desegregation Needed Now." *Focus* (July):5–7.

Ortiz, A. and J. Yates (1983) "Incidence of Exceptionality Among Hispanics: Implications for Manpower Planning," *Journal of the National Association for Bilingual Education* 7:41–53.

Ortiz, Vilma (1986) "Changes in the Characteristics of Puerto Rican Migrants, from 1955 to 1980." *International Migration Review* 20 (Fall):612–628.

Padilla, Elena (1958) *Up from Puerto Rico*. New York: Columbia University Press.

Padilla, Felix (1985) *Latino Ethnic Consciousness: The Case of Mexican-Americans and Puerto Ricans in Chicago*. Notre Dame, IN: University of Notre Dame Press.

——— (1987a) "On The Development of Salsa Music in the Puerto Rican Community." Paper presented at the annual meeting of the American Studies Association, November.

——— (1987b) *Puerto Rican Chicago*. Notre Dame, IN: University of Notre Dame Press.

Pantoja, Antonia (1972) "Puerto Rican Migration." Preliminary Report to the U.S. Commission on Civil Rights of Puerto Ricans, January 31.

Paredes, Gustavo (1984) *Documentary on Latin Music*. New York: Latin American Musicians Association.

Pear, Robert (1984) "Immigration and the Randomness of Ethnic Mix." *New York Times* (October 2):A26.

Pedraza-Bailey, Sylvia (1985) *Political and Economic Migrants in America: Cubans and Mexicans*, Austin: University of Texas Press.

Peirce, Neal R. and Jerry Hagstrom (1979) "Two Years After Carter's Visit, Islands of Hope Dot the South Bronx." *National Journal* (October 6):1644–1648.

Pelto, Pertti, Maria Roman, and Nelson Liriano (1982) "Family Structures in an Urban Puerto Rican Community." *Urban Anthropology* 11 (1):39–57.

Pérez, Martín (1987) "Trabajadores Agricolas de Vineland, New Jersey." *Centro de Estudios Puertorriqueños Bulletin* 2 (1):27–35.

Pérez, Nelida and Amilcar Tirado (1986) "Boricuas en el Norte." *Revista de Historia* 2(3):128–166.

Perloff, Harvey (1950) *Puerto Rico's Economic Future*. Chicago: University of Chicago Press.

Petrovich, Janice and Sandra Laureano (1986) "Toward an Analysis of Puerto Rican Women and the Informal Economy." *Homines* 10 (1).

Pico, Fernando (1986) *Historia General de Puerto Rico*. Rio Piedras, Puerto Rico: Huracan-Academia.

Pico de Hernández, Isabel (1975) "The Quest for Race, Sex and Ethnic Equality in Puerto Rico." *Caribbean Studies* 14 (4):127–141.

Piore, Michael (1979) *Birds of Passage: Migrant Labor and Industrial Societies*. New York: Cambridge University Press.

Pitt-Rivers, Julian (1975) "Race, Color, and Class in Central America and the Andes," in Norman R. Yetman and C. Hoy Steele (eds.) *Majority and Minority*. Boston: Allyn & Bacon.

Podhoretz, Norman (1968) *Making It*. New York: Random House.

Portes, Alejandro and Robert L. Bach (1985) *Latin Journey: Cuban and Mexican Immigrants in the United States*. Berkeley: University of California Press.

——— and Saskia Sassen-Koob (1987) "Making It Underground: Comparative Material on the Informal Sector in Western Market Economies." *American Journal of Sociology* 93 (July):30–61.

——— and John Walton (1981) *Labor, Class and the International System*. New York: Academic Press.

Powers, Stephen and L. Wagner (1983) "Attributions for Success and Failure of Hispanic and Anglo High School Students." *Journal of Instructional Psychology* 10 (4):171–176.

Prewitt-Díaz, Joseph O. (1983) "A Study of Self-Esteem and School Sentiment on Two Groups of Puerto Rican Students." *Educational and Psychological Research* 3 (Summer):161–167.

Prieto, Claudio (1984) Racial/Ethnic Distribution of Degrees Conferred in Institutions of Higher Education. Albany: New York State Department of Education, Office of Educational Policy, Bureau of Post Secondary Research.

Puerto Rican Council on Higher Education (1986) *Puerto Rican Council on Higher Education Newsletter* (April): 7–8.

PRCDP (1965) *Puerto Rican Community Development Project*. New York: Puerto Rican Forum.

Ramírez, Arnulfo G. (1985) *Bilingualism Through Schooling: Cross Cultural Education for Minority and Majority Students*. Albany: State University of New York Press.

Ramírez, Guillermo (1974) *El Arte Popular En Puerto Rico*. New York: Colección Montana.

Ramírez, M. (1981) "Language Attitudes and the Speech of Spanish-English Bilingual Pupils," in R. P. Duran (ed.) *Latino Language and Communicative Behavior*. Norwood, NJ: Ablex.

Ramírez, M. and A. Castañeda (1974) *Cultural Democracy: Bicognitive Development and Education*. New York: Academic Press.

Ramist, Leonard and Solomon Arbiter (1986) *Profiles, College-Bound Seniors, 1985*. New York: College Board.

Ramos, Henry A. J. and Marlene M. Morales (1985) "U.S. Immigration and the Hispanic Community: An Historical Overview and Sociological Perspective" *Journal of Hispanic Politics* 1 (1):1–17.

Rand, Christopher (1958) *The Puerto Ricans*. New York: Oxford University Press.

Ravitch, Diane (1972) *The Great School Wars of New York City, 1805–1969*. New York: Outerbridge & Lazard.

Regional Plan Association (1972) Linking Skills, Jobs and Housing in the New York Urban Region. New York: Author.

Reimers, Cordelia (1984a) "Sources of Family Income Differentials Among Hispanics, Blacks and White Non-Hispanics." *Americal Journal of Sociology* 89 (4):889–903.

——— (1984b) "The Wage Structure of Hispanic Men: Implications for Policy." *Social Science Quarterly* 65 (June).

Rendon, Mario (1984) "Myths and Stereotypes in Minority Groups." *International Journal of Social Psychology* 30 (Winter):297–304.

Reyes, Luis (1984) "Minority Dropouts: Systemic Failure in Inner City Schools." Paper presented at the II Seminar on the Situation of Black, Chicano, Native American, Puerto Rican, Caribbean and Asian Communities in the United States, sponsored by Casa de las Americas and the Centro de Estudios Sobre America, Havana, Cuba, December 4–6.

Reynolds, Lloyd G. and Peter Gregory (1965) *Wages, Productivity and Industrialization in Puerto Rico*. Chicago: Richard D. Irving.

Ricketts, Erol and Isabel Sawhill (1988) "Defining and Measuring the Underclass." *Journal of Policy Analysis and Management* 7 (2):316–325.

Ríos, Palmira (1985) "Puerto Rican Women in the United States Labor Market." *Line of March* 18 (Fall).

Rivera, Carmen (1986) "Research Issues: Post Hospitalization Adjustment of Chronically Mentally Ill Hispanic Patients." *Hispanic Research Center Bulletin* 9 (Spring).

Rivera, Edward (1983) *Family Installments: Memories of Growing Up Hispanic*. New York: Penguin.

Rivera, Eugenio (1987) "The Puerto Rican Colony of Lorain." *Centro de Estudios Puertorriqueños Bulletin* 2 (1):11–23.

Rivera, Monte (1984) "Organizational Politics of the East Harlem Barrio in the 1970s," in James Jennings and Monte Rivera (eds.) *Puerto Rican Politics in Urban America*. Westport, CT: Greenwood.

Rivera-Batiz, Francisco L. (1987a) "The Characteristics of Recent Puerto Rican

Migrants: Some Further Evidence." Paper presented at the meetings of the Puerto Rican Economic Association, May 1–2.

—— (1987b) "Is There a Brain Drain of Puerto Ricans to the U.S.?" *Puerto Rico Business Review* 12 (June/July):1–5.

Roberts, Tim, Jerry Hutton, and Maximino Plata (1985) "Teacher Ratings of Hispanic, Black and Anglo Students Classroom Behavior." *Psychology in the Schools* 22 (July).

Rodríguez, C. (1969) "Political Legitimacy." Master's thesis, Cornell University.

—— (1973) "The Ethnic Queue: The Case of Puerto Ricans." Doctoral dissertation, Washington University, St. Louis, MO.

—— (1974a) "Puerto Ricans: Between Black and White." *New York Affairs* 1 (4):92–101.

—— (1974b) "Puerto Ricans and the Melting Pot." *Journal of Ethnic Studies* 1 (4):89–98.

—— (1974c) "The Structure of Failure II: A Case in Point," *Urban Review* 7 (3):215–226.

—— (1975) "A Cost-Benefit Analysis of Subjective Factors Affecting Assimilation." *Ethnicity* 2:66–80.

—— (1979) "Economic Factors Affecting Puerto Ricans in New York," in History Task Force, Centro de Estudios Puertorriqueños, *Labor Migration Under Capitalism: The Puerto Rican Experience*. New York: Monthly Review Press.

—— (1981) "Triple Jeopardy and an Ethnic Studies Department," in George Mims (ed.) *The Minority Administrator in Higher Education: Progress, Experiences, and Perspectives*. New York: Schenkman.

—— (1984a) "Hispanics and Hispanic Women in New York State." Paper prepared for the First Legislative Research Conference, January 21, Albany.

—— (1984b) "Prisms of Race and Class." *Journal of Ethnic Studies* 12 (Summer):99–120.

—— (1988) "On the Declining Public Interest in Race." *Women's Studies Quarterly* (Fall/Winter).

—— (1989) "Race, Class, and Gender among Puerto Ricans in New York." Report submitted to the Inter-University Program for Latino Research/Social Science Research Council, University of Texas, January, Austin.

—— (in press) "Puerto Ricans and the Circular Migration Thesis." *Journal of Hispanic Policy*.

—— and Luis G. Rodríguez (1975) "The Health and Culture of Puerto Ricans: A Re-examination." Lehman College. (unpublished)

—— Virginia Sánchez-Korrol, and J. Oscar Alers, eds. (1984) *The Puerto Rican Struggle: Essays on Survival in the U.S.* Maplewood, NJ: Waterfront.

—— and Eliott Sclar (1983) "The South Bronx: A Failure or a Success of Public Policy and Management." Paper presented at the meeting of the Association for Public Policy and Management, October 21, Philadelphia.

Rodríguez, Richard (1982) *Hunger of Memory*. Boston: D. Godine.

Rodríguez, Richard F., Alfonso G. Prieto, and Robert S. Rueda (1984) "Issues in Bilingual/Multicultural Special Education." *Journal of the National Association of Bilingual Education* 8 (Spring):55–65.

Rodríguez Bou, Ismael (1966) "Significant Factors in the Development of Education in Puerto Rico," in *Selected Background Studies of the Status Commission Report*. Washington, DC: Government Printing Office.

Rogler, Charles (1972) "The Role of Semantics in the Study of Race Distance in Puerto Rico," in Eugenio Fernández-Méndez (ed.) *Portrait of a Society: Readings on Puerto Rican Sociology*. San Juan: University of Puerto Rico Press.

Rogler, Lloyd et al. (1983) *A Conceptual Framework for Mental Health Research* (Monograph No. 10). New York: Fordham University, Hispanic Research Center.

—— and Rosemary Santana-Cooney (1984) *Puerto Rican Families in New York City: Intergenerational Processes*. Maplewood, NJ: Waterfront.

—— R. Blumenthal, Robert G, Malgady, and Giuseppe Constantino (1985) "Hispanics and Culturally Sensitive Mental Health Services." *Hispanic Research Center Bulletin* 8 (July/October):3–4.

Rosen, Bernard (1959) "Race, Ethnicity, and the Achievement Syndrome." *American Sociological Review* 24:47–60.

Rosenberg, Terry J. (1974) *Residence, Employment, and Mobility of Puerto Ricans in New York City*. Research Paper No. 151. Chicago: University of Chicago, Department of Geography.

—— (1987) *Poverty in New York City: 1980–85*. New York: Community Service Society.

Rosenthal, Alvin S., Kevin Baker, and Alan Ginsburg (1983) "The Effect of Language Background on Achievement Level and Learning Among Elementary School Students." *Sociology of Education* 56: (October):157–169.

Rosenthal, Robert and Lenore Jacobsen (1968) *Pygmalian in the Classroom*. New York: Holt, Rinehart & Winston.

Ross, David F. (1976) *The Long Uphill Path: A Historical Study of Puerto Rico's Program of Economic Development*. San Juan: Editorial Edil.

Rothmyer, Karen (1984) "Mapping Out Moon's Media Empire." *Columbia Journalism Review* 23 (4):23–31.

Rutter, Michael et al. (1979) *Fifteen Thousand Hours: Secondary Schools and Their Effects on Children*. Cambridge, MA: Harvard University Press.

Ryan, E. and M. A. Carranza (1975) "Evaluative Reactions of Adolescents Toward Speakers of Standard English and Mexican American Accented English." *Journal of Personality and Social Psychology* 31 (5):855–863.

Salazar, Max (1984) "The Perseverance of a Culture," in C. Rodríguez, Virginia Sánchez-Korrol, and J. Oscar Alers (eds.) *The Puerto Rican Struggle: Essays on Survival in the U.S.* Maplewood, NJ: Waterfront.

Sánchez, José Ramón (1987) "Casas Ajenas: The Alienation of Power in the Housing of Puerto Ricans in New York City, 1945–80." State University of New York, Old Westbury. (unpublished)

—— (1988) "The Political Economy of Social Reproduction: Puerto Rican Labor, Housing and the State in New York City, 1948–80." State University of New York, Old Westbury. (unpublished)

Sánchez, María and Antonio M. Stevens-Arroyo, eds. (1987) *Toward a Renaissance of Puerto Rican Studies* (Social Science Monographs, Boulder, CO). Highland

Lakes, NJ: Atlantic Research and Publications. (Distributed by Columbia University Press)

Sánchez-Korrol, Virginia E. (1983) *From Colonia to Community: The History of Puerto Ricans in New York City, 1917–1948.* Westport, CT: Greenwood.

——— (1985) "In Search of Non-Traditional Women: Histories of Puerto Rican Women Preachers before Mid-Century." Paper presented at the meeting of the American Historical Association, New York.

Sandis, Eva E. (1970) "The Socioeconomic Characteristics of Puerto Rican Migrants," in Eva E. Sandis (ed.) *The Puerto Rican Experience.* New York: Selected Academic Readings.

Santana-Cooney, Rosemary and Alice Colón-Warren (1984) "Work and Family: The Recent Struggle of Puerto Rican Females," in C. Rodríguez, Virginia Sánchez-Korrol, and J. Oscar Alers (eds.) *The Puerto Rican Struggle: Essays on Survival in the U.S.* Maplewood, NJ: Waterfront.

Santiago, Carlos (1985) "The Changing Role of Migration in Puerto Rican Economic Development." Paper presented at the Yale Conference on Puerto Rican Migration, New Haven, CT, November 5.

——— (1987) "Hispanics in the Labor Force: A Survey of Recent Research and Recommendations for Economic Policy," in *Issues Relevant to the Labor Force in the Detroit Metropolitan Area* (Center for Urban Studies Monograph). Detroit: Wayne State University.

Santiago-Santiago, Isaura (1978) *A Community's Struggle for Equal Educational Opportunity: Aspira v. Bd. of Ed.* (Monograph No. 2, Office of Minority Education). Princeton, NJ: Educational Testing Service.

——— (1983) "Towards a Qualitative Analysis of Teacher Disapproval Behavior," in Ramona V. Padilla (ed.) *Theory, Technology, and Public Policy on Bilingual Education.* Rosslyn, VA: National Clearinghouse of Bilingual Education.

——— (1984a) "Dropouts or 'Pushouts'?" Puerto Ricans and School Policies." Paper prepared at the Roundtable on Puerto Ricans in the Continental United States, sponsored by the Johnson Foundation, March 22–24, Racine, WI.

——— (1984b) "Language Policy and Education in Puerto Rico and the Continent." *International Education Journal* 1(1):61–90.

——— (1986a) "The Education of Hispanics in the United States: Inadequacies of the American Melting Pot Theory," in Dietmar Rothermund and John Simon (eds.) *Education and the Integration of Ethnic Minorities.* New York: St. Martin's.

——— (1986b) "A Comparative Analysis of Instructional Strategies of Bilingual Teachers During Spanish/English Social Studies Lessons: Initial Findings." *Journal of the New York State Association for Bilingual Education* 2 (Spring):1–20.

——— (1987c) "Aspira v. Board of Education Revisited." *American Journal of Education* 95 (November).

Sassen-Koob, Saskia (1983) "Labor Migration and the New Industrial Division of Labor," in June Nash and María Patricia Fernández-Kelly (eds.) *Women, Men, and the International Division of Labor.* New York: SUNY-Albany.

——— (1986) "New York City's Growing Informal Economy: Comparing the Impact of Customized Production and Immigration." Paper presented at the 81st Annual Meeting of the American Sociological Association, New York, October 30.

—— (1986a) "New York City Economic Restructuring and Immigration." *Development and Change* 17:85–119.

—— (1988) *The Mobility of Labor and Capital*. New York: Cambridge University Press.

—— (1989) "New York City's Informal Economy," in A. Portes, M. Castells, and L. Benton (eds.) *The Informal Sector: Theoretical and Methodological Issues*. Baltimore: Johns Hopkins University Press.

Sawyers, Larry (1975) "Urban Form and the Mode of Production." *Review of Radical Political Economics* 8 (1).

Schill, Michael and Richard P. Nathan (1983) *Revitalizing America's Cities: Neighborhood Reinvestment and Displacement*. Albany: State University of New York Press.

Seda Bonilla, Edwin (1970) "Ethnic Studies and Cultural Pluralism." *The Rican* 1 (1):56–65.

—— (1977) "Who Is Puerto Rican: Problems of Sociocultural Identity in Puerto Rico." *Caribbean Studies* 17 (1–2):105–121.

Senior, Clarence (1965) *Strangers, Then Neighbors: From Pilgrims to Puerto Ricans*. Chicago: Quadrangle.

—— and Donald O. Watkins (1966) "Toward a Balance Sheet of Puerto Rican Migration," in *Status of Puerto Rico: Selected Background Studies* (prepared for the U.S.-Puerto Rico Commission on the Status of Puerto Rico). Washington, DC: Government Printing Office.

Sereno, Renzo (1945) "Cryptomelanism: A Study of Color Relations and Personal Insecurity in Puerto Rico." *Psychiatry* 10 (August):261–269.

Sexton, Virginia Cayo (1966) *Spanish Harlem: Anatomy of Poverty*. New York: Harper & Row.

Sibley, Elbridge (1942) "Some Demographic Clues to Stratification." *American Sociological Review* 8:322–330.

Smith, Donald H., chair (1987) *Dropping Out of School in New York State: The Invisible People of Color* (Report of the Task Force on the New York State Dropout Problem, Commissioned by the African American Institute of the State University of New York).

Soto, Elaine (1983) "Sex Role Traditionalism and Assertiveness, Puerto Rican Women Living in the U.S." *Journal of Community Psychology* 11 (October):346–354.

South Bronx Development Organization [SBDO] (1982) "Some South Bronx Highlights." September. (memorandum)

—— (1983) "Fact Sheet No. 1" (Human Services Unit). March.

—— (1980) *Areas of Strength, Areas of Opportunity: South Bronx Revitalization Program and Development Guide Plans*. New York: Author.

Sowell, Thomas (1981) *Ethnic America*. New York: Basic Books.

Stafford, Walter (1983) *Racial, Ethnic and Sexual Stratification and Affirmative Action Planning in New York's Public and Private Sectors*. Washington, DC: U.S. Commission on Civil Rights.

—— (1985) *Closed Labor Markets: Underrepresentation of Blacks, Hispanics, and Women in New York City's Core Industries and Jobs*. New York: Community Service Society.

Stahl, J. E. (1965) "Economic Development Through Reform in Puerto Rico." Doctoral dissertation, Iowa State University.

Sternlieb, George (1973) *Housing and People in New York City* (Report for the City of New York, available from the New York City Housing and Development Administration, Department of Rent and Housing Maintenance).

Stevens-Arroyo, Antonio and Ana María Diáz-Stevens (1982) "Puerto Ricans in the States: A Struggle for Identity," in Anthony G. Dworkin, and Rosalind J. Dworkin (eds.) *The Minority Report: An Introduction to Racial, Ethnic, and Gender Relations* (2nd ed.) New York: CBS College Publishing, Holt, Rinehart & Winston.

Stevenson, Gelvin (1980) "The Abandonment of Roosevelt Gardens," in Bronx Museum of the Arts, *Devastation/Resurrection: The South Bronx*. New York: Bronx Museum of the Arts.

———— (1986) "The Intensification of Capitalism: A New Context for Ethical Decisions." Paper presented at the meeting of the Presbyterian Church, U.S.A., Advisory Council of Church and Society.

Steward, Julian (1965) *The People of Puerto Rico*. Chicago: University of Illinois Press.

Tabb, William K. (1972) "Puerto Ricans in New York City: A Study of Economic and Social Conditions." Bureau of Labor Statistics, New York Regional Office. (unpublished)

Taeuber, Karl and Alma F. Taeuber (1967) "Recent Immigration Studies and Ethnic Assimilation." *Demography* 4(2):798–808.

Teichner, Victor J. and Gail W. Berry (1981) "The Puerto Rican Patient: Some Historical and Psychological Aspects." *Journal of the American Academy of Psychoanalysis* 9 (April):277–289.

Thiel, W. L. (1977) "The Impact of Minority Status on Self-Esteem and Cultural Values of Pre Adolescent Puerto Ricans." Doctoral dissertation, Loyola University of Chicago.

Thomas, Gail and Samuel A. Gordon (1983) *Evaluating the Payoffs of College Investments for Black, White and Hispanic Students*. Baltimore: Johns Hopkins University, Center for Social Organization of Schools.

Thomas, Piri (1967) *Down These Mean Streets*. New York: Knopf.

Thompson, Edgar T. (1975) "The Plantation as a Race Making Situation in Plantation Societies, Race Relations and the South: The Regimentation of Populations," in *Selected Papers of Edgar T. Thompson*. Durham, NC: Duke University Press.

Thurow, Lester (1986) "Latinos Enter Mainstream Quickly." *Los Angeles Times* (March 16):sec. IV, 1.

Tienda, Marta (1981) "Hispanic Origin Workers in the U.S. Labor Market: Comparative Analyses of Employment and Earnings." Department of Labor, Employment and Training Administration Grant, 9/70–10/81, Vol. 1, Report No. DLETA-21-55-79-27-2.

———— (1983a) "Market Characteristics and Hispanic Earnings: A Comparison of Natives and Immigrants." *Social Problems* 31 (October):59–72.

————— (1983b) "Nationality and Income Attainment Among Native and Immigran Hispanic Men in the United States." *Sociological Quarterly* 24 (Spring):253–272

————— (1985) "The Puerto Rican Worker: Current Labor Market Status and Future Prospects," in National Puerto Rican Coalition, *Puerto Ricans in the Mid '80s. An American Challenge.* Alexandria, VA: National Puerto Rican Coalition.

————— and Jennifer Glass (1985) "Household Structure and Labor Force Participation of Black, Hispanic, and White Mothers." *Demography* 22 (August):381–394.

————— and Patricia Guhleman (1985) "The Occupational Position of Employed Hispanic Women," in G. Borjas and M. Tienda (eds.) *Hispanics in the U.S. Economy.* New York: Academic Press.

————— and Leif Jensen (1986) "Poverty and Minorities: A Quarter-Century Profile of Color and Socioeconomic Disadvantages." Paper presented at the Institute for Research on Poverty conference, "Poverty and Social Policy: The Minority Experience," Arlie, VA: November 5–7.

————— and Ding-Tzann Lii (1987) "Migration, Market Insertion and Earnings Determination of Mexicans, Puerto Ricans, and Cubans." University of Wisconsin, Institute for Research on Poverty, DP# 830–87.

————— and Lisa J. Neidert (1984) "Language, Education and the Socioeconomic Achievement of Hispanic Origin Men." *Social Science Quarterly* 65 (June):519–536.

————— and Vilma Ortiz (1984) "'Hispanicity' and the 1980 Census." Center for Demography and Ecology, University of Wisconsin, Madison, CDE Working Paper 84–23.

Tobias, Sigmund, Carryl Cole, Mara Zibrin, and Vera Bodlakova (1982) "Teacher-Student Ethnicity and Recommendations for Special Education Referrals." *Journal of Educational Psychology* 74 (February): 72–76.

Torres, Andrés (1988) "Human Capital, Labor Segmentation, and Inter-Minority Relative Status: Black and Puerto Rican Labor in New York City, 1960–80." Doctoral dissertation, New School for Social Research.

Torruellas, Rosa (1986) "The Failure of the New York Public Educational System to Retain Hispanic and Other Minority Students" (statement submitted to the New York State Black and Puerto Rican Legislative Caucus, March 24, 1986). *Centro de Estudios Puertorriqueños Newsletter* (June).

Treiman, Donald and Heidi Hartmann (1981) *Women, Work and Wages: Equal Pay for Jobs of Equal Value.* Washington, DC: National Academy Press.

Treviño, Fernando M. (1987) "Standardized Terminology for Hispanic Populations." *American Journal of Public Health* 77 (January):69–72.

Triandis, Harry C., Gerardo Marín, Judith Lisansky, and Héctor Betancourt (1985a) "Simpatía as a Cultural Script of Hispanics." *Journal of Personal Social Psychology* (Fall).

————— Gerardo Marín, C. Harry Huri, Judith Lisansky, and Victor Ottati (1985b) "Role Perceptions of Hispanic Young Adults." *Journal of Cross-Cultural Psychology* 15 (September):297–319.

Tumin, Melvin and Arnold Feldman (1961) *Social Class and Social Change in Puerto Rico.* Princeton, NJ: Princeton University Press.

U.S. Bureau of the Census (1970) "Subject Report Series, Persons of Spanish Origin," *1970 Census of Population*. Washington, DC: Government Printing Office.

────── (1982) *Persons of Spanish Origin by State: 1980* (Supplementary Report PC80-S1-7, August). Washington, DC: Government Printing Office.

────── (1984) *Development of Race and Spanish Origin Questions for the 1990 Census* (Background statement, Office of the Director, December). Washington, DC: Government Printing Office.

────── (1985) "Population Characteristics," in *Current Population Reports* (Series P-20, No. 403). Washington, DC: Government Printing Office.

U.S. Commission on Civil Rights (1972) *Demographic, Social, and Economic Characteristics of New York City and the New York Metropolitan Area* (Hearings on the Civil Rights of Puerto Ricans, staff report, February). Washington, DC: Government Printing Office.

────── (1976) *Puerto Ricans in the Continental United States: An Uncertain Future*. Washington, DC: Government Printing Office.

────── (1983) *Teachers and Students: Differences in Teacher Interaction with Mexican American and Anglo Students* (Report 5, Mexican American Education Study). Washington, DC: Government Printing Office.

U.S. Congress, Senate (1970) Hearings before the Select Committee on Equal Educational Opportunity, 91st Congress. Part 8, Equal Educational Opportunity for Puerto Rican Children (November 23–25). Washington, DC: Government Printing Office.

U.S. Department of Labor (1974) "The New York Puerto Ricans: Patterns of Work Experience," in Adalberto Lopez and James Petras (eds.) *Puerto Rico and Puerto Ricans*. New York: Schenkman.

U.S. Department of Labor, Bureau of Labor Statistics (1972) *The New York Puerto Rican: Patterns of Work Experience* (Regional Report 19, Poverty Area Profiles). Washington, DC: Government Printing Office.

────── (1986) "Key New York Trends and Puerto Rican Prospects." Paper presented by the director of the Bureau of Labor Statistics to the Puerto Rican Research Exchange, February 21.

────── (1987) *Area Manpower Survey* (New York Regional Office, September 18 and December 1). Washington, DC: Government Printing Office.

U.S. Immigration Commission Reports (1911) Vols. 1, 2, 8 (U.S. Congress, Document No. 282, 61st Congress, 2nd Session), Washington, DC: Government Printing Office.

United States-Puerto Rico Commission on the Status of Puerto Rico (1966) *Status of Puerto Rico: Selected Background Studies Prepared for the Commission* and *Hearings—Senate Document No. 108* (Vols. 1–3). Washington, DC: Government Printing Office.

Uriarte-Gaston, Miren (1987) "Organizing for Survival: The Emergence of a Puerto Rican Community." Doctoral dissertation, Boston University.

Valdivieso, Rafael (1986) "Must They Wait Another Generation? Hispanics and Secondary School Reform." ERIC Clearinghouse on Urban Education, Teachers College, Columbia University.

Valentine, Bettylou (1978) *Hustling and Other Hard Work*. New York: Free Press.

Valentine, Charles A. (1968) *Culture and Poverty: Critique and Counter-Proposals*. Chicago: University of Chicago Press.

Van Middledyk, R. A. (1915) *The History of Puerto Rico*. New York: D. Appleton.

Varo, Carlos (1971) *Consideraciones Antropológicas y Políticas en Torno a La Enseñanza del "Spanglish" en Nueva York*. Río Piedras, Puerto Rico: Ediciones Librería Internacional.

Vásquez, Héctor (1971) "Discrimination Against Puerto Rican Professionals and Puerto Rican Pupils in New York City Public Schools." Paper presented at the Hearings on Minority Hiring Practices of the New York City Board of Education, January 27.

Vásquez, Jesse M. (1981) "Cultural Renaissance: Impressions of a Puerto Rican New Yorker in New Mexico." *Century: American Southwest Journal of Observation and Opinion* 1 (21): 18–20.

Vásquez Nuttal, E., Patricia Medeiros Landurano, and Patricia Goldman (1984) "A Critical Look at Testing and Evaluation from a Cross-Cultural Perspective," in Philip C. Chinn (ed.) *Education of Culturally and Linguistically Different Exceptional Children*. Reston, VA: Council for Exceptional Children.

Vazconcelos, José (1966) *La Raza Cósmica* (3rd ed.). Mexico City: Espasa-Calpe.

Veccoli, Rudoph J. (1970) "Ethnicity: A Neglected Dimension of American History." *American Studies in Scandinavia* 4.

Velez, William and Rajshekar G. Javalgi (1986) "Toward a Model Predicting Employment for the Puerto Rican Youth Segment." Paper presented at the annual meeting of the American Sociological Association, New York, August.

Veltman, Calvin J. (1981) "Relative Educational Attainments of Hispanic American Children, 1976." *Metas* 2 (Spring):36–51.

Verdugo, Richard R. (1986) "Educational Stratification and Hispanics," in Michael Olivas (ed.) *Latino College Students*. New York: Teachers College Press.

Vernon, Raymond (1960) *Metropolis, 1985*. Cambridge, MA: Harvard University Press.

Vigó, José A. (1976) "Racial Categories Among New York Puerto Ricans: A Semantic Study." (unpublished)

—— (1978) "A Semantic and Pragmatic Analysis of Puerto Rican Race Terminology." (unpublished)

Vivas, José Luis (1960) *Historia de Puerto Rico*. New York: Las Américas.

Wade, Peter (1985) "Race and Class: The Case of South American Blacks." *Ethnic and Racial Studies* 8 (April):233–249.

Wagenheim, Kal (1975) *A Survey of Puerto Ricans on the U.S. Mainland in the 1970s*. New York: Praeger.

——and Olga Jiménez de Wagenheim (1973) *The Puerto Ricans: A Documentary History*. New York: Praeger.

Wagley, Charles (1965) "On the Concept of Social Race in the Americas," in Dwight B. Health and Richard N. Adams (eds.) *Contemporary Cultures and Societies of Latin America: A Reader in the Social Anthropology of Middle and South America and the Caribbean*. New York, Random House. (Original work published 1959)

Wakefield, Dan (1959) *Island in the City*. Boston: Houghton Mifflin.

Waldinger, Roger (1985) "Immigration and Industrial Change in the New York City Apparel Industry," in G. Borjas and M. Tienda (eds.) *Hispanics in the U.S. Economy*. New York: Academic Press.

Warner, Lloyd and Leo Srole (1960) *The Social Systems of American Ethnic Groups*. New Haven, CT: Yale University Press.

Warren, Bruce (1970a) "The Relationship Between Religious Preference and Socio-Economic Achievement of American Men." Doctoral dissertation, University of Michigan.

―――― (1970b) "Socio-Economic Achievement and Religion: The American Case." *Sociological Inquiry* 40:13–55.

Weller, Neil J. (1960) "Religion and Social Mobility in Industrial Society." Doctoral dissertation, University of Michigan.

Wells, Henry (1969) *The Modernization of Puerto Rico*. Cambridge, MA: Harvard University Press.

Wessel, David (1986) "Growing Gap: U.S. Rich and Poor Increase in Numbers; Middle Loses Ground." *Wall Street Journal* (September 22):1.

Wilhelm, Sidney M. (1971) *Who Needs the Negro?* Garden City, NY: Doubleday-Anchor.

Will, Robert and Harold Vatter (1970) *Poverty in Affluence*. New York: Harcourt, Brace & World.

Williams, Eric (1945) "Race Relations in Puerto Rico and the Virgin Islands." *Foreign Affairs* 23:308–317.

―――― (1970) *From Columbus to Castro: The History of the Caribbean, 1492–1969*. New York: Harper & Row.

Wiseman, Carter (1981) "Little House on the Rubble." *New York* (June 1):54–55.

Wolff, Eric R. (1982) *Europe and the People Without History*. Berkeley: University of California Press.

Women's City Club of New York (1977) *With Love and Affection: A Study of Building Abandonment*. New York City: Author.

Wright, Pamela and Rafaela Santa Cruz (1983) "Ethnic Composition of Special Education Programs in California." *Learning Disability Quarterly* 6 (Fall): 387–394.

Wurzel, Jaime (1983) "Differences Between Puerto Rican and Anglo Secondary School Students in Perception of Relational Modalities." *International Journal of Intercultural Relations* 7(2):181–190.

Yetman, Norma R. and C. Hoy Steele, eds. (1975) *Majority and Minority*. Boston: Allyn & Bacon.

Yong, Arthur and F. Hohn Devaney (1982) *Sheltering Americans: New Directions of Growth and Change*. Washington, DC: U.S. Bureau of the Census.

Young Lords Party and Michael Abramson (1971) *Palante: Young Lords Party*. New York: McGraw-Hill.

Zavala, Iris M. and Rafael Rodríguez (1980) *The Intellectual Roots of Independence: An Anthology of Puerto Rican Political Essays*. New York: Monthly Review Press.

Zavala-Martínez, Iris (1981) "Mental Health and the Puerto Ricans in the United States: A Critical Literature Review and Comprehensive Bibliography,"University of Massachusetts Department of Psychology. (unpublished.)

Zenón Cruz, Isabelo (1975) *Narciso Descubre Su Trasero*. Humacao, Puerto Rico: Editorial Furidi.

Zentella, Ana Celia (1981) "Language Variety Among Puerto Ricans," in Charles Ferguson and Shirley Brice Heath (eds.) *Language in the U.S.* Cambridge: Cambridge University Press.

INDEX

ABOUT THE AUTHOR

Clara Rodríguez grew up in the South Bronx and earned her Ph.D. in sociology from Washington University, St Louis. Formerly a Dean at Fordham University, she spent 1988 as a visiting scholar at the Massachusetts Institute of Technology and is present Associate Professor of Sociology at Fordham. Professor Rodríguez is the author of numerous articles on the state of Puerto Ricans in the United States and is currently working on research supported by the Rockefeller Foundation.